ETHNIC CONFLICT IN AFGHANISTAN

Causes and Resolutions

ETHNIC CONFLICT IN AFGHANISTAN

Causes and Resolutions

Dr Ajit Kumar Singh

GYAN

First Published, 2018

Published by

Gyan Publishing House
5, Ansari Road
Daryaganj, New Delhi-110002
Phone: 9811692060
E-mail: books@gyanbooks.com

Printed at: G. Print Process, Delhi.

Cataloging in Publication Data—DK

Courtesy: D.K. Agencies (P) Ltd. <docinfo@dkagencies.com>

Singh, Ajit Kumar, author.

Ethnic conflict in Afghanistan : causes and resolutions / by Dr. Ajit Kumar Singh.

pages cm

Includes bibliographical references.

ISBN 9788121213431 (HB)

1. Ethnic conflict—Afghanistan. 2. Afghanistan—Politics and government. I. Title.

LCC HN670.6.Z9S62 2017 | DDC 305.8009581 23

Contents

Acknowledgements

This book would not have seen the light of the day without inexhaustible patience, constant encouragement, able and scholarly guidance and personal interest of my Ph.D. supervisor Dr Sharad Kumar Soni. I express my deep sense of gratitude to him for channelising my potentials in the right direction. I lack words to express my gratitude to him.

I express my sincere gratitude to the departed soul of Professor Dawa T. Norbu under whose guidance I completed my M.Phil. Dissertation, the first move towards achieving the desired goal.

I think I am very lucky that I work under Dr Ajai Sahni who has always been a guiding light and source of inspiration to *stand out in a crowd*.

I gratefully acknowledge my family members and friends with a deep sense of gratitude for their boundless encouragement, moral support and everything I asked for, during the pursuit of my writing. I dedicate this book to my mother (Smt. Damyanti Singh), father (Shri Girish Nandan Prasad Singh), brothers (Anil and Amit), sister-in-laws (Archana and Priya), and nephews (Agastya and Amartya). Soni, my wife,; and Akshita and Aishni, my two little gems; need special mention.

Finally, having been privileged in receiving encouragement and support, I own my responsibility for all the error or omissions in this work.

Ajit Kumar Singh

New Delhi
11th May 2016

Acknowledgement

Abstract

The world is passing through a phase of conflicts. Most of the nations, across the globe, are engaged in one conflict or the other. Notably, a large number of these conflicts are ethnic in nature. South Asia, one of the least developed regions, and home to multiple ethnic groups, is also engulfed by such conflicts. One of the South Asian countries, also the part of Central Asia, Afghanistan, since its inception, has witnessed several conflicts. However, the multi-ethnic nation plunged into an ethnic conflict in the beginning of 1990s and has since been looking for a resolution. In fact, it was in 1989 after the withdrawal of Soviet forces from Afghanistan that Afghanistan witnessed a period of unrest and ethnic conflict leading to a protracted civil war. This resulted in the collapse of the entire state structure. Although the Soviet backed government led by President Mohammad Najibullah tried to restore peace and order in the country his efforts were defeated by the warring factions of different ethnic groups who wanted to establish their supremacy. Several rebel groups formed a governing coalition, called the Islamic Council of Mujahideen and elected Burhanuddin Rabbani as the interim President of Afghanistan in 1992. But the Rabbani government's failure to checkmate the growth of ethnic groups further aggravated the situation. The Taliban, a group of Pashtuns preaching radical Islam, ousted the Rabbani government in 1996. During the reign of the Taliban, the Pashtun and non-Pashtun divide gave a fillip to ethnic conflict leading to the failure of state structure.

The end of the Cold War and the subsequent demise of the erstwhile Union of Soviet Socialist Republics (USSR), also known as Soviet Union, created a New World order. The state of Afghanistan was at a critical juncture. Its neighbouring states like Pakistan and Iran took advantage of it and made sincere efforts to influence the Afghan situation according to their own needs. However, neither the big powers like the United States (US) and Russia nor the world organisations like the United Nations (UN) had shown keen interest in Afghanistan. It was the September 11, 2001, also known as 9/11, incident that drew the attention of the world community towards Afghanistan. The Taliban misrule, ethnic strife, Islamic fundamentalism and terrorist infrastructure in Afghanistan compelled the world leaders, policy-makers and security analysts to describe it as a "failed state". The world community gave importance to state structuration and reconstruction in Afghanistan after the downfall of Taliban.

The book has been divided into six chapters including introductory and concluding chapters. In the first chapter titled "**Introduction**" ethnic conflicts in South Asia have been discussed in detail, besides surveying a wide ranging literature.

In chapter two titled "**Ethnic Conflict in Theoretical Perspective**" an attempt has been made to understand the term 'ethnicity' as well as the theories dealing with it. In the process, Concepts of Nationalism and Concept of State have also been dealt with apart from their relations with ethnicity. Moreover, various theories of Ethnicity as well as different aspects of ethnic conflict in theoretical perspective have been dwelt upon with the sole aim of understanding the subject under study comprehensively. In particular, the viability of the existing ethnic conflict theories in Afghanistan has also been examined.

Chapter three titled "**Society, State and Polity in Afghanistan**" have dwelt upon Afghan society, process of state formation and different phases of Afghan politics. This chapter has also dealt with the current political situation in Afghanistan.

The chapter titled **"Conflict In Afghanistan"**, which is the fourth chapter of the book, has discussed in detail about the outbreak of conflict in the aftermath of the 1978 coup. Beginning with the discussion on the 1978 coup the chapter goes on to deal with the Russian invasion, role of the Mujahideens, the withdrawal of the Red Army, the subsequent rise of Taliban. The chapter in the end deals with current security scenario in Afghanistan.

In chapter five titled **"External Conditioning of the Conflict"** the role of neighbouring countries as well as the distant powers in conditioning the conflict in Afghanistan has been discussed. Different phases of foreign intervention in Afghanistan have been looked into. The impact of these interventions have been analysed in detail.

The sixth and the final chapter titled **"Conclusion"** apart from producing the findings of this book has made some recommendations for the conflict resolution in Afghanistan.

This book has attempted to bring out various factors responsible for the growth of ethnic conflict and its repercussions on the State structure in Afghanistan. To that end, one may find that the theory of ethnic conflict and theory of structuration has been examined in a broader framework to apply in the case of Afghanistan so as to understand the whole scenario of Afghan society and state during the period of this research study and its aftermath.

The conclusions that can be drawn here indicate that today most of the nations, across the world, are engaged in one conflict or the other, though a large number of these conflicts are ethnic in nature. A multi-ethnic nation, Afghanistan, which has plunged into an ethnic conflict in the beginning of 1990s has since been looking for a resolution to become a peaceful society and state without having any prejudices whatsoever. While dealing with different aspects of ethnic conflicts in South Asia in general and Afghanistan in particular, this research study has discovered that the whole South Asian region has for long faced a complex ethnic conflict. Whereas some of these conflicts have subsided with the passage of time there are many which still have the potential to destabilise the whole region. The conflict in Afghanistan is one of them. The partial survey of available literature has established the fact that despite having innumerable pioneering work in the field, dearth of substantive work continues to exist.

After studying ethnic conflict in theoretical perspective several findings have been made. First, it has been reaffirmed that the complexity involved with the term 'ethnicity' has not been resolved in totality. The various attempts to reach to a definite definition, consequently, have also failed. Secondly, after surveying various theories and approaches of ethnicity, it has been found that no single theory is complete in itself and a combination of various theories can only help us understand better the phenomenon of ethnic assertions. In turn, no universally accepted theory of ethnicity has been propounded. Moreover, scholars have failed to bring forward a universally accepted theory of ethnic conflict which can be made applicable to all ethnic conflicts. Consequently, these theories fail to tell us when an ethnic conflict will break out in one particular region. This proves that ethnic conflict is a complex phenomenon.

The analysis of the state, society and polity in Afghanistan has emphasised the fact that the fragmented society of Afghanistan has always remained an obstacle in the formation of a strong united nation state. The country has witnessed interregnum quite often than not. However, for the first time in Afghanistan's checkered political history there has been a transfer of power which is truly democratic following the recent presidential elections. As the new government is a truly multi-ethnic government as Dr Mohammad Ashraf Ghani Ahmadzai belongs to the dominant Pashtun group, while the Chief Executive Dr Abdullah Abdullah is a Tajik, it now seems Afghanistan at last is on the path of formation of a democratic State in which the polity will be truly representative of all the sections of the society. Nevertheless, there is a long way to go for the conflict resolution.

The research findings point to the understanding that the conflict that has engulfed Afghanistan has its root in the developments that took place during the later years of President Mohammad Daud Khan. The deteriorating ties between Daud and the USSR resulted in a Soviet backed coup in 1978. The Coup changed the dynamics of Afghan polity and subsequently Afghanistan plunged into a conflict with compounding complexities. Ethnic conflicts in Afghanistan, which were not so prominent during the Soviet occupation of the country, are entirely different from the conflicts in other country in the region. Notably, while most of the other conflicts have either subsided, the conflict in Afghanistan continues to endanger the peace in the region. All attempts to conflict resolution seem to have failed as Afghanistan continues to be in turmoil. Evidently, while the rest of the world has focused its attention towards bloodbath in the Arab World, where the Islamic State of Syria and al Sham (ISIS), now rechristened as Islamic State, has created havoc, Afghanistan is plunging deeper into chaos.

Indeed, external forces have played a big role in the emergence of conflict in Afghanistan. They have, in fact, got the opportunity to do so as Afghanistan for most part of its existence has lacked unity among its people. All these interventions - political and military - have an adverse impact on the conflict in Afghanistan. While the first great game involving Afghanistan drew Afghanistan in a war which was not all in its own creation, the second great game pushed the country in the prolonged conflict. The landing of the foreign troops in the aftermath of the 9/11 attacks complicated the situation further as the policy was not well implemented. In the meantime, the continuous inflow of foreign *jihadis* (religious warriors) multiplies the problem further.

America's 'drawdown' is taking place at a time when a troubled Afghanistan has been tainted by large-scale corruption (the country ranked 174th out of 176 in the 2012 Corruption Perceptions Index), and capacities for governance remain deeply suspect. Though apprehensions of an abrupt collapse, comparable to events in the aftermath of the Soviet withdrawal in 1989, have receded, the uncertainties of the situation are monumental. Worse, the future of Afghanistan remains as intimately tied to global peace and stability as has been its recent past. If the Western powers leave chaos behind in this unfortunate country, it is likely to follow them home in their baggage trains.

As already emphasised, this study brings into sharp focus some key points which concerned with the period beyond 2001. Post-2001 period is significant in the sense that any study on ethnic conflict and state structure in Afghanistan would remain incomplete unless it is examined in the context of current scenario so as to reach a conclusion for the possible solution of the conflict. As it is, the research findings suggest that after the ouster of the Taliban from power in 2001, the ethnic conflict that had pushed the Afghan nation at the brink of structural collapse took the form of Islamist terrorism. The situation though was not alarming in early years. Regrettably, however, the Taliban with the help of people at the helm of affairs in Islamabad regrouped. In fact, Islamabad took the advantage of the fact that the international community became less focused on Afghanistan after the collapse of Taliban regime. Islamist militancy picked up. Taliban was on surge. Perturbed by the resurgence of Taliban, the US President Barack Obama in December 2009 called for surge in Forces strength. In fact, the new AfPak policy of Obama backfired. His call for surge in Forces along with the assertion that troops withdrawal will begin emboldened the spirits of Taliban. The Taliban felt that they have succeeded in defeating the foreign forces and now they have the chance to 'strengthen' their hold. They upped their ante.

The situation in Afghanistan highlights the fact that thousands of people are being killed on a yearly basis in terrorism-related violence that is going unabated. The numbers clearly suggest that Afghanistan is currently under the hold of Islamist terrorism. The Taliban have returned and now controls large swathe of Afghan territory. Indeed, varying media sources estimate that the Taliban now dominates an estimated 40 to 60 per cent of Afghanistan. Despite this harsh reality, the foreign troops began their stipulated withdrawal. From the peak of 132,457 troops on July 26, 2011, the number came down to mere 41,124 as on September 3, 2014. Moreover, almost the entire foreign contingent is in non-combat role now. Despite Afghan National Defence and Security Forces (ANDSF) demonstrating their capabilities in a number of successful operations, tremendous vulnerabilities are increasingly visible. It has failed to stem the spread of the Taliban.

Meanwhile, ending months of uncertainty, a day after the formation of the National Unity Government, on September 30, 2014, Afghanistan signed two separate security pacts with the US and the North Atlantic Treaty Organisation (NATO). The pacts which will allow the US and the NATO Forces to continue training and advising the ANDSF, as well as to continue assisting the ANDSF in counterterrorism operations, were eagerly awaited by the world community which was worried over the negative repercussions of premature withdrawal of troops.

Interestingly, the agreement nowhere mentions about the strength of US Forces that will remain within Afghanistan after December 31, 2014, when the process of withdrawal will be completed. It is, however, assumed that around 10,000 US troops will remain stationed. Notably, US President Barack Obama, on May 27, 2014, had announced, "Today, I want to be clear about how the United States is prepared to advance those missions. At the beginning of 2015, we will have approximately 9,800 U.S. service members in different parts of the country, together with our NATO allies and other partners. By the end of 2015, we will have reduced that presence by roughly half, and we will have consolidated our troops in Kabul and on Bagram Airfield. One year later, by the end of 2016, our military will draw down to a normal embassy presence in Kabul, with a security assistance component, just as we've done in Iraq".

Meanwhile, on the same day, September 30, 2014, Afghanistan signed an agreement with the NATO. The agreement, called Status of Forces Agreement (SOFA), again did not mention the number of NATO personnel that will remain in Afghanistan after December 31, 2014. However, as per various media reports, around 2000 NATO troops will remain stationed. It means the number of foreign troops operating in Afghanistan will come down to around 12,000 from the current 41,000, mostly in non-combat role. Consequently, it remains a huge challenge for the much depleted Foreign Forces to assist the ANDSF to take on the Taliban.

It is in this context that what is important to address the biggest concern for peace in Afghanistan is - Pakistan's nefarious design in Afghanistan. The US need to realise the Pakistani game. It is pertinent to mention here that the man who was responsible for the 9/11 attacks, al Qaeda founder Osama bin Laden was found and killed not in the rugged terrains of Afghanistan, where he was believed to have taken shelter, but deep inside Pakistan.

In his final address to Afghanistan's Parliament on March 15, 2014, former President Hamid Karzai declared, in an obvious reference to Pakistan, that the US could bring peace to Afghanistan if it went after terrorist sanctuaries and countries that supported terrorism. Also, on several occasions in the past the US officials have acknowledged that Pakistan is engaged in destabilising role. Major General Stephen Townsend, who commands US and NATO Forces in eastern Afghanistan, noted, "Until the Pakistanis do something about the safe havens, that's going to be a problem. (Terrorists) can recruit and train and equip and prepare to launch in Pakistan."

It seems the BSA has taken note of that. As per Annexure A of the agreement, "Agreed Facilities and Areas", include Kabul, Bagram, Mazar-e-Sharif, Herat, Kandahar, Shorab

(Helmand), Gardez, Jalalabad, and Shindand. Notably, most of these areas are close to Pakistani territory. Also, the BSA has brought this aspect of Afghan problem within its ambit under the head External Aggression (Article 6),

"On a regular basis, the Parties shall consult on potential political, diplomatic, military, and economic measures that could form part of an appropriate response in the event of such external aggression or the threat of external aggression against Afghanistan. Consultations shall seek to develop a list of political, diplomatic, military, and economic measures".

The BSA alone, however, cannot ensure peace in Afghanistan given the extent of Pakistani involvement.

On the other hand, the US feels that it needs Pakistan's help to exit from the land-locked Afghanistan at any cost. In return, it is trying to give some legitimacy to Pakistan's Taliban proxies – the 'Pakiban' as some commentators now describe them – in Kabul, via their recognition in Doha. Kabul did make an indirect reference to Pakistan's role in the context of the Doha office controversy, noting, 'the latest developments show that foreign hands are behind the Taliban's Qatar office'. The US, however, publicly acknowledged, on June 21, 2013, the 'constructive role' played by Pakistan in bringing Taliban and the US administration closer to reconciliation. The US Ambassador to Pakistan Richard Olson stated that 'We are working closely with Pakistan. Pakistan played a constructive role in the opening of Taliban office in Doha. This is a big step and we greatly appreciate Pakistan's support'.

Over the long term, the US seeks an assurance from the Taliban too that its Forces will not attack convoys carrying equipment and weapons of US Forces who are preparing to leave Afghanistan. The present US initiatives are driven, overwhelmingly, by fears of a chaotic flight of its Forces in the last phases of the drawdown, under focused attack by the Taliban. In its moment of desperation Washington has, once again, fallen back on its unreliable 'principal ally', Pakistan, restoring the prime supporter of the Taliban and of terrorism in Afghanistan to a central role at the most sensitive phase of the 'transition'. Though there are arguments that 'the Taliban is changing', as claimed by Masoom Stanikzai, head of the Afghan Government's High Peace Council secretariat, it is useful to recall that the Malim Shah Wali, the head of the High Peace Council in the southern Province of Helmand, was killed by the Taliban as recently as on May 1, 2013. The US faith in Pakistan and a 'peaceful' Taliban is wishful thinking, and will only plunge Afghanistan, and the wider South Asian region, into a deeper and lasting chaos.

Unless the Taliban's safe sanctuaries and infrastructure of support in Pakistan are dismantled, Pakistan-backed Islamist extremists will continue to wreak havoc in Afghanistan. Similarly, the political stability is the need of the hour. The lack of political sagacity on the part of the new National Unity Government will prove more disastrous for the socio-economic condition of the country.

Significantly, according to the United Nations World Food Programme (WFP), food insecurity in Afghanistan increased from 29 per cent in 2007 to 33 per cent in 2012, with 20 per cent of the population "severely food-insecure". "The situation in Afghanistan will become more challenging as international troops withdraw, aid levels decline and elections take place. The resulting insecurity could impede humanitarian access to 8.8 million food-insecure and undernourished people, a third of the population", WFP said. On January 15, 2014 Afghanistan's Ministry of Finance signed a USD 50 million grant agreement with the World Bank for a project that provides technical and financial support to thousands of the country's poorest households to help lift them out of extreme poverty by 2018.

What we find during this research is that Afghanistan is the largest producer and cultivator of opium in the world, accounting for 74 per cent of the global opium production in 2012. Launched by former President Karzai in 2007, the Good Performers Initiative, which is supported by the US, has been rewarding provinces which show progress in their eradication efforts with USD 1 million for development projects annually. Until last year, 17 of Afghanistan's 34 provinces were each awarded USD 1 million for being poppy-free. However, by the end of 2013, two northern provinces - Balkh and Faryab - lost their poppy-free status, according to a joint report by the United Nations Office on Drugs and Crime and the Government of Afghanistan, released in November 2013. In the failed state index for 2014, Afghanistan stands at seventh out of 178 countries. Similarly, according to Corruption Perception Index, 2013, Afghanistan is at eighth position out of 177 countries and territories.

To sum up, ethnic conflict is not a new phenomenon as it is considered to be as old as the mankind. Ethnic conflict has leapt onto centre stage due to the structural changes brought about by the end of the Cold War and colonialism. These structural changes have promoted ethnic conflict. The colonial powers and the independent states succeeding them declared that each and every person had an "ethnic identity" that determined his or her place within the colony or the post-colonial system. Since ethnic conflict is a complex phenomenon, there is no single approach that will work to its resolution. In fact, it is a case-by-case story. In the case of Afghanistan, ethnic conflicts, which were not so prominent during the Soviet occupation of the country, are now entirely different from the conflicts in other country. There have been cultural and external factors that had prompted the ethnic divisions in Afghanistan.

One may agree that the State plays an important role in resolving ethnic conflict. From time to time, the international system reorders itself normally in the aftermath of a major conflict. Recent events indicate that a new ordering principle is required. A state facing ethnic conflict (or for that matter any conflict) needs to be structured and for that a definite way has to be adopted. Afghanistan is a country in which nationalism is a sentiment expressed only in the face of great external pressures. On the individual level, an Afghan is torn between the one direction enforced by his society and the other by his faith. Islam, though the most prominent example of a common identity, has served as a weak foundation for national unity and has presented certain moral contradictions to the individual. One might argue that these circumstances have had the greatest impact on the contemporary history of Afghanistan.

During the period of this research it is hard to find any clear-cut resolution to the Afghan conflict, though recent political developments in Afghanistan, particularly after the election, points to a positive future scenario. However, we must not forget that even in the absence of foreign threat, the country is riddled with inner division and conflict. Any plan of action, therefore, must work from the inside out; meaning we must first solicit a change in the Afghan identity before we can expect any change in the behaviour that it creates. Only a strong nation-state will be able to create any sense of national identity. The world community must make every effort to help Afghanistan create such an entity. Hope for Afghanistan lies in its unification, and hence through changes in identity and loyalty, its people can hopefully experience some period of peace after so much conflict. Today, Afghanistan is at the cross road. If the world community fails to address the issues concerning Afghanistan in an appropriate manner there is every likelihood of Taliban's or its proxies returning to power in Kabul. If it happens, the country might plunge into another round of ethnic conflict.

This book is based on my doctoral thesis.

Chapter - 1

Introduction

The world is passing through a phase of conflicts. Most of the nations, across the globe, are engaged in one conflict or the other. Notably, a large number of these conflicts are ethnic in nature. South Asia, one of the least developed regions, and home to multiple ethnic groups, is also engulfed by such conflicts. One of the South Countries, also the part of Central Asia, Afghanistan, since its inception, has witnessed several conflicts. However, the multi-ethnic nation plunged into an ethnic conflict in the beginning of 1990s and has since been looking for a resolution. In fact, it was in 1989 after the withdrawal of erstwhile Union of Soviet Socialist Republics (USSR), also known as Soviet Union, forces from Afghanistan that Afghanistan witnessed a period of unrest and ethnic conflict leading to a protracted civil war. This resulted in the collapse of the entire state structure. Although the Soviet backed government led by President Mohammad Najibullah tried to restore peace and order in the country his efforts were defeated by the warring factions of different ethnic groups who wanted to establish their supremacy. Several rebel groups formed a governing coalition, called the Islamic Council of Mujahideen and elected Burhanuddin Rabbani as the interim President of Afghanistan in 1992. But the Rabbani government's failure to checkmate the growth of ethnic groups further aggravated the situation. The Taliban, a group of Pashtuns preaching radical Islam, ousted the Rabbani government in 1996. During the reign of the Taliban, the Pashtun and non-Pashtun divide gave a fillip to ethnic conflict leading to the failure of state structure.

The end of the Cold War and the subsequent demise of the Soviet Union created a New World order. The state of Afghanistan was at a critical juncture. Its neighbouring states like Pakistan and Iran took advantage of it and made sincere efforts to influence the Afghan situation according to their own needs. However, neither the big powers like the United States (US) and Russia nor the world organisations like the United Nations (UN) had shown keen interest in Afghanistan. It was the September 11, 2011, also known as 9/11, incident that drew the attention of the world community towards Afghanistan. The Taliban misrule, ethnic strife, Islamic fundamentalism and terrorist infrastructure in Afghanistan compelled the world leaders, policy-makers and security analysts to describe it as a "failed state". The world community gave importance to state structuration and reconstruction in Afghanistan after the downfall of Taliban.

Ethnic Conflict in South Asia

The region comprises of eight countries. These include Afghanistan, Bangladesh, Bhutan, India, Maldives, Nepal, Pakistan, and Sri Lanka.

Societies in all these countries except Maldives are multi-structure. Ethnic identities are formed in each country on the basis of caste, language, religion, race and region. There are majority and minority groups in each country. These ethnic groups have cross-country affiliations because of historic-political and geo-economic inter-linkages in the region. It has indeed made ethnic cauldron of South Asia quite complex (Upreti, 2001).

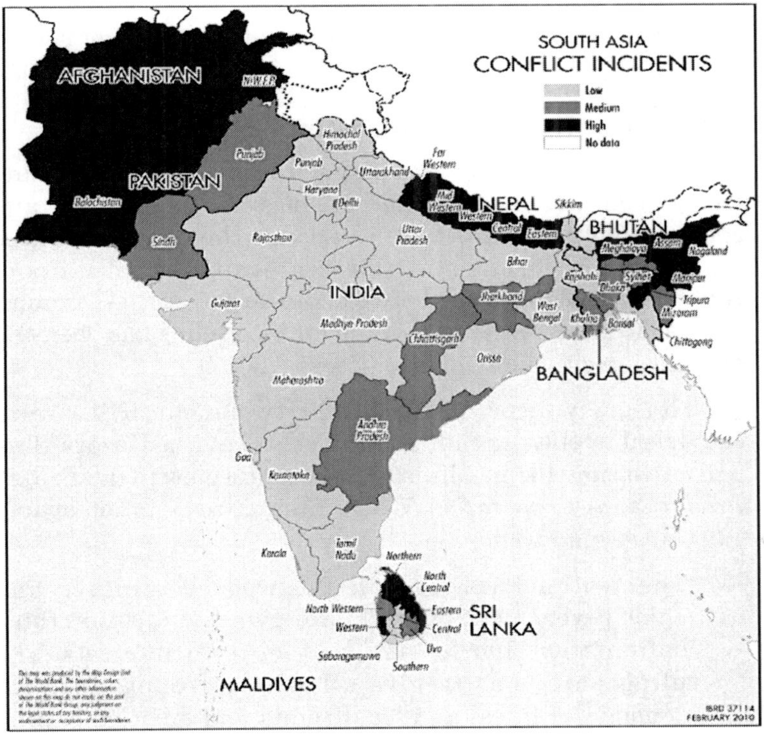

Source: VOX, CEPR's Policy Portal,
http://www.voxeu.org/sites/default/files/image/ghani%20fig%202(1).jpg

Figure 1.1. Conflict Incidents in South Asia.

The "domestic conflicts" in the region is entrenched in its tumultuous and fragmentary progression of "state-and nation-building" (Muni, 2013).

There are several factors which lead to a conflict. While some conflicts arise out of the "role of global powers", there are conflicts which emerge out of the disorder in the "internal political" situation. There are conflicts which result out of the disruptive acts of "non-state" actors (Muni, 2013). Moreover, a single conflict in itself can have all these facts. The ethnic conflict in Afghanistan is an appropriate example of such a conflict.

Ethnic Conflict in Afghanistan

Afghanistan was an area plagued with chronic unrest and violent conflicts. Due to the lack of a strong nation state, conflicts have arisen between various ethnic groups. These ethnic groups form the highly segregated social units of Afghanistan. The conflict between the largest of these groups, the Pashtuns, and the remaining ethnic groups has been one of great ferocity and violence (Reeves, 2007).

The grievances of the minority nationalities were expressed openly by Sultan Ali Keshtmand, a Hazara-Shia and a two-time Prime Minister. In an interview to the *British Broadcasting Corporation* (BBC), after his resignation in July 1991 Keshtmand said,

> "The Watan Party is still Pushtoon dominated and senior government officials are trying to stir up ethnic confrontation and tension for their own interests. The ruling party has to give all ethnic groups their fill economic, political and legal rights and must go beyond tokenism. The only way to bring a lasting solution to the conflict in Afghanistan is through a confederation of ethnic based administration, perhaps on the Swiss model" (Yunas, 1997).

After the withdrawal of forces belonging to the Soviet Union from Afghanistan in 1989, Afghanistan witnessed a period of unrest and ethnic conflict leading to a protracted civil war. This resulted in the collapse of the entire state structure. The Soviet backed government led by President Mohammad Najibullah tried to restore peace and order in the country. But his efforts were defeated by the warring factions of different ethnic groups who wanted to establish their supremacy. Several rebel groups formed a governing coalition, called the Islamic Council of Mujahideen and elected Burhanuddin Rabbani as the Interim President of Afghanistan in 1992. But the Rabbani government's failure to checkmate the growth of ethnic groups further aggravated the situation. The Taliban, a group of Pashtuns preaching radical Islam, ousted the Rabbani government in 1996. During the reign of the Taliban (1996-2001), the Pashtun and non-Pashtun divide gave a fillip to ethnic conflict leading to the failure of state structure.

Meanwhile, a New World Order came into existence as the Cold War ended. The Soviet Union had disintegrated. The state of Afghanistan was at a critical juncture. Her neighbouring states like Pakistan and Iran took advantage of it and made sincere efforts to influence the Afghan situation according to their own needs. However, neither the big powers like the US and the new nation Russia nor the world organisations like the UN had shown keen interest in Afghanistan. The 9/11 attacks, drew the attention of the world community towards Afghanistan. The Taliban misrule, ethnic strife, Islamic fundamentalism and terrorist infrastructure in Afghanistan compelled the world leaders, policy makers and security analysts to describe it as a "failed state". The world community gave importance to state structuration and reconstruction in Afghanistan after the downfall of Taliban.

However, all such attempts seem to have failed as Afghanistan continues to be in turmoil presently. While the rest of the world has focused its attention towards bloodbath in the Arab World, where the Islamic State of Syria and al Sham (ISIS), now rechristened as Islamic State, has created havoc, Afghanistan is plunging deeper into chaos (Singh, 2014).[1]

Ethnic Conflict in Bangladesh

Bangladesh is neither a multi-ethnic, nor a multi-cultural, multi-lingual and multi-religious country. The 166 million population comprises of 98 per cent Bengalis (CIA World Factbook, 2014). Unsurprisingly, the problem of ethnicity is not that a big issue in the country. Nevertheless, ethnic conflict does exist, more so in the area known as Chittagong Hill Tracts (CHT).

The violence in the region is endemic since 1978. It was at that point of time that the Bangladesh Government had decided to "inhabit Bengali speaking people" in the CHT completely disregarding the views of the indigenous people (Roy, 2010). Several hundreds of people have been killed. More number of them have been forced to leave their houses. Property worth millions has been destroyed in the violence which is the outcome of this discord.

The *Government of United Kingdom* in its *Foreign Travel Advice (Bangladesh)* describes the situation in the region: Security in the Chittagong Hill Tracts continues to be a cause for concern... There are regular reports of violence and other criminal activities, particularly in the more remote areas.

According to local media reports, in July 2013 alone, at least eight "indigenous leaders" were killed in such violence (IRNA, 2013).

Ethnic Conflict in Bhutan

Bhutan is a multi-ethnic, multi-cultural, multi-lingual and multi-religious country. Bhutans' officially recognised population of about 1733,643, has two broad categories: the original inhabitants termed as the Drukpas (of the north), and the Lhotshampas (of the south). The Drukpas comprises of the three ethnic groups - Ngalongs, Sarchops and Khengs. The Lhotshampas are immigrants of Nepali origin. The Drukpas form 50 per cent of the population, followed by ethnic Nepalese 35 per cent and indigenous or migrant tribes 15 per cent (CIA World Factbook, 2014).

Ethnic conflict in Bhutan constitutes between the Ngalong-dominated State and the Lhotshampas. The Ngalongs are basically Tibetan origin people, who migrated into Bhutan in the ninth and tenth centuries. They follow the Drukpa Kagyuppa sect of Mahayana Buddhism and speak Dzongkha - the national language of Bhutan (Muni, 2013).

New social forces that stood for entered into a protracted struggle with the traditional forces represented by religious orthodoxy. This triggered off a political crisis in 1964 when the *Lonchem* (Prime Minister) Jigmie Palden Dorji, who symbolised the spirit of modernisation, was assassinated. The assassination was followed by a *coup d'etat* against the king by a group of dissident officials. These two incidents and the resistance offered by the traditionalists compelled King Jigme Dorji Wangchuck to enter into an alliance with them. The formation of this alliance on the one hand stifled the process of modernisation and on the other excluded the ethnic groups other than Ngalongs from the arena of politics. In the process, the Bhutanese state became an Ngalong-dominated mono-ethnic one (Khan, 2009).

Not surprisingly, profound umbrage developed among the ethnic Nepalese by the 1990s as the Buddhists who were in majority denied "political representation" to the Nepalese. The resultant violent environment forced a large scale displacement among the Nepalese who escaped to refugees encampments in Nepal (BBC, 2014). As it has happened in several cases in the past these refugee camps became breeding ground for rebellious forces. The prominent among those include: The Bhutan Communist Party (Marxist-Leninist-Maoist), the Bhutan Tiger Force and the United Revolutionary Front of Bhutan. These groups threatened Bhutan's security for some time.

According to the *South Asia Terrorism Portal* (SATP), which has the largest database on conflict in South Asia, the country recorded a total of eight civilian fatalities between 2004 and 2008 in violence perpetrated by these groups. There have been no recorded fatalities in such incidents thereafter. However, as noted South Asia Counter Terrorism Expert Ajai Sahni points out "the issue of the Ngolops (Bhutanese refugees of Nepali origin), who had been pushed back into Nepal, remained substantially unresolved" (Sahni, 2014).

While growing international pressure has forced Bhutan to accept the idea of repatriation of some refugees, non-Bhutanese and Bhutanese with criminal and subversive records will certainly be excluded, accounting for a sizeable and potentially volatile chunk of the refugee population. Bhutan also fears that the repatriated groups may be 'infected' by the Nepalese Maoists.

Indeed, the Bhutanese Home Secretary, Dasho Penden Wangchuk, stated on September 23, 2006,

> "It is a confirmed fact that there is today a growing nexus between Maoists and the people in the camps in eastern Nepal...We also have information confirming radical elements from the camps in Nepal having received armed training from the Maoists" (Kuensel, 2006).

Yet, the Government of Bhutan needs to understand that the southern Bhutan problem is a political one which has to be tackled accordingly.

Ethnic Conflict in India

India assumes central place in South Asian state system. A symbol of unity in diversity, India, the second most populated country after China, with the current population standing at 1.2 billion (CIA World Factbook, 2014), is home to several religious, caste and ethnic groups.

Though the country is plagued by various types of conflict, ethnicity-based insurgencies are endemic in India's north-east. The region includes Arunachal Pradesh, Assam, Manipur, Meghalaya, Mizoram, Nagaland, and Tripura. The SATP has recorded a total of 20,722 deaths (including 9993 civilians) in ethnic violence in this region since 1992.

When the violence was at its peak, multiple insurgent/ terror groups operated in the region. The prominent among those included United Liberation Front of Asom (ULFA), National Democratic Front of Bodoland (NDFB), United National Liberation Front (UNLF), People's Liberation Army

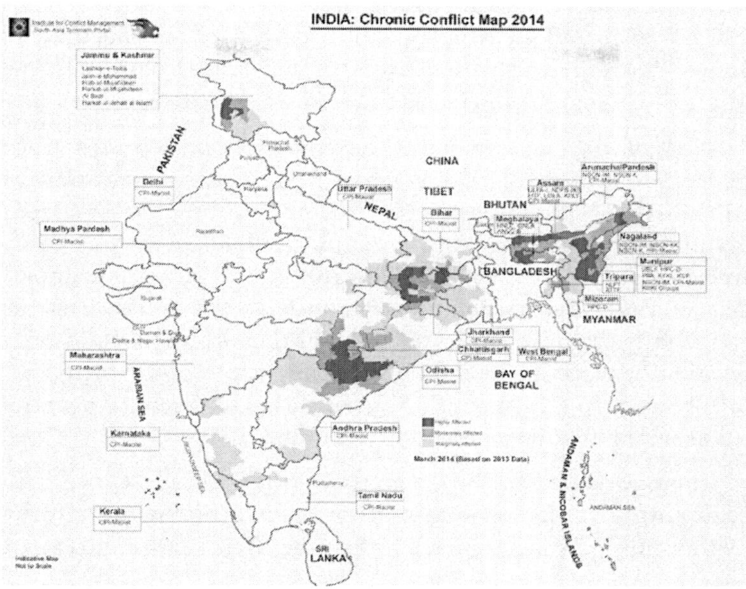

Source: India: Chronic Conflict Map 2014, South Asia Terrorism Portal http://www.satp.org/satporgtp/countries/india/database/conflictmapindia.htm

Figure 1.2. Chronic Conflict in India, 2014.

(PLA), Achik National Volunteer Council (ANVC), Hynniewtrep National Liberation Council (HNLC), National Socialist Council of Nagaland-Isak-Muivah (NSCN-IM), National Socialist Council of Nagaland-Khaplang (NSCN-K), National Liberation Front of Tripura (NLFT), All Tripura Tiger Force (ATTF), Hmar People's Convention- Democracy (HPC-D).

As per the *Union Ministry of Home Affairs* (MHA), *government of India*, several of these groups have either surrendered and are in talks with the government both at the Centre and in the respective States. However, violence has come down considerably. The States of Mizoram, Tripura and Arunachal have more or less restored peace. Nevertheless, splintered or breakaway factions of these groups continue to operate in rest of the States, like Assam, Manipur, Meghalaya and Nagaland. According to the MHA's list of banned terror groups, out of 36 such groups, 11 operate in the northeast alone. Therefore, despite registering some respite from violence the region continues to be in a state of turbulence.

Most of the scholars are of the view that while redrawing the region's administrative map the issue of prevailing multiplicity of ethnic, cultural, religious and linguistic groups was not addressed properly and that has led to an insecure environment in the region. For instance Hangmi argues, "One of the major problem areas is that the North-east is territorially organised in such a manner that ethnic and cultural specificities were ignored during the process of delineation of state boundaries in the 1950s, giving rise to discontentment and assertion of one's identity" (Hangmi, 2013).

Corroborating the argument, Sahni stresses that "the redrawing of political maps after India's partition" in an abysmal manner is at the core of the conflict (Sahni, 2012).

Ethnic Conflict in Nepal

Like most of the South Asian Countries, Nepal also is a multi-ethnic, multi-cultural, multi-lingual and multi-religious country. According to the *CIA World Factbook, 2014* report, the 30 million population of Nepal is divided into 125 caste/ethnic groups. The prominent among those include, Chhettri 16.6 per cent, Brahman-Hill 12.2 per cent, Magar 7.1 per cent, Tharu 6.6 per cent, Tamang 5.8 per cent, Newar 5 per cent.

While the Maoist movement which led to civil war in Nepal begun in 1996 when Pushpa Kamal Dahal *alias* Comrade Prachanda led Communist Party of Nepal-Maoist (CPN-M), declared "People's War" in Nepal "by attacking police stations in the Rukum and Rolpa Districts in north-western Nepal" (Nepal Backgrounder, SATP), the issue of ethnicity had plagued the nation much before. Not surprisingly, while the armed rebellion by the Maoists came to an end with the signing of the agreement between the seven-party alliance government and the Communist Party of Nepal-Maoist at midnight on

November 7, 2006, the ethnic imbroglio continues to haunt the nation.

According to the *Nepal Conflict Report* released by the *United Nations High Commissioner for Human Rights*, the country witnessed "at least 13,000 people dead and 1,300 missing between 1996 and 2006". Moreover, the SATP which commenced compiling data on insurgency-related fatalities in Nepal since March 2000 recorded a total of 13,000 deaths, including 1192 civilians and 2255 Security Force Personnel, till November 2006.

Issue of identity "based on ethnicity, caste, language, religion and regional identity" has been the hallmark of almost all the movements in Nepal (Lawoti and Hangen, 2012).

The outfits operating in the Terai region of Nepal, which is the epicenter of ethnic conflict, "targeted both the state and the Maoists, polarising Terai citizens along ethnic issues" that many believe have not been addressed adequately (Mandal, 2011).

Nepal is divided into three regions: the Himalayan, Hilly and Terai regions. It is the Terai region which faces ethnic problem. The Terai is located along Nepal's the Southern border with India, and the name is used interchangeably with Madhesh, and its people are described as Madheshis or Madheshyas. twenty-three per cent of Nepal's total land area of 147,181 square kilometers and approximately 30 to 40 per cent of the population falls within this region. Out of the country's 75 Districts, 20 are located in the Terai, including, from east to west, Jhapa, Morang, Sunsari, Saptari, Siraha, Dhanusha, Mahottari, Sarlahi, Rautahat, Bara, Parsa, Chitwan, Nawalparasi, Rupandehi, Kapilvastu, Dang, Banke, Bardiya, Kalaiya and Kanchanpur.

Indeed, violence in the Terai escalated after the Government of Nepal signed a peace agreement with the Communist Party of Nepal-Maoist in 2006 to end a 10 years civil war. Groups targeting both the State and the Maoists, polarising citizens along ethnic issues largely unaddressed during the civil war, pushed the region towards mayhem.

Analysis of the data indicates that the Terai, which hosts most of the 125 caste/ethnic groups reported in Nepal's 2011 Census Report, is the hot bed of violence, even though some groups, such as the Bhagat Singh led Janatantrik Terai Mukti Morcha, have handed over their weapons to the government following the signing of the four-point deal in August; as well as the Samyukta Janatantrik Tarai Mukti Morcha's decision to come over ground. Though they represent a large portion of the Nepali population, the Madheshis lack proportional representation in government and have long experienced discrimination by Kathmandu as well as the dominant ethnic groups in Nepal. The failure to address these issues is claimed as the justification of violence by the armed Madheshi groups.

Meanwhile, while most of the contentious issues related to the drafting of the new constitution have been sorted out, the issue of ethnic-based federalism continues to be a big obstacle. Significantly, the issue of federalism has divided the nation. The biggest concern is whether to go for single identity based federalism or multiple identity based federalism. While the Unified Communist Party of Nepal-Maoist (UCPN-M) and its ally United Democratic Madheshi Front (UDMF), are in favour of single-ethnicity based federalism, the ruling alliance of Nepali Congress (NC) and Communist Party of Nepal-Unified Marxist Leninist (CPN-UML) have rejected their option.

CPN-UML Vice Chairman Bam Dev Gautam thus noted that NC and CPN-UML proposed (the) multi-ethnic federal model. Here, the NC diluted its earlier stand of opposing ethnicity based federalism in toto, arguing that state restructuring should be based on economic and administrative viability and on geography. The number, size, naming and mapping of the federal States has also evaded unanimity. While the UCPN and its ally UDMF insist that the 14-state model or 10-state model suggested by the Parliamentary Committee on State Restructuring and the State Restructuring

Commission, respectively, should be adopted, the NC and CPN-UML proposed a 11 and 12 States model, respectively. Moreover, the Madheshi leaders reiterated their strong opposition to create multiple provinces in the Terai, and stuck to their long standing demand for a "single autonomous Madhesh province".[2]

Ethnic conflict in Pakistan

According to the *CIA World Factbook*, the 196 million population in the country is primarily divided into four major ethnic groups. These include 44.68 per cent Punjabis, followed

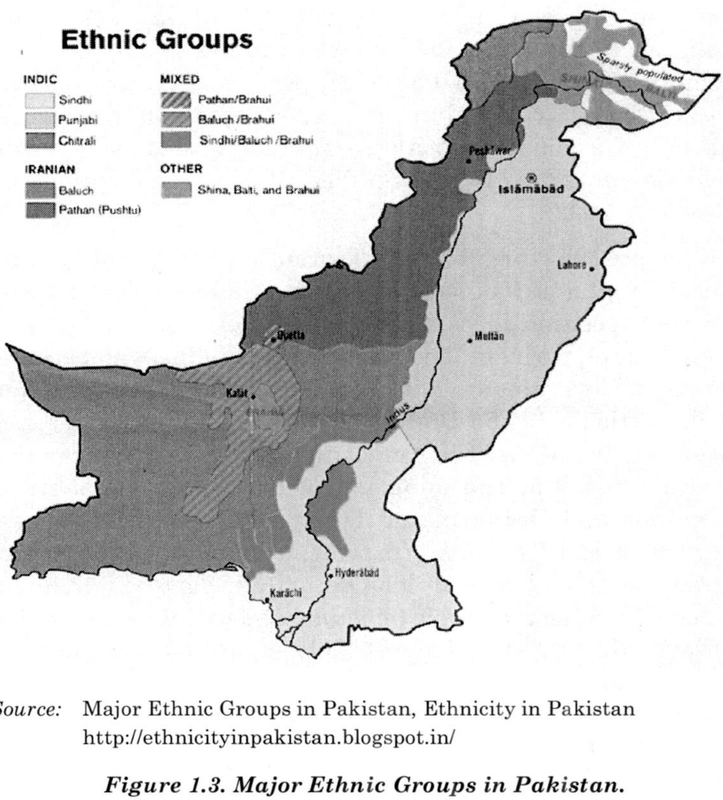

Source: Major Ethnic Groups in Pakistan, Ethnicity in Pakistan http://ethnicityinpakistan.blogspot.in/

Figure 1.3. Major Ethnic Groups in Pakistan.

by Pashtun (15.42 per cent), Sindhi (14.1 per cent), Sariaki (8.38 per cent), Muhajirs (7.57 per cent), Balochi (3.57 per cent), and others 6.28 per cent.

Since 1947, there has been constant tension in all these ethnic groups as the authorities at the helm continue to remain bias towards Punjabi people. Pakistan which has already experienced one division faces the possibility of further disintegration due to constant ethnic tension, particularly in Sindh and Balochistan. The ethnic conflict in Pakistan which started from the Sindh region has now engulfed the whole country. According to scholars the States, repressive attitude towards the *Muhajirs*[3] led to the emergence of conflict in Sindh. As they were in the lead role of freedom struggle for Pakistan, after independence they found themselves in preeminent position in Pakistani politics (Prakash, 2011). Arguing further Minahan writes, "They [mohajirs] were naturally in a dominant position as they opposed to the regional identities professed by the Sindhis, Pathans and Punjabis" (Minahan, 2002).

Despite this, the Mohajir's position of preeminence in the political realm of Pakistan eroded gradually. The Punjabis' took their position as the most dominant class at the Federal level. At the provincial level it was the Sindhis who became dominant. Governments both at the Federal and the Provincial level, particularly the Provincial Government took several anti-Mohajir actions. The "imposition of the Sindhi language in education and the adoption of the Sindh (Teaching, Promotion and Use of Sindhi Language) Act in 1972"[4] was one of such acts. The *mohajirs* protested violently. They were opposed by the others. For long period, the clashes remained confined between the people (*mohajirs* and non-*mohajirs*) only. However, the State acted repressively against *mohajirs* during one particular incident of 1985. Violence spiraled thereafter. Clashes between Police and *mohajirs* became frequent. Mohajir Quami Movement (MQM) leader Altaf Hussain became a prominent figure in this ethnic strife thereafter.

Pashtun groups in Pakistan want to separate NWFP [North West Frontier Province, now known as Khyber Pakhtunkhwa] from Pakistan and become part of Afghanistan. Bloch insurgency aims at independence of Balochistan Province from Pakistan (Bukhari, 2013).

The problem is more acute in Balochistan. Significantly, the World Report 2014 released by *Human Rights Watch* (HRW) notes,

> "The human rights crisis in the mineral-rich province continues unabated. As in previous years, 2013 saw enforced disappearances and killings of suspected Baloch militants and opposition activists by the military, intelligence agencies, and the paramilitary Frontier Corps. Baloch nationalists and other militant groups stepped up attacks on non-Baloch civilians. The military continued to resist government reconciliation efforts and attempts to locate ethnic Baloch who had been subject to 'disappearances'. Successive Pakistani governments have appeared powerless to rein in abuses by the military and both sectarian and nationalist militant groups. As a result, many members of the Hazara community and non-Baloch ethnic minorities under attack by militants fled the province or country, while Baloch nationalists have continued to allege serious abuses by the military" (HRW, 2014 report).

Islamabad continues with its old policy of pitting one communal or ethnic group against the other, with the government facilitating the mass settlement of 'outsiders' in South Balochistan through a range of policies such as allocation of land holdings to migrants from other Provinces, including preferential allocation to ex-Army personnel, in order to change the demography of the region and weaken Baloch separatism. This has created a sense of siege among Balochis in the region, precipitating ethnic violence.

Meanwhile, Saraiki nationalists want a separate province for the people bound together in linguistic ties and living in central areas of the country Constant demand of their rights and its constant denial results in frustration that ultimately pushes an ethnic group to the path of rebellion.

The *Country of Origin Information Report* (Pakistan) by the *United Kingdom Border Agency* the Pakistan Home Department in its February 14, 2012, report had observed that "target killings still continue in most parts of the country and major reasons behind these are sectarian, demographic changes, easy access to illicit weapons, mistrust among ethnic groups, family enimities and business rivalries".

Ethnic Conflict in Sri Lanka

The population of Sri Lanka (21 million) may be divided into four main groups. These primarily include Sinhalese (73.8 per cent), Sri Lankan Moors (7.2 per cent), Indian Tamil (4.6 per cent), Sri Lankan Tamil (3.9 per cent), other 0.5 per cent, unspecified 10 per cent (CIA World Factbook, 2014).

The most dominant of these, the Sinhalese who speak in Sinhalese follow Buddhism. The ethnic group which is next in terms of population is the Tamil speaking Sri Lankan Moors who are descendants of Arab and Indian Muslims. Believers in Hinduism who peak Tamil, the Indian Tamils are another of the significant ethnic groups of Sri Lanka. Likewise, the Sri Lankan Tamils are "predominantly Hindu and speak Tamil" (Ghosh, 1995).

At the core of the conflict are the Sinhalese and the Tamils. When the Tamils who live in the northeastern region felt that their rights are being curtailed and they are being marginalised by the dominant Sinhalese, they formed several organisations to fight against the 'injustice'.

Later, many of these outfits merged and formed Tamil United Front (TUF) in 1972. Subsequently, in 1976, the TUF rechristened itself as Tamil United Liberation Front (TULF). Several other groups were also in existence. With the passage of time, all such groups lost their steam.

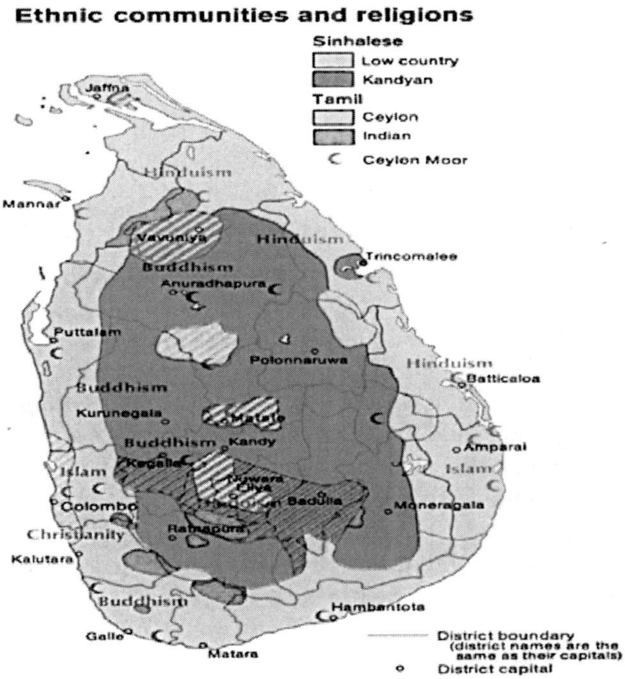

Source: Sri Lanka: Tamil Tigers on Verge of Extinction?, Bellum, A Project of the Stanford Review http://bellum.stanfordreview.org/? p. 436.

Figure 1.4. Ethnic Communities in Sri Lanka.

However, Velupillai Prabhakaran's Liberation Tigers of Tamil Eelam (LTTE) formed in 1976 and which at one point of time was "the only terrorist group which once possessed its own 'Military' – Tigers (infantry), Sea Tigers (sea wing) and Air Tigers (Air Wing), in the world, began its armed campaign in Sri Lanka for a separate Tamil homeland in 1983"[5] continued with its disruptive act. It fought four wars with the Sri Lankan Government which accounted for at least 100,000 deaths.

Finally, the Sri Lankan President Mahinda Rajapakse took the credit of ending the Eelam in May 2009. He was so determined that he had told Roland Buerk of the BBC in an interview published on February 21, 2007, that "I don't want to pass this problem on to the next generation" (BBC, 2007).

President Rajapakse appears to have made clear declarations in seeking an inclusive solution to the country's ethnic crisis. While announcing the LTTE's defeat in Parliament on May 19, he declared,

> "This is our country. This is our mother land. We should live in this country as children of one mother. No differences of race, caste and religion should prevail here. The war against the LTTE is not a war against Tamil people. Our aim was to liberate our Tamil people from the clutches of the LTTE. Protecting the Tamil speaking people of this country is my responsibility. That is my duty. All the people of this country should live in safety without fear and suspicion. All should live with equal rights. Those who live abroad and supported the terrorists with funds, if they have any love for their own people, should not help terrorism again. I call on all who have left our motherland due to terrorism, especially the Tamil people, to return. We shall resettle all those who have been freed from being hostages in very welcome surroundings. Similarly, it is necessary that the political solutions they need should be brought to closer to them faster than any country or government in the world would bring. I seek the support of all political parties for that solution. Time is now raising a new challenge before us. It is the challenge of building the motherland" (Sri Lanka President Website).

However, any solution to the ethnic conflict in Sri Lanka remains as elusive as ever. Colombo on the other hand feels it has a mandate which cannot be challenged. While commenting on the Tamil National Alliance (TNA) winning a majority of local authorities' elections in the Tamil areas and the consequent necessity of devolution of powers, Basil Rajapakse, Senior Advisor to the President, stressed that the President has a bigger mandate not to give those powers to anyone who are not accepted by a larger majority in the country. Claiming that that the 'political solution talk is simply irrelevant, Defence Secretary Gotabhaya Rajapakse, observed, that "we don't have to talk about solution and various things any longer, because we have ended this terrorism in Sri Lanka. We have a Constitution. If there is further amendment needed then government can speak with the elected representatives. Now we have representation from these areas" (Singh, 2011).

Ethnic Conflict in Maldives

Maldives, the least populated South Asian country, with its population standing at 393,595 comprises of three ethnic groups - South Indians, Sinhalese, Arabs (CIA World Factbok, 2014). Though there is very little evidence of ethnic strife, religious extremism is spreading alarmingly. "The growth of Islamic radicalism in Maldives can be traced to the beginning of the last decade. Like in Bangladesh, Pakistani *jihadi* (religious warriors) groups like Lashkar-e-Taiba (LeT) have been making inroads to indoctrinate young men in a conservative Sunni society, that has been bogged down with slow growth, political authoritarianism (until 2008, certainly) and mushrooming *madrassas* (seminaries) with Arab funds" (Bagchi, 2012).

Indeed, the region has for long faced complex ethnic conflict. While some of these conflicts have subsided with the passage of time there are many which still have the potential to destabilise the whole region. The conflict in Afghanistan is one of them. It is in this background that a few available literatures on the main subject under research have been surveyed in the section below.

Notes

1. Ethnic conflict in Afghanistan has been discussed in detail in Chapter 4.
2. This portion of analysis on conflict in Terai has been taken from this researcher's own publications. See, Ajit Kumar Singh, "Terai Simmering", SAIR, Vol. 9, No. 39, April 4, 2011; Ajit Kumar Singh,

"Chronic Uncertainty", SAIR, Vol. 11, No. 23, December 10, 2012; Ajit Kumar Singh, "So Near, Yet So Far", Vol. 10, No. 47, May 28, 2012.

3. According to the Immigration and Refugee Board of Canada Government, Muhajirs [also spelled Mohajirs or Mojahirs] refers to the descendants of people who migrated to Pakistan following India's partition in1947. Muhajir can be translated as "immigrant" or "refugee".
4. Pakistan Backgrounder, South Asia Terrorism Portal, http://www.satp.org/satporgtp/countries/pakistan/backgrounders/index.html.
5. Liberation Tigers of Tamil Eelam (LTTE), South Asia Terrorism Portal, http://www.satp.org/satporgtp/countries/shrilanka/terroristoutfits/LTTE.HTM.

Chapter - 2

Ethnic Conflict in Theoretical Perspective

In order to identify and subsequently address the conflicts arising out of ethnic division an attempt has been made in this chapter to understand the term 'ethnicity' as well as the theories dealing with it. In the process Concepts of Nationalism and Concept of State have also been dealt with apart from their relations with ethnicity. Moreover, various theories of Ethnicity as well as different aspects of ethnic conflict in theoretical perspective have been dwelt upon with the sole aim of understanding the subject under study comprehensively. In particular, the viability of the existing ethnic conflict theories in Afghanistan has also been examined.

Definition of Ethnicity

The timing of the origin of the term 'ethnicity' itself is contested. The term 'ethnicity' found expression in the liberal principles of self-determination at the Treaty of Versailles (1815 AD). "Its first usage is attributed to the American sociologist, David Riesman, in 1953" (Eriksen, 2002:4). Nevertheless, according to American sociologists Nathan Glazer and Daniel Moynihan, the term 'ethnicity' is relatively new. It was in 1972 that 'ethnicity' was first for the first used as a term in the Oxford English Dictionary. "The word 'ethnic', however, is much older" (Eriksen, 2002:4). "It is derived from the Greek *ethnos* (which itself emerged from the term *ethnikos*), which originally meant 'heathen' or 'pagan' (Williams, 1976). It slowly began to refer to racial characteristics from the middle of the fourteenth century. The progression continued until the middle of the nineteenth century. Further on, the term coincided with tribe, group, nation or people (Eriksen, 2002: 4).

Not surprisingly, there have been several attempts to define the term 'ethnicity'. However, the political scientists have failed to evolve one single definition. Hutchinson and Smith thus write: The term 'ethnicity' is new; the sense of kinship, group solidarity, and common culture to which it refers is as old as the historical record. Ethnic communities have been present in every period and continent and have played an important role in all societies" (Hutchinson and Smith, 1996). Indicating that the term is new, it has been said that 'ethnicity' is a product of modern politics (Bukhari and Ahmad, 2013).

"According to Webster's Third New International Dictionary 'ethnicity' ordinarily refers to certain quality or affiliation based on hereditary as well as cultural considerations" (Regmi, 2003). James Kellas defines ethnicity as a "state of being ethnic, or belonging to an ethnic group" (Kellas, 1991).

For American sociologist Milton Gordon, the feeling of "people hood" shaped by "common race, religion, national origin, history or a combination of all of these" define the term 'ethnicity' (Reed, 1986: 10).

According to Eriksen, "Ethnicity is an aspect of social relationship between agents who consider themselves distinctive from members of other groups with whom they have a minimum or regular interaction. It can thus also be defined social identity (based on a contrast vis-à-vis others) characterised by metaphoric or fictive kinship. Ethnicity refers both to aspects of gain and loss in interaction, and to aspects of meaning in the creation of identity. In this way it has a political, organisational aspect as well as symbolic one. Ethnic groups tend to have myths of common origin and they nearly always have ideologies encouraging endogamy" (Eriksen, 1993).

Ethnic Group

It is through ethnicity that people associate themselves with a larger group. According to Laurence Steinberg, "Membership of an ethnic group tends to be associated with and ideologies of shared cultural heritage, ancestry, history, homeland, language or dialect, and with symbolic systems such as Ethnic group religion, mythology and ritual, cuisine, dressing style, physical appearance, etc" (Steinberg, 2014).

The cultural, linguistic, ritualistic, behavioural and religious characteristics of an ethnic group remain more or less the same or in other terms these are the uniqueness of an ethnic group.

John Hutchinson and Anthony D. Smith opine that ethnic groups or 'ethnies', as they call them, have these six traits: "A common proper name to identify and express the essence of community; a myth of common ancestry that includes the idea of a common origin in time and place and that gives an ethnic group a sense of imaginary kinship; shared historical memories or shared memories of a common past or pasts, including heroes, events and their commemoration; one or more elements of a common culture, which normally include religion, customs or language; a link or attachment with the motherland; and a sense of solidarity on the part of some sections of the ethnic group" (Hutchinson and Smith, 1996).

According to Farley, "[An ethnic group is] a group of people who are generally recognised by themselves and the others as a distinct group, with such recognition based on social or cultural characteristics" (Zhu, 2007).

Similarly, Paul Brass defined ethnic groups in terms of distinct social and cultural category (Petersen, 2007). Theodorson and Theodorson defines an ethnic group as, "A group with a common cultural tradition, a sense of identity which exists as a sub-group of a larger society. The members of an ethnic group differ with regard to certain cultural characteristics from the other members of their society" (Theodorson and Theodorson, 1969).

Francis, however, pointed out that although every ethnic group has a distinctive culture, this distinctive culture or a common cultural pattern doesn't automatically constitute an ethnic group (Francis, 1998).

Shibutani and Kawn gave an authoritative definition which subsequently established the lines of enquiry into research on ethnicity. They observed, "An ethnic group consists of those who conceive of themselves as being alike by virtue of their Common ancestry, real or fictitious, and who are so regarded by others" (Shibutani and Kawn, 1965).

According to Guibernau and Rex, "Ethnic groups tend to have myths of common origin, and they nearly always have ideologies encouraging endogamy, which may nevertheless be of highly varying practical importance" (Guibernau and Rex, 2010).

Eriksen writes, "Since the 1960s, ethnic groups and ethnicity have become household words in Anglophone social anthropology" (Eriksen, 1993).

Obviously, scholars have failed to agree on one definition and consequently one theory for the term.

Meanwhile, according to the United Nations,

> "The specific ethnic and/or national groups of the population which are of interest in each country are dependent upon individual national circumstances. Some of the criteria by which ethnic groups are identified are ethnic nationality (i.e., country or area of origin, as distinct from citizenship or country of legal nationality), race, colour, language, religion, customs of dress or eating, tribe or various combinations of these characteristics. In

addition, some of the terms used, such as 'race', 'origin' or 'tribe', have a number of different connotations. The definitions and criteria applied by each country investigating ethnic characteristics of the population must, therefore, be determined carefully and with the involvement of or consultation with representatives of the groups which it desires to categorise. By the nature of this topic, these categories and their definitions will vary widely from country to country; therefore, no internationally accepted criteria are possible. Because of the difficulties of interpretation which may occur, it is important that, where such data are collected, the basic criteria used should be clearly explained so that the meaning of the classification will be readily apparent. It is also suggested that the primary classification consist of only a few broad categories, leaving open the possibility of a more detailed breakdown for important tribal or other groups where these are relevant" (UN Document)[1].

Types of Ethnic Group

Several scholars are of the opinion that the classification of types of ethnic groups depends largely on locus of group organisation, degree and nature of self-awareness in ethnic organisation, structural location in interethnic relations and the generational factor (Isajiw, 1993). Thus, an ethnic group can be divided into numerous types: primary and secondary ethnic groups, folk-community and nationality-community ethnic groups, dominant majority and subordinate minority ethnic groups, and immigrant or 'young' and established or 'old' ethnic groups" (Magocsi, 1999).

Primary and Secondary Ethnic Group

There is a distinct division even between Primary and Secondary Ethnic groups. Several authors have attempted to highlight this dissimilarity. The scholars are of the opinion that ethnic group which survive at the place of its origin is the Primary Ethnic Group. When an ethnic group changes its place of origin it takes form of a Secondary Ethnic Group. It has been found that while many primary ethnic groups have formed out of the secondary ethnic groups the vice versa have also happened (Isajiw, 1993).

Folk-Community and Nationality-Community Ethnic Group

As in the case of Primary and Secondary ethnic groups, there exist a division between the Folk-Community and Nationality-Community Ethnic Groups. According to Magocsi, a group of people having a peasantry background and whose social standing vary a little fall in the category of Folk-Community. On the other hand, there exists sharp division in the social status of people who are the members of Nationality-Community Ethnic Group (Magocsi, 1999). For Isajiw, members of the Nationality-Community Ethnic Group "are culturally highly self-aware". He is also of the same opinion about the members of the Folk-Community ethnic groups (Isajiw, 1993).

Dominant Majority and Subordinate Minority Ethnic Groups

Several opinions have been formed about the existing distinction between these two types of ethnic groups also. According to Magocsi, it is not the numerical strength but the power a group exercises which determines it status as majority or minority ethnic group. Notably, the society's primary foundation is decided by the culture of the ethnic group which is in dominant position. The group in minority lives with that reality (Magocsi, 1999).

Immigrant or 'Young' and Established or 'Old' Ethnic Groups

There is confusion among the scholars in defining these two types of ethnic groups. According to Isajiw, an ethnic group which constitutes of people who are "predominantly of the first - the immigrant - generation, and whose second generation is either small in size or young in age" is Immigrant or young ethnic group. On the other hand, an ethnic group which has "established in the larger society, i.e. they have at least a high proportion of adult second and adult third or consecutive generations" (Isajiw, 1993).

Evaluating Ethnicity

Several attempts using different approaches have been made in over last two decades to evaluate Ethnicity. Basically there are two main approaches to understand the ethnic phenomena.

Primordialist Approach

First, "the primordial approach to ethnic identities and ethnicity considers common descent as the more important factor, for primordial loyalties can be activated more easily than rational principles and organisations founded upon them" (Regmi, 2003). The term Primordialism was coined by Shils (1957) and further developed by Clifford Geertz (1963) who explained it as follows,

> "By primordial attachment is meant one that stems from the 'givens' - or, more precisely, as culture is inevitably involved in such matters, the assumed 'givens' - of social existence: immediate contiguity and kin connection mainly, but beyond them the givenness that stems from being born into a particular religious community, speaking a particular language, and following particular social practices. These congruities of blood, speech, custom and so on are seen to have an ineffable and at times overpowering coerciveness in an out of themselves" (Geertz, 1963).

The social psychological nature of the primordial perspective forms the basis for a generalised sense of group consciousness. Ethnicity becomes a powerful identity merging the individual with the group. It is important to note that the primordial approach doesn't conceptualise ethnicity in terms of immutable human characteristics.

Situational/ Subjective/Instrumental Approach

The second approach is Situational/Subjective/ Instrumental Approach. The "main emphasis is on the members' perception of being different from others and the implications of this for the groups' present status and predicament and to the understanding of contemporary realty, but they do not offer any final answers. They are often no more than grand exercises in the reconstruction of the past; the definition and redefinition of situations to explain the present; and strategies for achieving a desired future" (Regmi, 1995).

Ethnic Identity

Vermeulen and Govers (1997) argue that ethnic identity can be distinguished from other social identities. They view ethnic identity as an identity which can be distinguished from other social identities by a belief in a common origin, descent, history and culture. Though, they also acknowledge the difficulty in distinguishing an ethnic identity from other type of identities. The authors have proposed a way out of problem by viewing ethnicity as a variable, rather than in dichotomous terms.

According to Mukherjee and Ramaswamy, "The upsurge of regionalism and ethnonationalism the world over in recent decades and the continued assertion for effective political power at local levels not only in the third world, but also in the industrially advanced democracies have made it clear that, assumptions about modernisation and assimilation have been proved facile, even facetious" (Mukherjee and Ramaswamy, 1994-95).

As a social phenomenon, ethnicity has evolved from historical and socio- territorial specificities which vary from country to country, situation to situation. However, there are some common structural sources, which can be derived from the common underlying trends in different societies and which can be held responsible for the upsurge of ethnicity.

Accordingly, the ethnic phenomenon which includes issues such as, 'ethnic identity,' 'ethnic mobilisation'/'ethnic assertions,' and 'ethnic conflict,' has become the subject of much theoretical enquiry in social sciences under different disciplines in the last five decades (Kanbur, 2009).

Language, a common territory and religious beliefs may further contribute in varying degrees to ethnic identity (Bukhari and Ahmad, 2013).

According to Afkhami, "Ethnicity describes a collective identity and is based on the assumption that a collectivity has its roots in common ancestry, heritage, religion, culture, nationality, language and a territory. In the contemporary world everybody is assumed to have an ethnic identity" (Afkhami, 2012). Ethnicity is, thus, often linked with a fixed ethnic identity. However, it is being increasingly challenged because the idea of ethnically homogenous nation states. Ethnicity is also defined in terms of a social construct specific to a social and historical context. However, despite the contested definition of ethnicity, ethnic identities do have a "material foundation" and exist in modern societies as "social forces". "Ethnicity can explain inequalities in our societies and is therefore crucial to capture ethnic identities" (Afkhami, 2012).

Ethnicity and Nationalism

There is a strong relation between Ethnicity and Nationalism. According to Eriksen, "Like ethnic ideologies, nationalism stresses the cultural similarity of its adherents and by implication it draws boundaries vis-à-vis others, who thereby become outsiders" (Eriksen, 2002). "The distinction between the two may therefore appear to be one of degree, not one of kind - particularly since many political movements are commonly perceived as being both nationalist and ethnic in character" (Eriksen, 1991).

Ethnicity and State

As in case of Nationalism, there is a strong relation between Ethnicity and State. The mutual association linking the state and ethnicity is a genuine one. The complexity crops up when the state finds that it is incapable to enforce its "ethnicised codes" on a set of people which has obtained a separate ethnic realisation adequate to create its own cultural imitation. Under such situation, which arises more often than not, conciliation is agreed where state decides to share the state with other groups. In some cases, when such ethnic groups reside in area which is contiguous, they even demand for secession. In that case it becomes difficult for the state to fulfill the demand and the conflict prolongs (Schopflin, 2000).

Ethnic Conflict

The complexity involved with conflicts related to ethnicity makes it difficult to evolve one single approach towards it. For this reason each individual conflict should be studies in its own respective context. An ethnic conflict can arise out of several reasons. The demands from people involved in such conflicts vary from seeking greater autonomy to the extent of fighting for secession from their respective States.

Evidently, not all ethnic movements result in violent conflicts. However, most of them develop into a conflict.

Aspects of Ethnic Conflict

The societies, which are ethnically diverse, carry various degrees of conflict. Though they are distinct, they have some commonalities. For instance, Cohen says,

> "Men may and do certainly joke about or ridicule the strange and bizarre customs of men from other ethnic groups, because these customs are different from their own. But they do not fight over such differences alone. When men do fight across ethnic lines it is nearly always the case that they fight over some fundamental issues

concerning the distribution and exercise of power, whether economic, political, or both" (Cohen, 1974).

According to Sommer, "A rather controversial view on the causes of ethnic conflict is the *clash of civilisations* thesis as brought forth by Samuel Huntington. The author states that the mere presence of ethnic diversity can cause conflict due to insurmountable differences in values between the different cultures of the world" (Sommer, 2009).

Ethnic Conflict and Diversity

According to the *Human Development Report* (HDR) 2004, "The world's nearly 200 countries contain some 5,000 ethnic groups. Two-thirds have at least one substantial minority - an ethnic or religious group that makes up at least 10 per cent of the population" (HDR, 2004). In his monumental work, *Ethnic Structure and Cultural Diversity around the World: A Cross-National Data Set on Ethnic Groups*, James D. Fearon identifies, "820 ethnic and 'ethnoreligious' groups in 160 countries" (Fearon, 2003).

Considering the sample as a whole, he finds that "the 'average country' has about five ethnic groups that are larger than 1 per cent of the population, with half of the world's countries having between three and six such groups (this is the inter quartile range). Tanzania, with 23 groups, tops the list, while Papua New Guinea, with zero, is the somewhat anomalous minimum" (Fearon, 2003). What he discovers is that about 70 per cent of the countries all over the world have an ethnic group that makes an absolute majority of the population. This is despite the fact that "the average population share of such groups is only 65 per cent and only 18 per cent of countries are homogenous in the weak sense of having a group that claims 9 out of 10 residents. The average size of the second largest group, or largest ethnic minority, is surprisingly large, at 17 per cent" (Fearon 2003). Fearon has summarised his study in the following table:

Table 2.1. Descriptive Statistics on Ethnic Groups larger than 1 per cent of country population (by Region)

	World	*West*	*NA/ME*	*LA/CA*	*Asia*	*EE/FSU*	*SSA*
Countries	160	21	19	23	23	31	43
Percentage Total		.13	.12	.14	.14	.19	.27
Groups Percentage Total	819	6	70	81	109	141	350
Groups/country	5.11	3.24	3.68	3.52	4.74	4.55	8.14
Standard Deviation	3.54	2.41	2.14	.93	3.62	2.5	5.04
Max. groups	23c	9	9	6	13	12	23
Min. groups	0d	1	1	2	0	1	2
Avg. pop. Share of largest group	.65	.85	.68	.69	.72	.73	.42
Av. pop. Share of second largest group	.17	.09	.19	.21	.16	.15	.2
% countries with a group ≥50%	.72	1.00	.84	.78	.82	.90	.30
% countries with a group ≥90%	.18	.57	.21	.17	.18	.13	0

Notes: (a) Includes Australia, New Zealand and Japan. (b) Includes Sudan. (c) Tanzania. (d) Papua New Guinea is coded as having no ethnic groups that meet the 1% threshold. [NA: North America, ME: Middle East, LA: Latin America, CA: Central Asia, EE/FSU: Eastern Europe/ Former Soviet Union (EE/FSU), SSA: Sub-Saharan Africa].

Intensity of Ethnic Conflict World Wide

Several scholars have tried to assess the intensity of ethnic conflict worldwide. While some have tried to argue that the intensity of such conflicts are on decline using the quantitative data provided by several agencies involved in compiling of data, others are of the opinion that the intensity is on rise.

Dunaway in his work, *Ethnic Conflict in the Modern World-System: The Dialectics of Counter-Hegemonic Resistance in an Age of Transition*, have used the empirical data provided by the *Minorities at Risk Project* (2002) to analyse the intensity of ethnic conflict. He forms the opinion that it will be erroneous to conclude that "there is a dramatic increase in ethnic conflict since the end of the Cold War". He, nevertheless, concedes that "ethnification and indigenism are inherent structural contradictions" of the contemporary world that will not weaken (Dunaway, 2003).

On the other hand, Wimmer and Cederman in their work, *Ethnic politics and armed conflict: A configurational analysis of a new global dataset* attempts to argue that among all the conflicts ethnic conflicts are more worrisome and numerically high.

Table 2.2. The Conflict Dataset: 1946-2005

<table>
<tr><td></td><td colspan="3">Ethnic Conflicts</td><td>Non-Ethnic Conflicts</td><td>Total Conflicts</td></tr>
<tr><td>Secessionist</td><td colspan="3">56</td><td>3</td><td>59</td></tr>
<tr><td>Non-Secessionist</td><td colspan="3">54</td><td>101</td><td>155</td></tr>
<tr><td>Total</td><td colspan="3">110</td><td>104</td><td>214</td></tr>
<tr><td rowspan="2"></td><td>20</td><td>64</td><td>26</td><td rowspan="2" colspan="2"></td></tr>
<tr><td>Fought in the name the groups in power</td><td>Fought in the name of powerless or discriminated groups</td><td>Fought in the name of groups with local autonomy</td></tr>
</table>

As is evident from the table, 110 of the 214 armed conflicts between 1946-2005, were ethnic in nature. More worryingly, 59 of these conflicts were of secessionist character (Wimmer and Cederman, 2005). It is a well known fact that secessionist conflicts are more deadly.

Currently, conflicts are raging in almost all parts of the world. Number of countries involved in wars stands at 62 (Wars in the World 2014) and most of these conflicts are ethnic in nature. Ethnic conflict is prevalent in the entire South Asian region, more prominently in Afghanistan[2] and Sri Lanka.

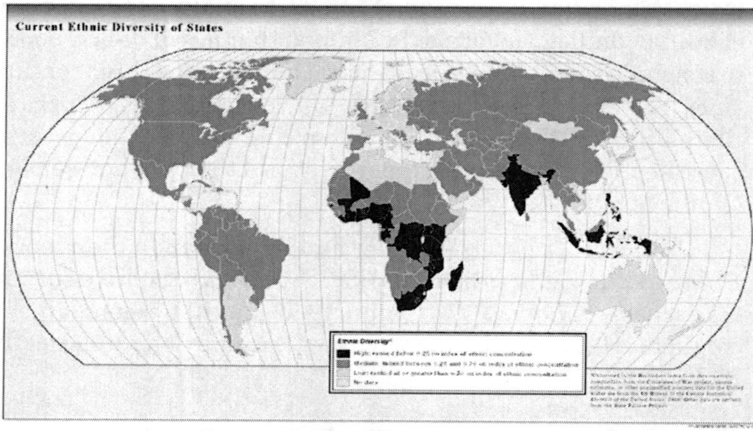

Source: Family Guardian, http://famguardian.org/subjects/Politics/Articles/GlobalTrends2015/753977.gif

Figure 2.1. Current Ethnic Diversity of States.

In an attempt to understand and subsequently address the conflicts arising out of ethnic division it is important to have an understanding of the theories of ethnic conflict propounded so far. The viability of the existing ethnic conflict theories in Afghanistan's present situation is also of importance.

Theorising 'Ethnicity'

There have been several attempts by scholars to theorize 'ethnicity'. However, there is not a single mutually agreed theory. It is not even expected given the fact that the term 'ethnicity' itself has several definitions. Nevertheless, some theories have been propounded and the prominent among those include the following:

Modernist Theory:

One of the better theories of ethnicity is the Modernist theory. According to Gurnam Singh, "Modernisation means the attainment of relatively higher levels of variables; such as education, per capita income, urbanisation, political participation, industrial employment, media participation, secularisation, gender equality etc" (Gurnam Singh, 1998). According to this school of thought, in the course of development, the ethnicity based identity will fade away. People will lose their local, parochial identities and loyalties in order to identify themselves with the larger economic and political unit, the nation, argues Karl Deutsch.

The contradictions of modernisation came to the fore with the passage of time and both the developed as well as developing countries witnessed the upsurge of mobilisation of people on ethnic basis. Modernisation theory provides an insight into ethnic assertions in present times. However, the predictions or projections made by the modernisation theorists have not come true as modernisation doesn't explain the ethnic occurrence in its entirety.

Consequently, it is desirable to search for economic and political rationalisations. It is a well known fact that all the developments in social sphere are defined by the politico-economic aspects. One such approach is the political-economy approach. This approach is generally considered to be either associated with or influenced by Marxism.

Marxist Theory

The protagonists of Marxism were more interested in the class struggle under capitalism than in the ethnic issues. The Marxist theory considered ethnic groups as an unnecessary distraction, if not inhibitors to economic and political progress. Marxism underscored the fundamental incompatibility between the appeal of ethnonationalism and the seemingly more powerful, persuasive and important command of class-based interests. Yet, Stack Jr. says that the history of ethnonationalism documents or proves the primacy of ethnic bonds (Stack, 1986).

The neo-Marxists however, recognise that ethnic groups are in a state of constant flux. Ethnic groups can't be solely responsible for ethnic conflicts; the contradictions of the wider society in which ethnic groups may or may not be significant actors should also be probed in. Smith argues that the emerging 'new orthodoxy' (neo-Marxists conflict theories) ultimately conceptualises ethnicity as a 'transitional phenomena' (Smith, 1981).

In addition to Marxists, a section of liberal scholars also believe in politico-economic explanation of ethnic assertion.

Politico-Economic Approach Theory

This theory has been interpreted differently by two different schools of thought - liberal and Marxist. The major point of contention between the two sides is over the issue of assigning importance on aspects of economic activity.

Relative Deprivation Theory

Ted Robert Gurr explains relative deprivation "as a gap between the expectations and perceived capabilities of person vis-à-vis his economic situation, political power, and social status in relation to others". This theory has immense importance in analysing ethnicity in a world where development is uneven.

Resource Competition Theory

The problem of ethnicity arises due to unequal distribution of resources, benefit and influence between different ethnic groups (Upreti, 2002). Glazer and Moynihan state, "The strategic efficacy of ethnicity as a basis, for asserting against government has its counterpart in the seeming case whereby government employs ethnic category as a basis for distributing its rewards" (Ahemed, 1996).

Resource competition model however has been criticised by Paul Brass on the basis that treating an ethnic group as just another type of interest group is an error. Brass, instead suggests the elite-competition theory (Narang, 1995).

Elite Competition Theory

Paul R. Braas is among the pioneers who have dealt with this theory. The scholars dealing with this theory are of the opinion that the competition among the elites of the society lead to ethnic conflict. In fact, the elite competition and the actions of "ethnic entrepreneurs" drive ethnic conflict. Elites manipulate ethnic identities in their quest for power. It is they who "construct" ethnic conflict (Brass, 1997).

Kruger, quoting Brass, states, "Ethnic self consciousness, ethnically-based demands, and ethnic conflict can occur only if there is some conflict either between indigenous and external elites and authorities or between indigenous elites" (Kruger, 1993).

Cultural Deprivation Theory

This theory is based on the assertion that many minority ethnic groups are fearful of losing their identity to the majoratrain culture. Consequently, such ethnic groups, if they feel they are segregated, rise against their respective states. Democratic set up of governance, however, provides them the leeway as it allows them to affirm their culture.

External Factors Theory

According to this theory, most of the conflicts which are ethnic in nature owe their sustenance to external destabilisers. It is noteworthy to mention that it is with the help of foreign powers that the groups involved in such activities get the access of arms and ammunition. Moreover, those powers provide them the financial aid needed for their sustenance. Yet, it is the internal factors which bring the conflict to the fore, only to be given thrust by the foreign powers. Afghanistan is a great example of this.

Realistic Group-Conflict Theory

One of the best known theories of inter-group conflict has been leveled as Realistic Group Conflict Theory. According to this position, inter-group "hostility arises because opposing groups are competing for scarce external resources and group action is instrumental in winning the zero-sum game". This theory is applicable to situation where one group is acting to deny another group, access to valued resources, and commandeering these resources for its own group members (Aronson and Wilson, 2009).

Rational Choice Theory

Situated far from primordialism is the rational choice approach adopted above all by Michael Hechter and Michael Banton. This theory reflects both, normative and structuralist explanation because both ignore the role of individual preferences. Hechter and Banton built models on the basis of individual pursuit of public goods. Ethnic organisations, the repository of information are joined by members of the group as long as the members are individually benefited (Hutchinson and Smith, 1996).

After surveying various theories and approaches of ethnicity, we find that no single theory is complete in itself and a combination of various theories can only help us understand better the phenomenon of ethnic assertions. However, broadly speaking that studies on ethnicity fall into two major categories: (i) primordialism and (ii) instrumentalism, and as Gurr (1993) states, "The first treats ethnic nationalism as a manifestation of persisting cultural identity based on a primordial sense of ethnic identity, the second regards ethnicity as an exercise in boundary maintenance (Wimmer, 2008).

Theories of Ethnic Conflict

There is no one single abstract theory of ethnic conflict. Several scholars have propounded different theories from time to time. While some of the propounded theories have emphasised on cultural aspect of the conflict, some others have stressed upon the biological aspect of the conflict. Indeed, most of them have failed to take into account the fact that ethnic conflicts vary in nature and it is unlikely that one theory will prove valid for all the conflicts.

Numerous schools of thought press forward contradictory theories of ethnic conflict with a range of "permutations and combinations". There are quite a lot of subjects on which they diverge, but the divergences can be abridged to "hard views versus soft views" of ethnic conflict, with 'hard' and 'soft' referring to the nature of group affiliations and the ends of conflict behaviour (Horowitz, 1998).

Suggesting the ideal theory of ethnic conflict, James D. Fearon and David D. Laiting, state, "A good theory of ethnic conflict should be able to explain why, despite the greater tensions, peaceful and cooperative [ethnic] relations are by far more typical outcome than is large scale violence" (Fearon and Laiting, 1996).

Some of the most prominent theories of ethnic conflict have been discussed below:

Indivisible Territory Theory

Indivisible Territory Theory was propounded by Monica Duffy Toft. Explaining the Theory she writes, "Territory is a *sine qua non* of the state and can be an irreducible component of ethnic identity. The control over territory may become a matter of survival and, consequently, an indivisible issue. When both sides in a conflict regard control over a disputed territory as indivisible, violence is likely" (Toft, 2003).

To develop this theory she has surveyed the Russian conflict with Chechens and Tatars as well as Georgia's conflict with Abkhaz and Ajars. According to her the two states - Russia and Georgia - interrelate with two constituent ethnic groups aggressively in quest of greater autonomy and control over their homelands. These conflicts provide an excellent "laboratory because they offer variation on both the independent and the dependent variables (for example, settlement patterns and violence due to ethnic conflict)" (Toft, 2003).

Security Dilemma Theory

Security Dilemma Theory, originally described by Robert Jervis, is also known as Offense Defense Theory. The two important variables in the theory are "the offence-defense balance – whether it is easier to take territory or to defend it, and; offense defense distinguishability – whether the forces that support offensive missions are different from those that support defensive missions". The fundamental forecasts relating to the "offence-defense balance are that as the advantage of offense increase, the security dilemma becomes more severe, arms races become more intense, and war becomes more likely" (Brown, 2004).

Explaining the theory, Monica Duffy Toft, states, one thing which is adequate to one state's protection will seem, and over and over again be, "offensive to its neighbours" as the neighbouring state aspire to remain "autonomous and secure". It is expected that those countries which will feel offended will respond by attempting to reinforce their own arrangements. States can set off theses response even if they have no "expansionist inclinations". "This is the security dilemma: what one does to enhance one's own security causes reactions that, in the end, can make one less secure" (Toft, 2003).

Security Dilemma Theory is one of the basic concepts of International Relations. It is a highly valued theory that has been used to explain multiple cases in world history. In this 'new world disorder', there is a growing concern that ethnic conflicts are so contagious that a conflict in one region can easily stimulate another elsewhere (Kuppevelt, 2012).

Not surprisingly, an attempt is now being made to realise the security threat and find out ways to manage it. Stephen Ryan states, "Multi-ethnic states are likely to continue to be a feature of politics both within and between sovereign states".

The Security Dilemma Theory "will be able to integrate many diverse understandings of ethnic conflict from different schools of International Relations theory" (Tang, 2011).

According to Security Dilemma Theory there are two major factors in accounting for the wave of contemporary ethnic conflicts. These include: The trend towards 'democratisation' in previously authoritarian countries has given more scope for ethnic minorities to freely assert their perceived rights; Increasing international concern for human rights, especially those of minorities—now tends to override more conventional concerns for sovereignty and non-interference in a country's internal affairs (Singh, 2002).

Several scholars have applied Security Dilemma Theory to address the issue of ethnic conflicts in both Serbia and Croatia. The theory has also been applied to explain the cause of conflict in Russia and Ukraine.

Ethnic Nepotism Theory

Ethnic Nepotism Theory was propounded by Tatu Vanhanen. Explaining Ethnic nepotism he writes,

> "Our behavioural predisposition to ethnic nepotism evolved in the struggle for existence because it was rational and useful. It is reasonable to assume that ethnic nepotism is equally shared by all human populations. Consequently, all human populations and ethnic groups have an approximately equal tendency to resort to ethnic nepotism in interest conflicts. It explains the otherwise strange fact that ethnic interest conflicts appear in so many countries where people belong to clearly different ethnic groups, and that ethnic interest conflicts have emerged within all cultural regions and at all levels of socioeconomic development. It would be difficult to imagine any cultural explanation of ethnic conflicts that could explain the appearance of these conflicts across all cultural boundaries" (Vanhanen, 1999).

His study based on three hypotheses examines ethnic conflict in 148 countries. For this purpose he has used several indices. One of the indices is the Index of Ethnic Heterogeneity (EH). Another is the Index of Ethnic Conflict (EC).

Table 2.3. Region-wise EH and EC Index

Area	*Countries*	*EH<11*	*EC<11*	*Diff*	*EH>10*	*EC>10*	*Diff*
Europe	38	11	10	-1	27	28	1
W. Hemisphere	24	7	8	1	17	16	-1
Asia/ Oceania	42	3	6	3	39	36	-3
Africa	44	3	4	1	41	40	-1
Totals	**148**	**24**	**28**		**124**	**120**	

Vanhanen's study to a greater degree established his forecast that any nation with an EH over 10 would experience noteworthy ethnic conflict. Indeed, 118 out of the 124 countries with an EH level higher than 10 witnessed major ethnic conflict. On the contrary only two countries, which recorded an EH of ten or less witnessed such conflicts.

Taking help of another index, used by him in an earlier study, the Index of Democratisation he argues that "ethnic nepotism leads to ethnic interest conflicts in all societies independently from their level of socioeconomic development or from the degree of democracy because all human populations share the same behavioural predisposition to ethnic nepotism" (Vanhanen, 1999).

The theory has been applied to understand the conflicts in India.

Social Identity Theory

It was first projected by Tajfel (1978, 1979) and afterward by Tajfel and Turner in 1979. This theory that endeavours to clarify "cognitions and behaviour with the help of group-processes" is social-psychological theory (Trepte, 2006).

It proposes that uneven allocation of resources lead to conflict when the subsidiary set of people discards its earlier acknowledged "negative self-image and with it the status quo", and move in the direction of the growth of a "positive group identity". "When social identity based on intergroup comparisons is unsatisfactory, individuals will either strive to leave the group for a better identity or make their own group more positively distinct, thus causing conflict" (Zartman, 1998).

Some scholars are of the view that this theory presents a "promising evolutionary theory of groups". "Social Identity research shows that people are highly prone to identifying themselves with groups. There is a tendency to conceptualize both ingroups and outgroups as more homogeneous than they really are" (Macdonald, 2001).

Donald Horowitz has applied the Social Identity Theory to explain ethnic conflicts in Africa, Asia, and the Caribbean.

Genetic Similarity Theory

Genetic Similarity Theory propounded by J. Philippe Rushton is an extension of W. D. Hamilton's theory of kin selection and Anthony D. Smith's theory of ethno-symbolism Rushton has applied this theory to "explain the lethality of the conflicts between Tutsis and Hutus in Rwanda, Hindus, Muslims and Sikhs in the Indian subcontinent, and Croats, Serbs, Bosnians and Albanians in the former Yugoslavia, or even the level of animosity between Blacks, Whites and Hispanics in the US" (Rushton, 2005). The theory goes past "kin recognition by proposing mechanisms that assess phenotypic similarity as a marker for genetic similarity" (Macdonald, 2001).

Power Transition Theory

It's another theory of ethnic conflict. A. F. K. Organski who established the theory in 1958 describes a hierarchical in which states are differentiated by their power resources

(Lekme, 2002). The theory at first published in *World Politics* (1958), Organski's text book, was propounded with objective to examine "the cyclic condition of wars, and how transition of power in terms of machtpolitik affects the occurrence of these wars (Goldstein, 2012). As Toft observes, "Power matters, and so shifts in power matter; but what matters most is how relevant actors perceive the consequences of shifts in power" (Kegley, 2012). After testing the theory in numerous countries, including Afghanistan, Sri Lanka, and Yugoslavia, Toft concludes that this theory is a "promising framework for understand civil war".

Symbolic Politics Theory

The Symbolic Politics Theory was propounded by Murray Edelman. The theory, in contrast to the restricted rationalist theory, provides added precise explanation of ethnic conflict. It holds responsible "both elite politics and the socialisation of competing identities" for the eruption of intense hostility. Symbolic theory's assumption, which builds on psychological human motivations over pure rational calculation, prevails across three core concerns within the study of ethnic conflict. According to Green this theory can be applied to comprehend ethnic politics much more appropriately (Green, 2012).

Consociatational Theory

The Consociatational Theory was formulated and developed by some of the world's leading political scientists – most notably Arend Lijphart. Other prominent contributory scholars include Hans Daalder, Luc Huyse, Gerhard Lehmbruch, and others. The "theory is an empirically grounded normative theory that – through promoting power sharing of a specific kind – promises a democratic solution to societies confronted by durable ethnic division and political conflict. Today it is generally accepted that consociationalism is 'the dominant model of managing ethnically divided societies'" (Taylor, 2009). The theory was applied to understand the conflict in Northern Ireland.

The Enemy System Theory

Developed as a model to elucidate the intricacy of "group behaviour", predominantly in reference to "antagonistic group relationships" the theory was proposed in the late 1980s by a group of psychiatrists and international relations practitioners. The theory is based on the assumption that "humans have a deep-rooted psychological need to dichotomise and to establish enemies and allies". Notably, this theory has been used extensively to examine "intractable conflict". For instance, the Cold War in the early 1990s prior to the disintegration of the Soviet Union, terrorism in Northern Ireland, have been studies using this theory (Cunningham, 1998).

Human Needs Theory

The theory based on the supposition that humans have essential desires that needs to be fulfilled in pursuit to preserve stable societies was developed in the 1970s and 1980s as a "generic or holistic theory of human behaviour" (Cunningham, 1998). Indeed, John Burton writes,

> "Now we know that there are fundamental universal values or human needs that must be met if societies are to be stable. That this is so thereby provides a non-ideological basis for the establishment of institutions and policies. Unless identity needs are met in multi-ethnic societies, unless in every social system there is distributive justice, a sense of control, and prospects for the pursuit of all other human societal developmental needs, instability and conflict are inevitable" (Burton, 1991).

To sum up, the complexity involved with the term 'ethnicity' has not been resolved in totality. The various attempts to reach to a definite definition, consequently, have also failed. In turn, no universally accepted theory of ethnicity has been propounded. Moreover, scholars have failed to bring forward a universally accepted theory of ethnic conflict which can be made applicable to all ethnic conflicts. Consequently these theories fail to tell us when an ethnic conflict will break out in one particular region.

This proves that Ethnic conflict is a complex phenomenon. Ethnic conflict is a case-by-case story. Ethnic conflicts in Afghanistan, which were not so prominent during the Soviet occupation of the country, are entirely different from the conflicts in other country.

Conflict Resolution

State plays an important role in resolving ethnic conflict. Some of the methods adopted by multiethnic states are:

I. Methods for Eliminating Differences in Culture and Identity

These policies all share the same general goal—either reduce the ethnic and cultural diversity in the state, or seek to overcome it by building a supra-ethnic identity based around the nation as delimited by state boundaries.

A. Genocide (Direct or indirect killing of an ethnic minority).
B. Forced Mass-Population Transfers (Ethnic cleansing).
C. Secession.
D. Assimilation.
E. Civic Integration.

II. Methods for Managing Differences in Culture and Identity

In contrast to the options above, these policies seek to accommodate ethnic minorities in the state. Goal is to maintain or even intensify ethnic, cultural and regional differences in the state, and hopefully create stability and cohesion.

A. Federalism/Regional Autonomy.
B. Power-Sharing.
C. Multiculturalism/Cultural Pluralism.
D. Affirmative Action.

Indeed, the global structure reorders itself at regular interval more so in the aftermath of a major conflict. It is done along with an attempt to evolve and impose innovative set of regulations to safeguard states from the causes of the conflict. "Because 'great power war' has been the proximate cause of past restructuring, great power war has been the ordering the principle for international (and national) rules and institutions" (Hayes and Barnett, 2002). Events like 9/11 fall in the category of 'major conflict'.

According to Waslekar (1996), the process of conflict resolution passes through many phases. These include:

- Sensing the problem
- Defining the problem
- Judging the present situation (unilateral action on resolution)
- Developing commitment to resolution
- Selecting the process of resolution
    - Direct negotiation
    - Facilitated negotiation
    - Third Party meditation
- Preparing for the resolution exercise
- Arranging the resolution
    - Stating the problem
    - Developing options
    - Reaching Agreement
- Implementing the agreement

Once the conflict is resolved, or during the course of resolving the conflict, the process of State structuration should begin so that there is no return of violence.

State Structuration

A state facing ethnic conflict (or for that matter any conflict) needs to be structured and for that a definite way has to be adopted. To understand the process of state structuration, this theory has to be looked into. Indeed, the theory aspires to elucidate "social practices across space and time by viewing action and social structure as inextricably linked by their interdependency". For him, "human agency and social structure each act as an enabling condition of the other" and therefore "social subjects and social systems are continually reproducing and reforming each other" (Miller, 2003).

Anthony Giddens has suggested this theory to understand the process of constitution of society. Since state represents a large number of societies, this theory can also be applied in the process of state structuration. When we talk of state structuration we could take different groups (here in this case ethnic groups) as human agency and state as a social structure.

In this process of state structuration external powers also start playing role, as in case of Afghanistan, on the pretext of their responsibility to bail out the 'failed state' from crisis.

Notes

1. Concepts and Definitions, Ethno cultural characteristics United Nations Statistics Division, http://unstats.un.org/unsd/demographic/sconcerns/popchar/popcharmethods.htm
2. Afghanistan became part of SAARC in 2007.

Chapter - 3

Society, State and Polity in Afghanistan

While the recorded history of Afghanistan dates back its existence to the period around 500 BC when the region was part of the Achaemenid Empire, there are evidences of urbanisation the region that began much earlier, anytime between 3000 BC and 2000 BC. According to some scholars, in the pre-history period, the people speaking Indo-European languages may have entered the Iranian plateau that includes most of today's Iran and Afghanistan, at about the middle of the second millennium BC. The languages used by them still stay alive in the form of Pashto and Dari. Similarly, the culture of Arabs, who invaded Afghanistan in later period, have a continuing imprint as Zoroastrianism, Macedonianism and Buddhism had disappeared long ago (IBPUSA, 2013).

Yet, there is another point of view which suggests that Afghanistan's history traverses over five thousand years and the Afghan people have made significant contributions to the emergence of many Central Asian empires (The Embassy of Afghanistan Washington, D.C. Website). Being the ancient centres of culture and civilisation Afghanistan has had varied cultural influences of from these outsiders such as Rome, Greece, Arabia, Iran, Central Asia, India, and China. In addition, great conquerors such as Chinggis Khan and

Timurlane who swept through Afghanistan during the thirteenth and fourteenth century, brought with them the desire to establish kingdoms there. They are known to have established cultural and scholarly communities in Afghanistan, particularly, during the Timurid dynasty, when poetry, architecture and miniature painting reached their highest point. As such, over a period of time, cultural diversity has left both the positive as well as negative impact on the Afghan society which, in turn, has also influenced the formation of state and hence the polity in Afghanistan.

Afghan Society

The society in Afghanistan is full of diversity. Mazhar writes, "Like most of the post-colonial states, throughout the history, Afghanistan has remained a 'multi-ethnic state', having more than 'one ethnic group, speaks too many languages, and has multiple and multi-layered identities'" (Mazhar, 2012). Unsurprisingly, there is clear social fragmentation in Afghan society. However, the semblance of unity in deeply divided multi-ethnic society of Afghanistan is visible because of the Islamic identity of the State. Martin Ewans thus writes,

> "Insofar as there has been a sense of unity in the country [Afghanistan], it is Islam, with its concept of community and universality (*umma*), which has superimposed itself on the ethnic diversity and provided the main focus of loyalty. Both in Pashtoon society and more widely throughout the nation, therefore much influence is exercised by *imams* or *mullahs*, who may not only have ritual, juridical, medical and educational roles at village and tribal level, but may also exercise an inspirational leadership, particularly when a confrontation with 'infidels', or a cultural threat to the faith is in question. This influence is all the greater in a society which is largely illiterate, traditional by instinct and mostly ignorant of modern ways of life" (Ewans, 2002).

Ethnic Composition

Afghan people are divided into multiple ethnic groups. While Pashtun forms the largest ethnic group, they are followed by Tajik, Hazara, Uzbek and others. Interestingly, 14 ethnic groups find representation in the national anthem of the country.

Table 3.1: Ethnic Groups in Afghanistan

Ethnic Groups	*Percentage of Population*
Pashtun	42
Tajik	27
Hazara	9
Uzbek	9
Aimaq	4
Turkmen	3
Baloch	2
Others	4

Source: Afghanistan, South Asia, The World Factbook, Library, Central Intelligence Agency https://www.cia.gov/library/publications/the-world-factbook/geos/af.html

Meanwhile, an attempt is being made to assess the accurate size and composition of the diverse ethnic groups living across the country. As of July 2014, according to the *CIA World Factbook* 2014 report, total population of Afghanistan is 31.82 million. An additional three million people have taken refuge in other countries, with 2.7 million of these residing in neighbouring Pakistan and Iran[1].

The Hindu Kush mountain range efficiently splits the country into northern and southern halves that also approximately overlap with divergent ethno-cultural zones (Asthana and Nirmal, 2009). The following map shows the geographical spread of the ethnic groups:

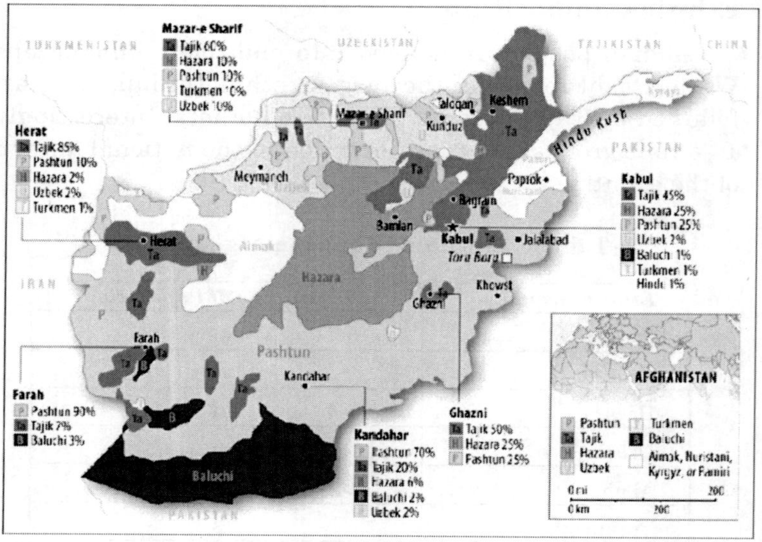

Source: Afghanistan: Politics, Elections, and Government Performance, Congressional Research Service. http://fas.org/sgp/crs/row/RS21922.pdf

Figure 3.1. Map of Afghan Ethnicities.

The Map 1 clearly illustrates that southern part of Afghanistan is primarily populated by Pashtuns. On the other hand, the Tajiks dominate the northern part. Likewise, the central plateau is inhabited by the indigenous. These areas are hence not only geographically separated but also widely divergent in terms of ethnic identity, social structures and religious and societal mores.

Pashtun

The Pashtuns are the populace who inhabit residing primarily in the region that lies between the Hindu Kush in north-eastern Afghanistan and the northern stretch of the Indus River in Pakistan. Constituting the bulk of the population in Afghanistan they "bore the exclusive name of Afghan" prior to the time when the term Afghan was used to refer to "any native of the present land area of Afghanistan" (Encyclopaedia Britannica, 2014). The majority of Pashtuns are the followers of Sunni denomination of Islam, while a small group are Shia.

Despite the fact that "Kinship" is an important issue "within the tribal social organisation", Pashtuns readily acknowledge that this "age-old bond is not as cherished as it was in the past" (Mazhar, 2012). The main tribal confederations of Pashtun include the Durranis, Ghilzais, Mohmands, Afridis and Yusufzais.

The traditional Pashtuns follow *Pashtunwali*, an unwritten code of ethics which means 'the way of the Pashtuns' or 'the code of life'. Mainly there are nine principles of *Pushtunwali.* One of the principles, *Me/mastin* (hospitality), states that it is essential for every Pashtun to affectionately greet their guests. On the other hand, *Badal*, another of the principles, provides people the right to dispute with those who are at odds with them or their family members. *lmnndari* (righteousness), urges the people to conduct in a moral way; while *Jsteqnmat*, asks for perseverance in whatever people do, from their studies to their beliefs. Another of the principles, *Ghayrnt*, gives people the right to protect their property and their individual as well as family honour. *Nnmus* means that men in all situations must guard women against danger. Other principles include *Tureh* (bravery); *Sabat* (loyalty), and *Nanawati* (Banting, 2002). Even non-Pashtun Afghans also follow many of its laws.

It is to be noted that Pashtuns are the most dominant group in the Afghan society and resultantly in politics.

Tajik

Mainly inhabiting the northeast region of Afghanistan, the Tajiks are primarily Sunni Muslims. Numerically, the second biggest ethnic group in Afghanistan, the Tajiks, according the assessment done by the *Minorities at Risk Project*, are strongly cohesive organisationally and have a relatively strong identity than the Pashtuns.[2] They are the major rivals of Pashtuns in the Afghan politics.

Hazara

The inhabitants of the mountainous region of Hazarajat (in central Afghanistan) Hazaras are believed to be the descendants of the Mongol warriors who came along with Chinggis Khan. The name 'Hazaras' has been taken from the Persian word *hazar*, which means 'thousand'. It is widely considered that Chinggis Khan's army was separated into groups of 1,000 warriors. While Hazaras are mainly Shia Muslims, some of them pursue Sunni or lsmaili, a branch of Shia (Banting, 2002).

Uzbek

According to the *Encyclopaedia Britannica,* 2014, the Uzbeks emerged out of a intermingling of ancient settled Iranian populations with a multiplicity of nomadic Mongol or Turkic tribes that marched into the area between the eleventh and the fifteenth century. The Uzbeks are primarily Sunni Muslims. Apart from agriculture, they are also engaged in Afghanistan's textile industry since its inception.

Aimaq

Aimaq are another ethnic group. Inhabiting in the north-western region of Afghanistan around Herat, are "transhumant pastoralists". One of the peculiarities of this group is that it spends the winter season in valley weaving carpet. Interestingly, the design differ from clan to clan (Philips, 2001). For the Aimaq, who are Hanafi Sunni Muslims, physical attribute is not a definite and precise pointer of ethnicity.

Turkmen

Inhabitants of north-eastern and north-western Afghanistan the Turkmen by tradition are "nomadic pastoral people" who raise sheep, goats, horses, camels, asses, and cattle for livelihood. However, a section of Turkmen are no more "nomadic pastoral people" as they are now engaged in agriculture. Though they follow Islam, the Turkmen are not as profoundly inclined by Islam as are the sedentary Turks (Encyclopaedia Britannica, 2014).

Baloch

Baloch or Baluch are another ethnic group. According to Gladstone the "Baluch society is tribal, highly segmented and centrally organised under powerful chieftains known as *sardars*" (Gladstone, 2001). According to the *Country of Origin Information Report* (Pakistan) by the *United Kingdom Border Agency* the Baluchis are the indigenous peoples of Baluchistan, which is split between the Pakistani province of Baluchistan and Iranian Baluchistan. Baluchis are largely Sunni Muslims, followers of the Hanafi School.

Other Ethnic Groups

Apart from the above-mentioned major ethnic groups there are other ethnic groups who have significant presence across Afghanistan. These ethnic groups include the Wakhis, the Nuristanis, etc. Followers of Ismaili Shia denomination, the Wakhi people have got their name from the place of their origin, the Wakhan, a narrow valley in the north-east of Afghanistan. It belongs to the Pamirian group.[3]

According to *World Directory of Minorities and Indigenous People*, the Nuristanis are those people who reached Afghanistan in an attempt to escape the eastward spread of Islam. The group which speak an unique Indo-European-language was, however, subjugated by Amir Abdur Rahman Khan in 1895-96 and were forced to discard their ancient religious belief in favour of Islam. Nuristanis primarily reside in the east of the country.[4]

Linguistic Composition

As Afghanistan is a multi-ethnic society, its populace is multi-linguistic too. Nearly 50 per cent of the people speak Afghan Persian or Dari (official), followed by 35 per cent who speak Pashto, 11 per cent who speak Turkic languages (primarily Uzbek and Turkmen), and the rest 4 per cent speak almost 30 minor languages (primarily Balochi and Pashai).[5]

Table 3.2: Linguistic Groups in Afghanistan

Linguistic Groups	*Percentage of Population in Descending Order*
Dari	50
Pashto	35
Turkic	11
30 minor languages	4

Source: Afghanistan, South Asia, The World Factbok, Central Intelligence Agency. https://www.cia.gov/library/publications/the-world-factbook/geos/af.html

Dari and Pashto are the official languages in Afghanistan (CIA World Factbook, 2014). The Turkic languages that include Uzbek, Turkmen, Balochi, Pashai, Nuristani, and Pamiri, have officially been declared as the third language spoken in those areas where the mainstream population lives. Dari is undoubtedly the lingua franca.

Religious Composition

Afghanistan is a predominantly an Islamic country. According to the *CIA World Factbook,* 2014, 80 per cent of people in Afghanistan are Sunni Muslims, followed by Shia Muslim (19 per cent), and other 1 per cent (including Hindus and Sikhs). Several Afghan Muslims, particularly many Sunnis, are practicing Sufis.

According to Mendoza, "Despite the fact that [Jamal al-Din] al-Afghani spent most of his early life in Afghanistan, pan-Islamism in its strictest sense did not take root in Afghanistan; rather, pan-Islamism sentiment was often manipulated by rulers in Afghanistan in the realm of foreign policy" (Mendoza, 2004).

Afghan State

The *ethnonym* Afghan has widely been used in reference to Pashtuns for over a thousand years.[6] The word Afghan appeared in a "Sessanian inscription" of the Third Century AD (Ewans, 2002). The name Afghanistan has been derived from "the *ethnonym* Afghan, originally in the loose meaning 'land of the Afghans' and referred to the Pashtun tribal areas south of the Hindu Kush"[7] around Sulaiman Mountains, land between the Amu Darya and the Indus River. Traversing through a long period of history, Afghanistan became a sovereign state in 1919.

Formation of Afghan State

The history of Afghanistan dates back to early periods. However, before eighteenth century, people of Afghanistan had never been firmly united to claim a separate political identity. Indeed, the unification of Afghanistan was achieved under Ahmad Shah Durrani who brought together the Pashtun tribes to set the foundation of Afghanistan in 1747. He was a powerful war-lord and a capable politician. After his coronation, he took the title of Durr-*i-Durran* (Pearl of The Age). Afghanistan which we presently know has come into being only during his reign. Once Ahmad Shah Durrani left the scene the country once again lost its way. Later on, the weakness of the Afghan State was exploited by the Tsarist Russia and British Indian Empire, who in their attempt to spread their area of influence reached to the borders of Afghanistan.

Afghanistan as a Modern State

It emerged as a modern state only in 1880 under the leadership of Abd al-Raahman Khan. Rahman who formed a state uniting different regions even attempted to refashion his empire by forming a regular Army and the society's "first institutionalised bureaucracy"[8].

Another characteristic of Rahman's rebuilding was his interest in technological improvement. According to the *Global Security Website* physicians, engineers (especially for mining), geologists, and printers were called from other countries with this purpose. His 'Government' apart from importing European machinery also promoted "establishment of small factories for soap, candles, and leather goods". He welcomed external counsel on "communications, transport, and irrigation"[9].

Afghanistan as a Buffer State[10]

In the nineteenth century when the two imperialist powers, namely Tsarist Russia and British India, were expanding their territories, they came close on the heels of Afghan border. Both of them wanted to gain influence over Afghanistan for their own benefit. But neither Tsarist Russia nor British India wanted to have direct control over Afghanistan for a number of reasons. To begin with, primarily the topographic conditions of Afghanistan were not conducive for foreign occupation. It has a large number of terrains, valleys and mountains. Once it had better road linkages but in the nineteenth century it was not easily accessible. So, both Tsarist Russia and British India stayed away from occupying the land and were interested in influencing Afghanistan from outside. Secondly, the climatic condition of Afghanistan posed serious challenges. Its chilly winter even today receives very little rain. Not only the little rain but also the absence of rivers make agricultural activities more difficult. This is also one of the key reasons as to why these imperialist powers were not interested in direct control of Afghanistan. Thirdly, the political conditions of Afghanistan have always been full of uncertainty. The different tribes and ethnic groups continued to fight among themselves to gain superiority. It is this volatile political condition, which made the task difficult for two imperialist powers to intervene and influence the conditions there. Fourthly, the economic health of the country in ancient times was much better than in the later periods. Being situated along the Great Silk-Route it drew attention of the ancient world and was highly benefited by trade, which was taking place at that time. But once Vasco-da-Gama discovered the sea-route to India, the flourishing Afghanistan economy took the U-turn. It lost its importance in world economic affairs and has since been suffering. This was also one of the reasons for the two powers for keeping themselves away from Afghanistan and carving it out as a buffer. And lastly, the Afghans were/are very rich both in social as well as cultural affairs. Since they are hard working and independence loving people they do not want anyone to rule over them. They have always fought to remain independent and whosoever has tried to rule them they took them to task. Once again a matter of grave concern for the Tsarist Russia and British India and therefore they remained outside Afghanistan as they were aware of the consequences.

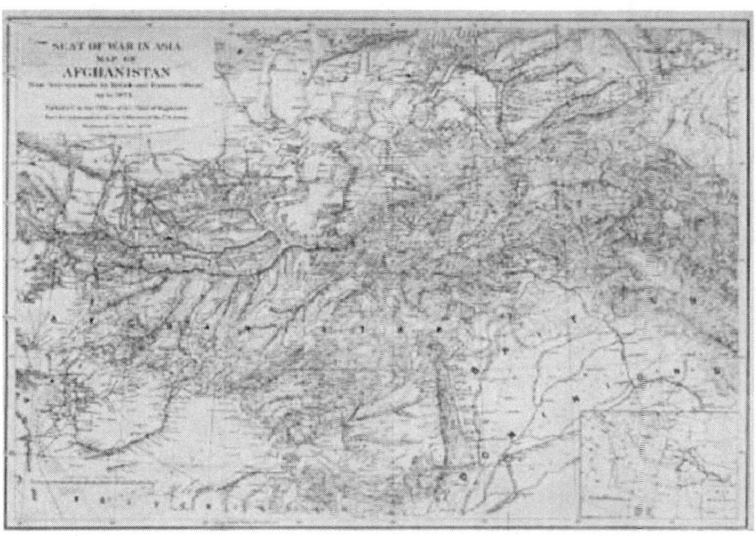

Source: Afghanistan 1914, Digital Map Collection, American Geographical Society Library, University of Wisconsin-Milwaukee Librarie. http://collections.lib.uwm.edu/cdm/singleitem/collection/agdm/id/505

Figure 3.2.Afghanistan 1878.

This is why they looked to create a 'buffer state' (a small country between two powers separating them or providing them some space in between their frontiers to avoid any direct hostility) in the form of Afghanistan rather than to have a direct control over it. Under such circumstances Afghanistan became the focal point of power rivalry. For as the Russians moved South, the British moved north-west. Ambitious Russians hoped to weaken the British grip at the straits by threatening their Indian Empire. Ambitious Britons hoped to defend India by setting up client states in Central Asia. Thus, began what Kipling called the 'Great Game' in this hitherto neglected area in the nineteenth century (Stephenson, 1969).

Source: Afghanistan 1914, Digital Map Collection, American Geographical Society Library, University of Wisconsin-Milwaukee Librarie, http://collections.lib.uwm.edu/cdm/singleitem/collection/agdm/id/506/rec/11

Figure 3.3. Map of Afghanistan and its Neighbours (1914).

After a protracted battle, both military and diplomatic, it was decided that the politically united Afghanistan could serve as a 'buffer' between the two (Dobson, 1895).

The 1907 Anglo-Russian convention was the final chapter in the delimitation of Afghanistan's international boundary. With this ended the rivalry between the two imperialist powers- Britain and Tsarist Russia-in the Central Asia region. Both these powers got their area of influence under their control, leaving apart Afghanistan with its boundaries more or less well defined.

Afghanistan after that played the role of a 'buffer' between these two powers who got themselves engaged in other areas being assured of hostility free zone in Central Asia. Afghanistan played the role of a buffer and was rewarded for its role. It became an independent country in 1919.

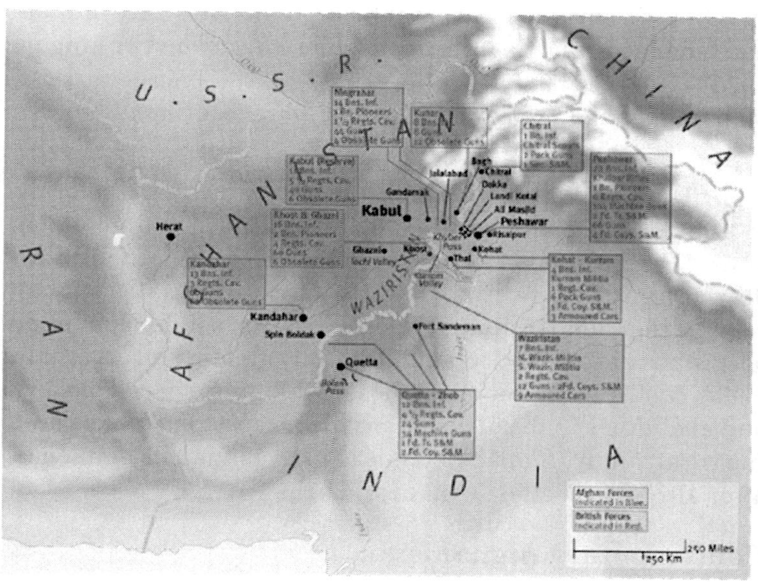

Source: Map of the Third Afghan War 1919, Military History Monthly, http://www.military-history.org/articles/map-of-the-third-afghan-war.htm

Figure 3.4: Map of the Third Afghan War (1919).

Afghanistan as an Independent State

Amanullah Khan who became the ruler after the killing of Habibullah Khan on February 20, 1919, attacked the British in May 1919. The fighting did not prolong as the two sides quickly agreed for peace. The primary reason behind this peace pact was the fact that while the Afghans were reluctant to protracted air attacks by the British on Kabul and Jalalabad, the British were disinclined to initiate a 'land war' "so soon after the bloodletting of World War I" (Alikuzai, 2013). According to various scholars the Afghans through the peace pact achieved what they could not have gained in war. Afghan became an Independent nation on August 19, 1919. Soon after Afghanistan established diplomatic relations with the Soviet Union in 1919; followed by Iran, Britain, Turkey, Italy, and France.

On the domestic front, in the paradigm shift, Amanullah had "changed his title from *amir* (chief) to *padshah* or king in 1923" (Dupree, 1980). Earlier, in 1826, the energetic Dost Mohammad had proclaimed himself *amir*, not *Shah*.

Several administrative reforms were carried during his reign. During Amanullah's time, there were sweeping reforms in political and judicial filed. These included the adoption of first constitution (1923); guarantee of civil rights (first by decree and then in the constitution); universal national registration and issuance of identity cards; establishment of a legislative assembly; creation of a court system and of secular penal, civil, and commercial codes; prohibition of blood money; and abolition of subsidies and privileges for tribal chiefs and the royal family. *Sharia* (Islamic law) reclaimed its eminence after 1923-24 rebellion (Alikuzai, 2013).

Contemporary Afghanistan

Today Afghanistan is a mountainous country stretching approximately 652,000 square kilometres. It shares its borders with China, Iran, Pakistan, Tajikistan, Turkmenistan,

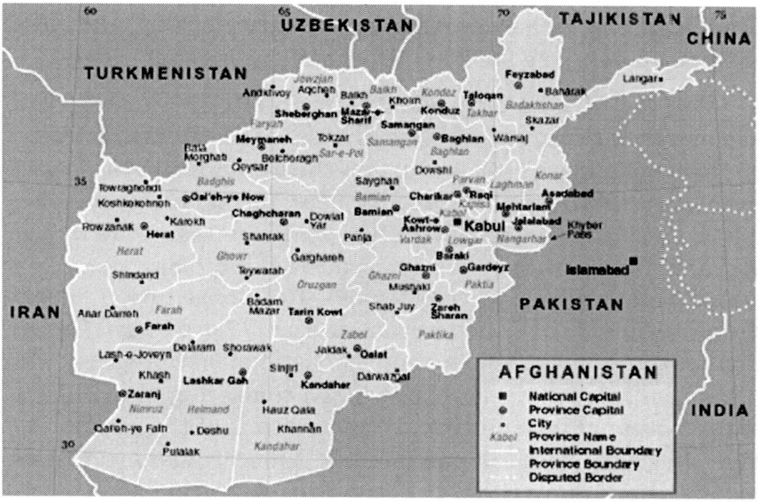

Source: "Afghanistan in Brief", Embassy of Afghanistan, Washington DC, http://www.embassyofafghanistan.org/page/afghanistan-in-brief

Figure 3.5: Map of Afghanistan.

Uzbekistan and a sector of the disputed territory of Jammu and Kashmir that is controlled by Pakistan. Roughly half of its territory is more than 2,000 metres above sea level.[11]

The Contemporary Afghanistan is known as Islamic Republic of Afghanistan. Locally it is known as Jamhuri-ye Islami-ye Afghanistan. According to the *CIA World Factbook* 2014 report, Afghanistan has 34 provinces. These include Badakhshan, Badghis, Baghlan, Balkh, Bamyan, Daykundi, Farah, Faryab, Ghazni, Ghor, Helmand, Herat, Jowzjan, Kabul, Kandahar, Kapisa, Khost, Kunar, Kunduz, Laghman, Logar, Nangarhar, Nimroz, Nuristan, Paktika, Paktiya, Panjshir, Parwan, Samangan, Sar-e-Pul, Takhar, Uruzgan, Wardak, and Zabul. Kablu is the National Capital.

Though the country had adopted and implemented several constitutions in earlier period, it drafted a new Constitution between December 14, 2003, and January 4, 2004. This

Constitution, which was signed on January 16, 2004, and later ratified on January 26, 2004, is in force at present.

The Country has Presidential form of Government. The bicameral National Assembly comprises of the *Meshrano Jirga* or House of Elders (102 seats, two-thirds of members elected from provincial councils for four-year terms, and one-third nominated by the president for five-year terms) and the *Wolesi Jirga* or House of People (no more than 250 seats; members directly elected for five-year terms). The Constitution allows the government to summon a constitutional *Loya Jirga* (Grand Council) on "issues of independence, national sovereignty, and territorial integrity". The *Loya Jirga* consisting of members of the National Assembly and chairpersons of the Provincial and District Councils can modify the "provisions of the Constitution" and put on trial the President. So far, no such *Loya Jirga* has been convened (CIA World Factbook, 2014).

The Chief of State is the President of the Islamic Republic of Afghanistan. Presently, Ashraf Ghani Ahmadzai is the President. The *Stera Mahkama* or Supreme Court is the Highest Court.

Afghan Polity

Throughout the early history, different tribes and ethnic groups within Afghanistan have fought among themselves to gain superiority. Unsurprisingly, the political conditions of Afghanistan have always been full of uncertainty. The nature of polity therefore has changed from time to time.

Ethnicity played the most significant role in the polity of Afghanistan. Throughout Afghanistan's history, all politics of Afghan governments have become ethnicised. All Pashtun rulers from, Ahmad Shah Durrani, to the last King, Mohammad Zahir Shah, favoured the Pashtuns. These leaders in order to establish a so called sovereign and a Unitary Government used a brutal regime apparatus toward non-Pashtun communities leading to a political environment full of bitterness. There have been very few non-Pashtun rulers.

Different Regimes

During its lost history Afghanistan has witnessed the ascendency of several rulers. Time and again, the individual rulers in their own capacities affected the Afghan polity. A chronological description of the rulers has been given below:

Ahmad Shah Durrani (1747-1772)

Indisputably one of the most compelling leader whoever ruled Afghanistan, Ahmad Shah was a seasoned warrior. Unsurprisingly, he had a "trained, mobile force of several thousand cavalrymen". Acknowledged in as Ahmad Shah Baba or 'father', Ahmad Shah during his rule always consulted with a council of eight or nine *sirdars* or sardars on all important issues. Each of those *sardars* was accountable for their own group. As he himself was a Durrani he favoured the Durranis, and particularly his own lineage, the Sadozai, he was assuaging to the other Pashtun chiefs as well (Alikuzai, 2013). Nevertheless, even before his death in 1772, his empire began to disentangle. It is considered that he was the one who founded Afghan polity.

Timur Shah (1772-1793)

The second son and designated heir of Ahmad *Shah*, Timur Shah, succeeded him.[12] Taimur like his father officially engaged other Durrani *sirdars* for advice (especially the chief of the powerful Muhammadzai, Painda Khan), but his style of functioning alienated his fellow Pashtuns. Despite the fact that he faced only two "major internal rebellions" during his long tenure of 20 years, "his turn away from the council of Durrani advisers to the Qizilbash guards began a process of alienation of the Sadozai rulers from their Pashtun subjects" (Baynard, 1986). He died suddenly in 1793. There was no noticeable change in the political domain during his regime.

Zaman Shah (1793-1800)

As Timur had not left a designated heir to the throne, his sons fought among themselves and that led to confusion over who would succeed him. Prominent among those included the sons of Timur who were the then governors of Qandahar, Herat, and Kabul, even though the later, Zaman, was the strongest contender. As Zaman got the support of Painda Khan, his appointment to the throne was guaranteed. Zaman, the fifth son of Timur, became *shah* at the age of 23 (Gladstone, 2003).

Zaman Shah had to meet several challenges. The primary of those included the implementation of the policy of "one monarch to rule all the Pashtun tribes". Unlike Ahmad *Shah*, Zaman *Shah* was resolute to the "harmonious council balance" which the hallmark of Ahmad Shahs regime. In the process he instead of adopting "multi-clan leadership" emphasised on new electing "representatives from his own lineage of the Sadozai tribe. Consequently, the Durrani leaders who were removed from the leadership began to plot in opposition to Zaman Shah (Runion, 2007). Eventually, he lost his throne in 1800. There were no significant political developments during his regime too.

Shah Mahmud (1800-1803)

Zaman was succeeded by his older brother Shah Mahmud. Shah Mahmud deposed his brother with the help of Fateh Khan, son of Painda Khan, "who had served as deputy to Ahmad Shah. Fateh Khan fled to Iran to pledge alliance support to a new ruler of Afghanistan, Mahmud Shah. Rebelling forces seized Qandahar from Zaman Shah" (Runion, 2007). His rule lasted only for three years (Baynard, 1986). There was no significant change in the political domain during his regime.

Shah Shoja (1803 to 1809)

Shah Shoja, another of Timur's son, took the reign in 1803. While he was attempting to impose his rule, he was forced to sign an agreement with the British. On June 7, 1809, he was forced by the British to sign a "Treaty of Friendship". The treaty incorporated a clause that stressed that Afghanistan would in future resist the "passage of foreign troops through his territories" (Gladstone, 2003). Though the treaty ensured the British support to Afghan ruler against external aggression, it led to internal rebellion and he was dethroned in 1809. He took exile in India. There was no significant change in the political domain during his regime.

Shah Mahmud (1809-1818)

Shah Mahmud came back to rule Afghanistan. He got his throne back as he succeeded in winning the support of Painda Khan's son, Fateh Khan. Fateh Khan at that point of time was in command of the Muhammadzai and had emerged as one of the most influential chief among the Durrani Pashtuns. However, in due course of time the relation between *Shah* Mahmud and Fateh Khan deteriorated. Due to some trivial reasons Fateh Khan was seized and blinded. Subsequently, Fateh Khan's 20 brothers (according to several estimates), who were in key positions all over Afghanistan, led the Muhammadzai in uprising. The youngest among them, Dost Mohammad, whose mother had been a Qizilbash, convinced his mother's tribesmen in Kabul to support him in removing the supporters of Mahmud Shah from Kabul. Forced to vacate Kabul, Mahmud and his followers took shelter in Herat. He along with his son Kamran continued to rule Herat though had been forced to concede the dominion of the Iranian monarch. Mahmud died in 1829. Kamran ruled the city until he was killed in 1842 (Baynard, 1986). There was no significant change in the political domain during his regime.

Multiple Rulers (1818-1826)

Afghanistan went through a phase of almost eight in which there were multiple leaders who were controlling different parts of the country. In fact, the fight was among the various sons of Painda Khan who fought among themselves for establishing their own preeminence. Meanwhile, Afghanistan in all practicality "ceased to exist as a single nation, disintegrating temporarily into a group of small units, each ruled by a different Durrani leader". Resultantly chaos prevailed across the country. Finally, in 1826 Dost Mohammad Khan emerged victorious and became the ruler (Alikuzai, 2013).

Dost Mohammad Khan (1826-1839)

Soon after establishing himself as the sole ruler he declared himself *amir*, not *shah*. Unfortunately for him, it was during his reign that the First Great Game – between Tsarist Russia and British Indian Empire - intensified. It had an adverse impact on Afghanistan and despite being an able administrator, Dost Mohammad, the first of the Muhammadzai rulers, failed to bring significant changes during his regime.

After fighting the British onslaught for a long period, Dost Mohammad lost his throne in 1839 to Shah Shoja, who had taken shelter in India after his removal from throne in 1809. Shoja was enthroned in Kabul by the Britishers.

Shah Shoja (1839-1842)

As Shah Shoja was enthroned in Kabul by the Britishers, the freedom loving Afghan people revolted against him. He failed to gain control in the areas which were outside the influence of the Britishers who had enthroned him. Shoja was finally assassinated in April 1842. There was no significant change in the political domain during his regime.

Months of uncertainty prevailed over Afghanistan. In between, Mohammad Akbar, son of Dost Mohammad secured local control.

Dost Mohammad Khan (1843-1863)

According to the *British Library*, "Dost Mohammed for the second time became the ruler of Afghanistan in April 1943. Soon, the first Anglo-Sikh war took place. In 1848-49, Second Anglo-Sikh War took place in which Dost Muhammad Khan allies with the Sikhs. In 1849 the British defeated the Sikhs and their allies and annex the whole of the former Sikh dominions. The whole of northern Afghanistan (except Badakhshan) submits to Dost Muhammad"[13].

Dost Mohammad died in 1863. There were some significant changes in the political domain during his regime.

Era of Uncertainty (1863-68)

There was an era of uncertainty following Dost Mohammad's death. His successor, Sher Ali Khan, failed to take control of Kabul till 1868. Notably, till that period Kabul remained under the control of Muhammad Afzal, another son of Dost Mohammad.

Sher Ali Khan (1868-1878)

Sher Ali who ultimately had managed to set up control over Kabul in 1868 came to know that the British were prepared to strengthen his regime supplying arms and funds. However, they were not assuring to provide anything else (Gladstone, 2003). Sher Ali was not interested. He was sensitive to the probable reaction in Afghanistan. As relations between the two sides started deteriorating, "a British force of around 40,000 fighting men was distributed into military columns which penetrated Afghanistan at three different points". He appointed his son, Mohammad Yaqub, as regent, and moved towards Moscow to seek Russian help, but failed to gain support. He died in February 1879 (Gladstone, 2003). There was no significant change in the political domain during his regime.

In the meantime, as a large portion of the country was under the control of the invading British forces, Yaqub signed the Treaty of Gandamak in May 1879 to thwart British invasion of the remaining of Afghanistan. As per the agreement the British provided an annual subsidy and unclear pledge of backing in case of foreign hostility. In return Yaqub surrendered control of Afghan foreign affairs to the British (Gladstone, 2003)*. He moved out of power centre in 1880.*

Abd al-Rahman Khan (1880-1901)

Abd al-Rahman Khan, son of Muhammad Afzal, came to the throne in 1880. A leader competent enough to assert his authority and uniting the people to reestablish the Afghan State which was in chaotic condition ruled for 21 long years. His efforts to "modernize and establish control of the kingdom", coincided with the efforts of the two imperial powers, who were fighting for their supremacy in the country, to delineate Afghanistan's modern borders. "Rahman turned his formidable energies to what turned out to be virtually the creation of the modern state of Afghanistan, while the British and the Russians, with the Afghans as bystanders, determined the borders of the Afghan state", explains Baynard (Baynard, 1986).

Rahman apart from establishing a nation from the "fractured regions comprising Afghanistan" also took several measures to modernise his kingdom by creating the first "institutionalised bureaucracy". Indeed, in spite of being considered as definitely dictatorial personality, Rahman called for a "Loya Jirgah", an assemblage of royal princes, important notables, and religious leaders". He also established a regular Army.

Several scholars are of the view that Rahman had three objectives. These included vanquishing the tribes; widening government influence through a strong and visible army, and strengthening the power of the ruler, the royal family as well as royal council, which "had only advisory powers". Tribal leaders, various advisers, and agency heads, as well as state secretaries for the important regions of the country constituted the royal council. The succession of his eldest son, Habibullah, to the throne on his father's death in October 1901 in a peaceful manner clearly demonstrated the fact that Rahman had succeeded in establishing full control (Gladstone, 2003).

Habibullah Khan (1901-19)

Habibullah Khan's enthronement was very smooth.

Despite the fact that he secured his position by "virtue of the support from the Army" formed by his father, Habibullah could not assert himself in the same authoritarian way as Abd al-Rahman Khan. Consequently, several religious leaders increased their influence during his rule. His cousin Mahmoud Beg Tarzi, a highly "educated and well-traveled poet and journalist", founded an Afghan nationalist newspaper and used it as a "platform for rebutting clerical criticism of Western-influenced changes in government and society" (Gladstone, 2003). Despite the fact that the two brothers were always at odds, Habibullah in the later years of his rule was forced to agree with Tarzi's demands for an end to British tutelage (Baynard, 1986). Habibullah was killed in mysterious circumstances on February 20, 1919.

Amanullah Khan (1919-1929)

Amanullah, the third son of Habibullah Khan succeed him. Indeed, he was the one who was in charge of Kabul when Habibullah was on the hunting expedition where he was eventually killed.

Amanullah who was in command of both the national treasury and the Army when the news of his father's death reached took a resolve to grab power, although his two older brothers and his uncle had equal claims. Within a few months he managed to win the support of the majority of tribal leaders. It helped him in establishing complete control over (Gladstone, 2003).

Tajik Ruler Habibullah Khan (January-October 1929)

Taking advantage of the chaos, a Tajik, who called himself Habibullah Khan, became the ruler. It was for the first time for a long time that Afghanistan was under a Tajik ruler. Other called him *Bacha-i-Saqqao* (Son of the Water Carrier). According to various descriptions, he was a deserter from the Afghan army; he had worked in Peshawar as a tea seller and then served 11 months in prison for housebreaking. He had participated in the Khost rebellion of 1924 and then had become a highwayman (Baynard, 1986). Very little is known about the period during which he ruled, but majority of historians concur that he could not have prolonged his stay in the throne under any condition as he was non-Pashtun. There was no significant change in the political domain during his regime.

Significantly, when Amanullah Khan failed in his attempt effort to reclaim his throne, the Musahiban brothers, who were also Muhammadzai Barakzai, emerged as the strongest contenders. There were five prominent Musabihan brothers. The eldest among them, Nadir Shah, who had served as minister of war under Amanullah for sometime (he had resigned as he disagreed with Amanullah's military and domestic reforms) led the fight. After facing several reverses, Nadir and his brothers finally raised a sufficiently large force (mostly from the British side of the Durand Line) and took Kabul on October 10, 1929. On October 16, Nadir Shah was proclaimed King Nadir Shah. The Tajik Habibullah fled Kabul, was arrested in Kohistan, and was executed on November 3, 1929, despite promises of reprieve (Baynard, 1986).

Mohammad Nadir Shah (1930-33)

Mohammad Nadir Shah took the throne of Afghanistan. He swiftly put an end to most of Amanullah Khans reforms. However, despite his attempt to strengthen the army it remained weak while the "religious and tribal leaders" gained power. A new constitution was promulgated in 1931. It included several of the principles of Afghan society. Though it appeared to institute a constitutional monarchy, it formed a royal oligarchy. Popular participation remained only and elusion (Alikuzai, 2013).

Despite the fact that he succeeded in pacifying religious elements with a "constitutional emphasis on orthodox religious principles", he also emphasized on the modernisation of

Afghanistan in material ways. However, this aspect was given less prominence. Construction of roads, especially the Great North Road through the Hindu Kush, was done and means of communication were improved. Commercial links were also established with other countries, and, "under the leadership of several leading entrepreneurs, a banking system and long-range economic planning were started". Schools, which had been closed during the disorder of the Tajik rule, were reopened. He even during the later years of his reign created a 40,000-strong force before his death in 1933, and he also established a military school and an arsenal. Significantly, he had inherited virtually no national army at all (Baynard, 1986).

Mohammad Zahir Shah (1933-73)

Mohammad Zahir Shah was the last king of Durrani dynasty. While in the first 30 years he acknowledged the guidance of powerful advisers in the royal family-his uncles for the first 20 years and his cousin, Mohammad Daud Khan, for another 10 years, in the last 10 years he established complete control.

During the first 30 years a lot of experiments were made with political system. National assembly elections definitely less controlled than ever before, resulted in the formation of 'liberal parliament' in 1949. However, the developments thereafter made the government to believe that the 'liberalisation' has worsened the situation; and therefore another election was held in 1952. In fact the elections in 1952 clearly demonstrated that experiment in open politics was over (Gladstone, 2003).

As Baynard notes,

> "In the wake of the failed political reforms of the 1949-52, came a major shakeup within the royal family. Since the advent of King Nadir Shah to the throne in 1929, Afghanistan had been ruled by the royal family as a united group. By mid-1953, however, the younger members of

the royal family (including perhaps the King himself) had challenged the dominance of the King's uncles, and in September 1953 the rift became public when the King's first cousin and brother-in-law, Daoud, became Prime Minister. Shah Mahmud, left his post, but he continued to proffer his support and advice to the new leaders. The change occurred peacefully, entirely within-and apparently with the consent of the royal family" (Baynard, 1986).

Prime Minister Mohammad Daud Khan, the first of the young, Western educated generation of the royal family to exert authority in Kabul by all standards, was an energetic leader whose succession to power brought several important changes in Afghanistan's policies, both domestic and foreign. However, he lost the confidence of the people. King Zahir Shah, who had the support of the royal family, in March 1963, asked Daud for his resignation on the ground that the country's economy was deteriorating as his policy of Pashtunistan is proving detrimental. As the armed forces were under his control, Daud definitely had the muscle to resist the king's demand for his resignation, but instead he accepted the demand and resigned. Muhammad Yousuf, a non-Pashtun, German educated technocrat, who had been serving as the Minister of Mines and Industries was named the new Prime Minister (Gladstone, 2003).

The development led to the strengthening of Zahir Shah's position. Nevertheless, the solitary accomplishment of the 1963 to 1973 decade was the 1964 constitution. The constitution-and the deliberations that produced it-demonstrated several interesting changes in political thinking. It banned the royal family, other than the King, from politics and government-a provision that was believed to be done with an aim at keeping Daud out of politics (Alikuzai, 2013).

Following the signing of the Constitution, free and fair elections were conducted in 1965. The reality that four PDPA [People's Democratic Party of Afghanistan (PDPA)] members won parliamentary seats implies that the "government efforts to intervene in the balloting to prevent the success of its leftist opponents were half-hearted". Notably, the PDPA formed on January 1, 1965, was "not an orthodox Marxist party but an entity created out of diverse leftist groups that united for the principal purpose of gaining parliamentary seats in the elections" (Banting, 1986).

Later on, some unwarranted developments led to removal of Yousuf from Prime Ministership. The King nominated another Prime Minister, Mohammad Hashim Maiwandwal.

In the meantime, Nur Mohammad Taraki, who was among one of the four elected PDPA members started the first major leftist newspaper, *Khalq* (Masses), "which lasted little more than a month before being banned by the Government" (Alikuzai, 2013) as it felt that it is instigating the student unrest. Significantly, three students had been killed when troops opened fire on students protesting at *Wolesi Jirga*. Consequently, political parties remained banned.

Not surprisingly, the parliament constituted following elections in 1969 was not as much representative as the earlier one. The prominent among the leftists who had won included Babrak Karmal and Hafizullah Amin (a mathematics teacher educated in the United States). By now, 1969, the PDPA had witnessed a significant divide, the faction of Babrak Karmal parting company ideologically with Taraki. The new group's newspaper *Parcham* (Banner) "operated from March 1968 until July 1969 when it was closed" (Alikuzai, 2013).

The political atmosphere in the aftermath of the 1969 elections was less interrelated. Polarisation between left and right amplified. Meanwhile, King Zhahir Shah, despite maintaining his popularity was criticised as a leader because of his method of governance. It was perceived that he was not supporting his own Prime Ministers. Legislative work had suffered. Indeed, "between 1969 and 1973, parliamentary elections and removal of the King, the parliament passed only one minor bill in the 1969-70 Session" (Alikuzai, 2013).

Two consecutive years of drought followed by a catastrophic famine in 1972 in which "as many as 100,000 Afghans may have perished" (Baynard, 1986), led to resentment in public. There were allegations about mishandling of foreign donations. On external front, "the Indo-Pakistani War and the secession of Bangladesh from Pakistan in 1971 was closely watched in Afghanistan, where interest in Pakistani politics was great and where the Pashtunistan issue always lurked near the surface of politics" (Baynard, 1986).

Amidst such a volatile environment, Daud executed a coup d'état that was under his consideration for more than a year in reaction to the 'anarchy and the anti-national attitude of the regime'. The coup was executed when the king was out of the country for medical treatment. Daud and a small military group took command without any significant resistance from any other quarter apart from the strong resistance which came from the regent, Abdul Wali (Alikuzai, 2013).

Mohammad Daud Khan (1973-78)

On July 17, 1973, Daud became the head of the State. Expectedly, he brought an end to the arrangement of monarchy and declared Afghanistan a Republic. Daud in 1975 established his own political party, the National Revolutionary Party, which was to be the focus of all political activity. A Loya Jirgah in January 1977 accepted Daud's constitution, which established a presidential, one party system of government (Baynard, 1986).

It is widely believed that Daud had got the support of USSR in his coup against King Zahir Shah. However, in due course of time he lost the support of both the communists within Afghanistan and the USSR.

Not surprisingly, on April 27, 1978, a *coup* commenced with rebel troop's marching towards the military base at Kabul International Airport. It developed gradually over the next 24 hours as the rebels fought with units trustworthy to Daud in and around the capital. Daud and most of his family were shot dead in the Presidential Palace on April 28, 1978. 231

years of rule by Ahmad Shah and his descendants thus came to an end.

Nur Mohammad Taraki (1978-79)

Nur Mohammad Taraki of the Khalq faction of the PDPA, who led the April 27-28 coup in 1978 formed the first Communist Government in Afghanistan. He established a single-party government, the "new-style" state of the Democratic Republic of Afghanistan, in which the executive completely subjugated the legislature (renamed, Revolutionary Council) and the judiciary.[14] Nur Mohammad Khan became the Chairman of the Revolutionary Council of the Democratic Republic of Afghanistan, the head of State on April 30.

According to the *Encyclopedia Britannica*,

> "Once in power, however, Taraki faced numerous problems. His Marxist land and social reforms led to violent demonstrations. Unable to end the growing unrest, he turned to the Soviet Union for assistance. Taraki also found himself on the losing end of a power struggle with Hafizullah Amin, a deputy prime minister and fellow member of the People's faction of the PDPA. In March 1979, Taraki was forced to name new Chairman of the Council of Ministers. He, however, continued to work as Chairman of the Revolutionary Council of the Democratic Republic of Afghanistan and PDPA general secretary. At the beginning of September 1979, Taraki traveled to Havana for a summit conference of nonaligned nations. Returning via Moscow, he was believed to have been advised by then Soviet President Leonid I. Brezhnev to eliminate Amin, whose anti-Islamic policy the Soviets felt was exacerbating the political situation in Afghanistan" (Encyclopedia Britannica, 2014).

Taraki's effort to have Amin killed failed, and Amin seized authority on September 14, 1979. Taraki was assassinated in the hostility. Although his death was declared on October 9, there were contradictory reports on the definite date of his death.

Hafizullah Amin (1979)

Hafizullah Amin who was first appointed Deputy Prime Minister in the Government of Nur Mohammad Tarkai, on March 27, 1979, claimed Taraki's position of Prime Minister. He 'allowed' Amin to function as President. At the time, the country was becoming more and more unsteady as Afghans disapproved the government's Marxist reforms, many of which seemed to weaken Afghanistan's customary Islamic culture. Later, on September 14, 1979, Amin overthrew Taraki and declared himself President. His nationalist views and efforts to get better relations with Pakistan and the United States, however, drew the distrust of the Soviet Union.[15]

"The country further fell into unrest, and the Soviets invaded Afghanistan on December 24, 1979. Amin was killed, and Babrak Karmal, of the Banner faction of the PDPA, was installed as President"[16]. The present conflict in Afghanistan has its root in this event. The details about the particular event and what followed then has been discussed in Chapter 4.

Current Political Status

In 1989, the Soviet Union withdrew from Afghanistan under relentless pressure by internationally supported anti-communist *mujahideen* rebels. A series of civil wars followed that saw Kabul finally falling in 1996 to the Taliban, a hardline Pakistani-sponsored movement that emerged in 1994 to end the country's civil war and anarchy. Soon after the 9/11, a US Allied and anti-Taliban Northern Alliance military action toppled the Taliban for sheltering slain al Qaeda founder Osama bin Laden (Cuhaj, 2012). In 2001, the UN-sponsored Bonn Conference established a process for political reconstruction that included the adoption of a new constitution, a presidential election in 2004, and National Assembly elections in 2005. In December 2004, Hamid Karzai became the first democratically elected president of Afghanistan and the National Assembly was inaugurated the following December (Cuhaj, 2012). Karzai was re-elected in August 2009 for a second term until he has been replaced by the new Afghan President Mohammad Ashraf Ghani Ahmadzai after the recently held Presidential elections in 2014.

Regrettably, however, political quibble returned to haunt the nation during the recent Presidential Elections. The first round of the Presidential Elections, held on April 5, 2014, failed to throw up a clear winner, but were fortunately devoid of controversy. Abdullah Abdullah, the former Foreign Minister, garnered 45 per cent of the total votes, followed by former Finance Minister Ashraf Ghani Ahmadzai, with 31.56 per cent votes. According to the demands of the Afghan Constitution, at least one of the candidates had to secure 50 per cent or more of the votes to be declared the winner. Consequently, second round of polls took place on June 14, 2014. Preliminary results on July 7, 2014, showed that Ashraf Ghani Ahmadzai, the runner up in the first round, got 56.44 per cent votes as against 43.56 per cent for Abdullah. While Ghani welcomed the results, Abdullah, who had urged postponement of the declaration of the preliminary results claiming that there were "unclean votes", declared, "I will accept the result when the clean votes are separated from unclean votes." Sayed Fazel Sancharaki, Abdullah's spokesperson, alleging widespread voting fraud, argued, "The level of participation in the second round was far lower than the first round, so how can the [election] commission announce that more than 7 million people participated? We have documents showing participation [in the second round] could not have exceeded 5.2 million. In some areas, there are more votes than people". Significantly, the number of votes cast in June exceeds the April vote by over 1.3 million. European Union chief election observer Thijs Berman on July 3, 2014, thus noted, "I have serious concerns about a significant number of polling stations. I have no conclusions on possible fraud because this you can only do when you have done an in-depth audit, but the indications are very worrying".

With Ghani displaying some reluctance, Abdullah's supporters, who felt that he had been cheated for the second time, as he was the runner up to Karzai during the first round of polls in 2009 as well, and did not contest the run-off elections, asked Abdullah to form a "parallel Government." Indeed, Abdullah even threatened to declare his own government, though he urged his frenzied supporters to give him time to negotiate. On July 8, 2014, he thus stated, "The people of Afghanistan have been asking us to announce our government today, and we can't disregard this right. I am not going to betray you — just give me time to defend justice, freedom, the rule of law and the people's right. Give me time".

Subsequently, however, better sense prevailed, as the two candidates agreed to an audit of votes. US Secretary of State John Kerry, who rushed to Afghanistan at the height of the political squabble, announced on July 12, 2014, "Both candidates have committed to participate in and stand by the results of the largest most possible audit. Every single ballot that was cast will be audited". Later, on July 17, 2014, the Afghan Election Commission begun the audit of 7.9 million votes cast in the June 14 run-off elections.

Significantly, after a protracted face off, an agreement to form a National Unity Government was signed between the two Presidential candidates - Dr Abdullah Abdullah and Ashraf Ghani Ahmadzai - on September 21, 2014. Ashraf Ghani Ahmadzai was subsequently sworn in as new President of Afghanistan on September 29, 2014. Abdullah Abdullah became the Chief Executive.

Thus, for the first time in Afghanistan's checkered political history there has been a transfer of power which is truly democratic. More importantly, it is a truly multi-ethnic Government as Ghani belongs to the dominant Pashtun group, while Abdullah Abdullah is a Tajik. It now seems Afghanistan at last is on the path of formation of a democratic State in which the polity will be truly representative of all the sections of the society.

Notes

1. UNHCR 2011 refugee statistics: full data, *The Guardian*, http://www.theguardian.com/news/datablog/2011/jun/20/refugee-statistics-unhcr-data
2. Assessment for Tajiks in Afghanistan, Minorities at Risk Project Data, http://www.cidcm.umd.edu/mar/assessment.asp?groupId=70003
3. Origin of Wakhi Ethnic Group, http://www.gojal.net/history_wakhies.htm
4. World Directory of Minorities and Indigenous People, http://www.minorityrights.org/5448/afghanistan/nuristanis.html
5. Afghanistan, South Asia, The World Factbook, Library, Central Intelligence Agency, https://www.cia.gov/library/publications/the-world-factbook/geos/af.html
6. Afghan (Ethnonym), *World Heritage Encyclopedia*, http://www.worldheritage.org/articles/Afghan_(ethnonym)
7. *Ibid.*
8. Abdur Rahman Khan "The Iron Amir" - 1880-1901, Global Security, http://www.globalsecurity.org/military/world/afghanistan/amir-abdur-rahman.htm
9. *Ibid.*
10. A large part of this portion has been taken from this researcher's own M.Phil. Dissertation titled, *Emergence of Afghanistan as a Buffer State between Tsarist Russia and British Indian Empire (19th C.)* submitted to the Jawaharlal Nehru University in 2003.
11. Afghanistan and the United Nations, UN News Centre, http://www.un.org/News/dh/latest/afghan/un-afghan-history.shtml
12. Ahmad Shah Durrani, Afghan Wiki.com, http://www.afghanwiki.com/en/index.php?title=Ahmad_Shah_Durran, accessed on July 4, 2013
13. Afghanistan 1843-1878: Sources in the India Office Records, British Library, http://www.bl.uk/reshelp/findhelpregion/asia/afghanistan/afghanistancollection/1843to1878/sources1843to1878.html
14. Constitutional History of Afghanistan, Encyclopedia Iranica, http://www.iranicaonline.org/articles/constitutional-history-of-afghanistan, accessed on September 2, 2014.
15. Hafizullah Amin, Encyclopedia Britannica, http://www.britannica.com/EBchecked/topic/20639/Hafizullah-Amin
16. *Ibid.*

Chapter - 4

Conflict in Afghanistan

The Conflict that has engulfed Afghanistan has its root in the developments that took place during the later years of President Mohammad Daud Khan. The deteriorating tie between Daud and the USSR resulted in a Soviet backed coup in 1978. The Coup changed the dynamics of Afghan polity and subsequently Afghanistan plunged into a Conflict with compounding complexities.

The 1978 Coup

The 1978 coup brought an end to Daud' regime. Daud failed to counter the coup despite having "well-trained armed forces, which remained loyal to him" all through his regime, because most of the military commanders and government workers were off duty as it was Thursday, a day before Friday, the Muslim day of worship. The entire episode is known as 'Sawr Revolution' as it took place in the Afghan lunar month of *Sawr* (Taurus) (Rubin, 2002).

Abdul Qadir Dagarwal of the *Khalq* faction of the PDPA, as the Chairman of the Military Council of the Armed Forces of Afghanistan led the rebel force. On April 27, as the troops began movement he took over as the Head of the State.

On April 30, he handed over power to a Revolutionary Council named by the formally 'united' PDPA. Nur Mohammad

Taraki of the *Khalq* faction of the PDPA became the President of the Revolutionary Council and Prime Minister. Babrak Karmal and Hafizullah Amin, who loathed each other, were also Politburo secretaries, members of the Revolutionary Council Presidium, and Deputy Prime Ministers (Rubin, 2002).

Meanwhile, Taraki promptly signed Decree No. 1, which proclaimed the establishment of the Democratic Republic of Afghanistan (Rubin, 2002). Thus, was formed the first Communist Government in Afghanistan. The Soviet Union expectedly announced massive support from the Government.

Afghan Reaction

As in the past, the freedom loving people of Afghanistan once again revolted against the puppet Government. Indeed, uprisings against the PDPA government were reported from most parts of Afghanistan. Consequently, the new PDPA government, soon announced and implemented a hostile doctrine against any political dissent, whether inside or outside the party.

Meanwhile, taking advantage of the chaotic situation, Hafizullah Amin, as mentioned in the previous chapter became the Head of the State on September 16, 1979. "His nationalist views and attempts to improve relations with Pakistan and the United States, however, drew the distrust of the Soviet Union"[1].

Soviet Intervention in 1979

'Perturbed' by the developments that were taking place inside Afghanistan and the role played by some other countries the Soviet Union invaded Afghanistan, on December 24, 1979. Amin, who was reluctant to hand over power peacefully to a Soviet approved leadership, was killed on December 27.

The Soviet Military operation is known as *Operation Storm-333*. In the course of the operation, Soviet Special Forces attacked and stormed the Tajbeg Palace, home of the royal family[2], in Kabul. According to Chant,

"[They] killed Amin and his 200 personal guards. Several other government buildings were seized during the operation, including those of the Ministry of the Interior, Internal Security Organisation and General Staff... *Operation Storm-333* cost the Soviet Forces 19 killed and about 50 wounded, the former comprising two men of the Alpha Group, three men of the Zenith Group, nine of the 'Muslim Battalion' and five of the paratroopers. The Afghan losses were in the order of 200 killed, 200 wounded and 1,700 captured" (Chant, 2012).

Rise of Babrak Karmal

Babrak Karmal who after his differences with Nur Mohammad Taraki had been sent abroad as Ambassador to Czechoslovakia, at the time of coup had taken exile in Russia.

In the aftermath of the killing of incumbent Head of State, Amin, by the invading Soviet Forces, on December 27, 1979, he became the President of the Revolutionary Council of the Democratic Republic of Afghanistan. Soon, *mujahideens* who got readily available support from the United States, China and Saudi Arabia started opposing Karmal and the Red Army in Afghanistan. The conflict that prolonged settled into a standoff, "although the Soviet Force, estimated at first at 30,000, grew to number 120,000. Though better armed and in control of the air, the Soviets were unable to defeat the rebels" (Pace, 1996).

Meanwhile, during the course of time, Moscow openly condemned Karmal, complaining that he was at fault for he has failed to quell the rebellion. Moscow also accused that Karmal for the prevailing poverty in the country. Ultimately, on November 24, 1986, Karmal was forced to resign (Pace, 1986).

Haji Mohammad Chamkani succeeded Karmal as President of the Revolutionary Council of the Democratic Republic of Afghanistan on November 24, 1986. He relinquished the post on September 30, 1987. "He was a non-communist. He was a tribal leader from the Paktia Province in Eastern Afghanistan" (Lentz, 2014).

Ascendance of Mohammad Najibullah

Mohammad Najibullah became the President of the Revolutionary Council of Afghanistan on September 30, 1987. Soon, a new constitution which offered for a "bicameral legislature" was promulgated. As per the new constitution, the representatives of the national assembly were to be "popularly elected". Members who were unattached with any official party were in preeminent position both inside the parliament and the government. The word 'democratic' was dropped from the name of the country, which thenceforth was known simply as the Republic of Afghanistan"[3].

Mohammad Najibullah assumed the post of President on November 30, 1987. He remained President till April 16, 1992.

Najibullah tried to get support for his government and for that he played the emotive Islamic card. Indeed, the 1990 constitution stated,

> "The republic of Afghanistan is an independent, unitary and indivisible and Islamic state. The sacred religion of Islam is the religion of Afghanistan. In the republic of Afghanistan no law shall run counter to the principles of the sacred religion of Islam and other values enshrined in this constitution"[4].

Najibullah, however, could not muster any support for his Government.

Meanwhile, the Soviets withdrew in 1989. "While direct Soviet assistance had ended, the Soviet Union still supported Najibullah with plentiful economic and military aid" (Alikuzai, 2013). Nevertheless, perturbed by the development, the Afghan Government gave more emphasis on reconciliation.

Things changed dramatically in December 1991. The USSR disintegrated. The new State, Russia, was facing economic crisis. Expectedly, it stopped funding the Afghan Government. Moreover, crisis within the Government intensified. Eventually, Najibullah resigned in April 1992. Apprehensive about his security, Najibullah took shelter inside the UN headquarters in Kabul. Regrettably, however, when Taliban succeeded to capture Kabul "in 1996, Najibullah is said to have been castrated by the Taliban, and was dragged behind a truck in the streets of Kabul, before he was publicly hanged" (Alikuzai, 2013).

He was succeeded by Abdul Rahim Hatef on April 16, 1992. He transferred power to Sibghatullah Mojadedi on April 28. Mojadedi remained in office till June 28.

Burhanuddin Rabbani representing *Mujahideens*

Burhanuddin Rabbani became President of Afghanistan on June 28, 1992, and remained in power till September 27, 1996, when the Taliban controlled Kabul. With Taliban storming into Kabul in September 1996, he went into exile and continued to claim Presidency. "He was still recognised as ruler of Afghanistan by the United Nations and some other countries until he formally handed over power to an Interim Government headed by Hamid Karzai on December 22, 2001"[5].

He was among one of the earliest founders of *mujahideens* movement in the late 1970s, right before the Soviet invasion of Afghanistan. Following the ouster of Najibullah Government in 1992, it was his forces, among many mujahedeen groups, that penetrated Kabul first.

Afghan *Mujahideens* and the Bloodbath

Soon after the formation of the Communist Government in Afghanistan in the aftermath of the 'Sawr Revolution', several Afghan *mujahideen* groups supported by USA, Pakistan, China, countries in the West, and the Arab world, primarily Saudi Arabia, revolted against the Government. These countries provided both financial and military support.

The role of foreign powers have been discussed in the Chapter 5, titled "External Conditioning of the Conflict."

In due course of time most of these groups coalesced into 11 major groups. These groups included the following[6],

Jebh-e-Nejat-i-Melli Afghanistan or Afghanistan National Liberation Front (ANLF): The ANLF is a moderate party established by Sibghatullah Mojadedi, a Pashtun. Principally secular, it got support from the tribes, the old social order and the Sufi orders of the South. It was very strong in the provinces of Kunar and Paktia provinces. It has Deobandi links.

Hezb-e-Islamie-i-Gulbuddin (HIG): The radical Islamist party HIG was formed with the objective to oppose the Daoud government was led by Gulbuddin Hikmatyar. Hikmatayar, a radical internationalist Pashtun, recruited profoundly from among the government secular school and Kabul religious school graduates. The party drew maximum support from Nuristan, Nangrahar and around Kabul. With the passage of time, dissent grew within the party, and it split as another two cofounders Burhanuddin Rabanni and Mawlawi Mohammed Yunis Khalis established their own factions.

Hezb-e-Islami-Khalis (HIK): Mawlawi Mohammed Yunis Khalis, a Tajik, who had migrated to Pakistan in 1973 after the Daud coup laid the foundation of this party. A hardcore anti-Shia leader Khalis belongs to Nangrahar Province. Among his trusted lieutenants were Abdul Haq, a Tajik, in Kabul, Haji Abdul Qadir in Nangrahar and Jalladuddin Hagani of Paktia Province. The party is fundamentalist moderate. Its recruits came from graduates of government schools, religious schools of the Gilhzai, Khugiangi and Jadran tribes as well as the Kabul and Kandahar regions. Its strength was in Nangrahar, Kabul, Kunar, Lowgar and Wardak provinces.

Harakat-e-Inqilab-i-Islami or Islamic Revolutionary Movement (IRMA): Formed by Mohammad Nabi

Mohammadi, IRMA, the party was moderate (traditional Islamist) and primarily Pashtun. It drew recruits from the private seminaries, liberal intellectuals, and the Andar, Gilhzai, Mahmund, Hotak, and Durrani tribes. Its strength was in Lowgar Province and the Helmand valley. General Yahyah Nawroz was one of its most famous commanders.

Jamiat-i-Islami or Islamic Society (JIA): The JIA was founded by a Tajik, Burhanuddin Rabanni, who escaped to Pakistan in 1974. His most trusted commanders were Ahmed Shah Masood, a Tajik, in the Panjshir valley and Ismail Khan, also a Tajik, in Herat Province. The party is primarily moderate fundamentalist and dominated by ethnic Tajiks, but has Uzbeks and Pashtun in its ranks. Its cadres came from the religious and secular government schools and northern Sunni religious schools and northern Sufi brotherhoods. Its force was in northern Afghanistan. It had members across Afghanistan but was particularly strong in Lowgar, Samangan, Faryab, Farah and Nimroz provinces. Masood later formed his own faction: Ittihad-e-Islami - Shura-e-Nazar Alliance, a military and political alliance of 130 northern commanders in the late 1980s.

Ittihad-I-Islami or Islamic Union for the Liberation of Afghanistan (IUA): The IUA, known as Etehad-e Islami (EIA) until 1981, was founded by Abd Al-Rab Abdul-Rassul Sayyaf, a Pashtun. The faction is combative fundamentalist and anti-Shia. The IUA was heavily financed by the Wahhabi sect out of Saudi Arabia. Sayyaf was known for recruiting motivated Arab youths for jihad in his organisation.

Mahaz-e-Melli or National Islamic Front of Afghanistan (NIFA): The NIFA was founded by Pir Sayed Ahmad Gailani, a Pashtun. This moderate party drew a number of former officers from the Afghan Army and moderate technocrats. This royalist party recruited from the landed aristocracy, the tribes and the Sufi brotherhood. The principal power base came from the Zadran, Mangal, Jaji, Ahmadzai, Tareen, Kochi, and Sulemankhel tribes. The party was mainly Pashtun and its strength was in Paktia, Paktika, Ghazni and Kandahar provinces.

Shura-iInqilab-iIttifagh-iIslami-i Afghanistan or Revolutionary Council of the Islamic Union of Afghanistan: It was a traditionalist Shia party led by Sayyad Beheshti. It recruited among the Hazara peasants and social elite. Many Afghan Army officers who deserted led its ranks. It had wide support in the Hazarajat and Ghazni Province.

Sazman-i Nasr-iIslami-yi Afghanistan or The Islamic Victory Organisation of Afghanistan: It was a radical Islamist party led by a council that recruited from young Hazara who were educated in Iran. This pro-Iran party was headquartered in Daykundi.

Harakat-i-Islami or Islamic Movement: It was founded by Ayatollah Asef Muhsini in Iran as a Shia faction. The party's orientation is traditionally Islamic. It recruited educated Shia from all ethnic groups. Its most famous commander was Mohammad Anwari who fought in the Turkmen valley west of Kabul.

Sepah-iPasdaran or Army of the Guardians of the Revolution: It was a radical Islamist party led by Akbari and Saddiqi. It had strong relation with the Iranian government. It had few fighters but drew from clerics who were disaffected with Behesti's Shura.

Evidently, the *mujahideens* were an exceptionally diverse lot, including ethnic Pashtuns, Uzbeks, Tajiks and others. Most of them were made up of Sunni Muslims, while some were Shia. The recruits were mainly "young Afghan men living in refugee camps"[7] in Pakistan.

In addition to the Afghan *mujahideens*, Muslims from other countries volunteered to join the *mujahideen* ranks. Arabs had joined the ranks of the *mujahideens*.

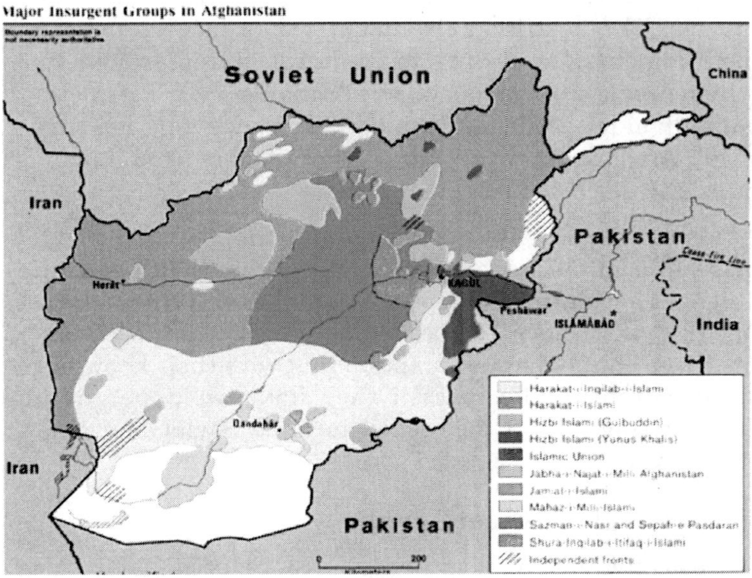

Source: Military Situation in Afghanistan, Afghanistan - Maps, Global Secuirty.org, http://www.globalsecurity.org/military/world/afghanistan/maps.htm

Figure 4.1. Major Insurgent Groups in Afghanistan during Soviet Invasion.

Unity among the *mujahideens* increased during the course of the conflict as they realised the might of the 'occupying Soviet Forces'. They were relentless in their attack on Soviet Forces and establishments of the government, puppet Government. On the other hand the Soviet Army with the help of the incumbent government continued its ruthless assault on the *mujahideens*.

The number of Afghan civilians killed during the decade long conflict (1979-89) stood approximately at 1.5 million (Lee, 2014). Moreover, 18,000 Afghan and over 14,500 Soviet troopers were also killed. The *mujahideens* suffered heavy casualties as they lost nearly 90,000 of their cadres (Taylor 2014). In total, approximately 2.72 million people died on Afghan land.

Moreover, around three million Afghans sustained injuries. The hostile environment led to large number of displacements. According to some estimates around five million people took refuge outside Afghanistan, while another two million left their native place and moved to other areas within Afghanistan in search of safety and started living as internally displaced persons.

Given the might of the Soviet Union, very few had imagined that the *mujahideens* could sustain their resistance for long. The *mujahideens*, on the other hand, were convinced that they will defeat the occupying forces. Their conviction was based on the their assumption that with their knowledge of the mountainous terrain they have an upper hand. Unsurprisingly, they succeeded to force Soviet for troop's withdrawal.

Withdrawal of Soviet Troops

Soon after the invasion, Soviet Forces realised that fighting the rebellious Afghan forces in the rugged terrains will be a difficult challenge. As the battle prolonged, the Soviet commanders felt requirement of more troops which the government was not in a position to provide. On the other hand, "morale in the Afghan military was low. Draftees deserted at the earliest opportunity, and the Afghan military dropped from its 1978 strength of 105,000 troops to about 20,000–30,000 by 1987. The Soviets attempted new tactics, but the resistance always devised counter tactics" (Encyclopaedia Britannica, 2014).

Meanwhile, Soviet Government's belief that it is fighting a losing battle became stronger when it started to emerge that the rebellious forces are getting direct support from outside forces, like US, Pakistan, Iran, and many other countries.

Significantly, the *mujahideens'* prospects improved greatly "towards the end of 1986 [as they] began to receive more and better weapons from the outside world - particularly from the United States, the United Kingdom (UK), and China via

Pakistan, the most important of these being the shoulder-fired ground-to-air missiles. The Soviet and Afghan Air Forces then began to suffer considerable casualties" (Gohari, 2000).

Not surprisingly, the Soviet Government which on many occasions in the past is reported to have discussed troop's withdrawal and stop looking for a military solution, but had never shown seriousness to the matter, got alarmed. It started looking for a way out.

Since the beginning of the Soviets invasion of Afghanistan, the US forced the USSR, through diplomatic channels to withdraw from Afghanistan. On the other hand, the Soviets, attempted to portray that they were not an occupying force and would leave Afghanistan once its security concerns were removed. The Democratic Republic of Afghanistan and the USSR had argued that Soviet forces had entered Afghanistan in order to protect the Afghan regime from foreign forces intervening – Pakistan supported *mujahideen* (Azam, 1993).

Meanwhile, with both the US and USSR agreeing, the UN had begun negotiations in 1982 to assist a Soviet withdrawal from Afghanistan. Pakistan and Afghan governments talked with the arbitration of the UN Secretary General's Special Representatives, Javier Perez de Cuellar and followed by Diego Cordovez. The talks were circuitous as Pakistan did not recognise the Democratic Republic of Afghanistan. The arrangement of negotiation had fundamentally been agreed upon by 1985 in which the US and the Soviet Union had dedicated themselves to guaranteeing the implementation of an accord leading to a withdrawal. Both the format and the substance of the agreement were designed to be acceptable to the Soviet Union and the Democratic Republic of Afghanistan (Azam, 1993).

By the commencement of 1987, the Soviets were resolute to withdraw. On the other hand the Soviet military insisted that Kabul should not be abandoned. Nevertheless, the Soviet leadership was convinced that resolution of cold war issues with the West and domestic restructuring were far more urgent than the fate of the Kabul government.

Pakistan which had a greater say and was in position of strength side-lined the *mujahedeen* and acted as their representative in all stages of arbitration.

Ultimately, on April 14, 1988, an accord was signed between Afghanistan and Pakistan, with the US and the USSR serving as guarantors. The accord came to be known as Geneva Accord.

The Geneva Accord had provisions for the timetable of the withdrawal of Soviet troops from Afghanistan. It facilitated the withdrawal of the Red Army from Afghanistan. It officially began on May 15, 1988 and ended by February 15, 1989. Lieutenant General Boris Gromov, who led the Soviet Forces at the time of the invasion, was the last trooper to leave.

Reporting about the accord BBC wrote,

The Soviet Union has signed an agreement pledging to withdraw its troops from Afghanistan. The pact, drawn up in negotiations between the United States, the USSR, Pakistan and Afghanistan, was signed in a United Nations ceremony in the Swiss capital, Geneva. It ends nine years of occupation by the Soviet Union, who intervened in 1979 to prop up the struggling communist government...Today's agreement provides for a gradual Russian withdrawal, phased over nine months. But critics have pointed out that it still allows the Soviet Union and the United States to continue arming the two sides in the Afghan civil war. Today's signing ceremony was itself fraught with complications and required some delicate negotiations to get all four parties around the table.

As the Afghan Mujahideens were neither party to the negotiations nor to the Geneva Accord, they refused to accept the terms of the agreement. Not surprisingly, the rebels attacked the withdrawing Soviet troop's convoy. In all, "523 Soviet soldiers were killed during the process of withdrawal"[8].

Emergence of Ethnic Conflict

Afghan Mujahideen were not in attendance in the procedure of the accord, though there were told about the developments infrequently and more importantly, poorly, by Pakistan. Pakistan actually acted as solicitor for Afghan resistance. Consequently, the war sustained even after the conclusion of the Soviet withdrawal.

Meanwhile, while some analysts believed that the withdrawal of Russian troops will lead to rapid demise of the Soviet-backed Najibullah Government, the contrary happened. Najibullah managed to retain power as he possessed the firepower to quell the internal rebellion. Najibullah Government managed to survive for three more years.

In the period after the withdrawal of the Red Army in 1989, the overall size of the Afghan armed forces stood at 329,000 men, 1,568 tanks, 828 armoured personnel carriers, over 4,880 artillery pieces of varying calibre, 126 combat aircraft and 14 military helicopters. Moreover, newly installed SCUD missile systems became a decisive tactical skill for Kabul to conduct its ongoing war with the mujahidin. Between October 1988 and February 1992, over 2,000 SCUD missiles were fired in Afghanistan, the single greatest attention of ballistic missiles launched in anger since the Second World War. Also, Soviet aid to the Najibullah regime was calculated by western observers in 1990 to amount to between two to six billion dollars annually (Marshall, 2006). It was enough for the Najibullah Government to thwart *mujahideens* threat.

The Najibullah Government also got the support of a section of the rebels. For instance, Abdul Rashid Dostum's warriors numbering 40,000 by 1991 joined the mainstream. This force was officially re-labelled the 53rd Division. It operated directly under Najibullah, bypassing the central Ministry of Defence. Forming the regime's sole mobile reserve after 1989, they emerged, in the assessment of one analyst, as 'the only formation capable of aggressive offensive operations' (Marshall, 2006).

Assured about his strength, Najibullah made several attempts for national reconciliation. But all his efforts were proved futile as the *mujahideens* had splintered into different groups.

In fact, soon after the Russian withdrawal, the *mujahideens*, who had joined forces to fight the 'occupying forces' split. Thus, began a prolonged ethnic conflict between several warlords.

Signs of disunity were visible during the course of Jalalabad Operation. Significantly, the external intelligence agency of Pakistan Inter-Services Intelligence (ISI), in the beginning of 1989, made an attempt to install a Pakistan-backed Government led by Gulbuddin Hikmatyar. Jalalabad was to be the capital.

Indeed, in March 1989 around 10,000 mujahidin under the tutelage of Pakistani ISI gathered outside Jalalabad, aided by pre-arranged defections from the Afghan 11th infantry division, and launched a long-lasting ground assault with the aim of seizing the town itself, creating an alternative governmental capital, and opening the road to Kabul. They, however, lost steam by April. By mid-May it became evident that they had suffered a severe battlefield defeat, incurring perhaps as many as 3,000 casualties (Marshall, 2006). Thousands of civilians were killed.

Significantly, Ahmed Shah Masood and Abdul Haq, the prominent mujahideen leaders stayed away from the operation. It was their belief that *mujahideens* lack the capacity to defeat the government forces in conventional war and take control of Jalalabad. In a clear sign of lack of unity among the *mujahideens* Masood claimed that he came to know about the operation through BBC. Criticising the approach of Pakistan and its Afghan followers in launching an attack without taking other *mujahideens* groups into confidence, Masood stated, "The damage caused by our [meaning the mujahideen forces] lack of a unified command is obvious. There is a total lack of coordination, which means we are not launching simultaneous offensives on different fronts. As a result the government can concentrate its resources and pick us off one by one. And that is what has happened at Jalalabad" (Camp, 2001-2002). Likewise, Haq argued, "How is that we Afghans, who never lost a war, must take military instructions from the Pakistanis, who never won one?"

Moreover, according to published reports, even during the 1980s, Hikmatyar's HIH "developed a reputation for attacking moderates, raiding caravans of other forces as well as relief organisations" (Fitzgerald and Gould, 2011). Hekmatyar was relentless in his opposition to Ahmad Shah Mascod that Washington "feared he might be a secret KGB [Komitet Gosudarstvennoy Bezopasnosti, Russian Spy Agency] plant whose mission was to sow disruption within the anti-communist resistance" (Coll, 2004). Notably, Hkmatyar had got continuous support from US through Pakistan.

In one such incident, in 1989 Gulbuddin Hikmatyar's forces carried out an attack directly targeting Ahmad Shah Masood and the senior leadership of Shura-e-Nazar. Though Masood escaped unhurt, around 30 of his men, including some close friends were brutally killed. Subsequently, Masood's Shura-e-Nazar was able to capture the attackers. As Masood was more interested in forging an unity among the *mujahideens*, instead of taking revenge by killing those who were captured.

Indeed, Ahmad Shah Masood was "the only Afghan leader with an integrated vision". He had once declared, "My message to Hikmatyar's people is that without a united front we cannot succeed, we cannot achieve anything in Afghanistan".

Meanwhile, Najibullah who had been able to thwart the mujahideens attempt to overrun his state, faced the recurrent problem of disunity within his party. The rift became evident. Unsurprisingly, Defense Minister, Shahnawaz Tanai, who belonged to the Khalq faction of the PDPA, "entering into secret talks with Gulbuddin Hekmatyar, [Tanai] launched a coup bid against the Kabul government on 6th March 1990 that came close to killing Najibullah himself' (Marshall, 2006). The oppression of the disaffected army men trustworthy to Tanai obligated the government in Kabul to increase rocket attacks on its own airfields, destructing 46 aircraft in the process, of which only 34 were later repaired. Tanai escaped to Pakistan, leaving behind him an establishment significantly weakened (Marshall, 2006). Consequently, the rift between the two factions reached at a greater level.

In the meantime, policies of "*perestroika* (restructuring) and *glasnost* (openness) were Mikhail Gorbachev's watchwords for the renovation of the Soviet body politic and society that he pursued as general secretary of the Communist Party from 1985 until 1991"[9], eventually led to the disintegration of USSR in 15 independent States (Shoemaker, 1970) in December 1991. This development proved detrimental for Najibullah Government as the new Russian Government could not continue the economic and political support for the Najibullah Government. Expectedly the Najibullah Government collapsed in April 1992.

According to the US Library of Congress 1997, complicity amid military leaders rapidly brought down the Kabul government. In mid-January 1992, within three weeks of the collapse of the Soviet Union, Ahmad Shah Masood became conscious of conflict within the government's northern command. General Abdul Momim, in charge of the Hairatan border crossing at the northern end of Kabul's supply highway, and other non-Pashtun generals based in Mazari-i-Sharif feared exclusion by Najibullah and substitution by Pashtun officers.

As the generals revolted the situation was taken over by Abdul Rashid Dostum, who held general rank as head of the Jozjani militia, also based in Mazar-i-Sharif. He and Masood reached a political conformity, together with another major militia leader, Sayyid Mansor, of the Ismaili community based in Baghlan Province. These northern allies consolidated their position in Mazar-i-Sharif on March 21. The coalition covered nine provinces in the north and northeast (US Library of Congress, 1997).

The government force was absent in the area between the northern allies and the major air force base at Begram, some seventy kilometers north of Kabul, as the disorder developed within the government in Kabul. By mid-April the air force command at Begram had capitulated to Masood. Kabul was defenseless, its army was no more dependable. Najibullah had lost domestic control instantly after he declared his willingness on March 18 to resign in order to make way for a neutral interim government (US Library of Congress, 1997).

As the government splintered into numerous factions it became difficult to accomplish a transfer of power. Najibullah tried to fly out of Kabul on April 17, but was stopped by Dostum's troops who controlled Kabul Airport under the command of Karmal's brother, Mahmud Baryalai. Retribution between *Parchami* factions was reaped. Najibullah took sanctuary at the UN mission where he remained in 1995. A group of *Parchami* generals and officials affirmed themselves an interim government for the purpose of handing over power to the mujahidin" (US Library of Congress, 1997)

Meanwhile, the Kabul interim authority invited Masood to enter Kabul as the new Head of State, but he held back. Masood ordered his forces, located to the north of Kabul, not to penetrate "the capital until a political resolution was in place. He called on all the senior Afghan party leaders, many then based in exile in Peshawar, to work out a political settlement acceptable to all sides and parties."[10]

Further, "with United Nations support, most Afghan political parties decided to appoint a legitimate national government to succeed communist rule, through an elite settlement"[11]. At that point of time, some *mujahideen* factions had begun their march to penetrate Kabul - Gulbuddin Hikmatyar's HIG from the south; Abd Al-Rab Abdul-Rassul Sayyaf's IUA from the west; the Mawlawi Mohammed Yunis Khalis led HIK from the east, etc.

However, following the call for unity Afghan *mujahideen* leaders met in Peshawar (Pakistan), for "establishing a broad coalition government inclusive of all parties. On April 24, 1992, the leaders in Peshawar agreed on and signed the Peshawar Accord"[12]. The Accord got support of all *mujahideen* parties. Even a section of the disposed Najibullah Government also supported it.

Subsequently, an interim government was formed. The government was headed by a Supreme Leadership Council. Sibghatullah Mojadedi was made the President for two months. As per the agreement Burhanuddin Rabbani succeeded him. The Defence Minister in the new government was Masood. Notably, following the Peshawar Accord Afghanistan became Islamic State of Afghanistan.

Meanwhile, despite being offered Prime Ministership Hikmatyar refused to sign the Accord. In fact, he sought to become the sole ruler of Afghanistan stating that coalition government in Afghanistan as it is going to be weak and incapable of stabilising the situation. In response Masood stated that all the parties had participated in *jihad* in Afghanistan, so they had to have their share in the government. Again, when Masood said that Kabul is ready to surrender, so instead of the fighting we should gather and the troops should not enter Kabul, they should enter later on as part of the government; Hikmatyar responded by saying, "We will march into Kabul with our naked sword. No one can stop us. Why should we meet the leaders? On this Masood retorted, "It seems to me that you don't want to join the leaders in Peshawar nor stop your threat, and you are planning to enter Kabul. In that case I must defend the people".[13] The divide was apparent.

Eventually, Masood ordered his forces to enter Kabul. On April 30, 1992, Kabul was under the command of the Interim Government. However, normalcy outside Kabul had not been restored. In fact, though he was forced to leave Kabul, Hikmatyar's Forces stationed itself just at the periphery of

Kabul from where they continued their artillery barrage inside Kabul. He was getting the support of Islamabad.

Meanwhile, Rabbani assumed office on June 28. Hikmatyar continued his assault against Afghanistan. "In January 1994, Hikmatyar joined forces with Dostum to oust Rabbani and his defense minister, Masood, launching full-scale civil war in Kabul. In 1994 alone, an estimated 25,000 were killed in Kabul, most of them civilians killed in rocket and artillery attacks"[14].

Describing this phase of conflict, Human Rights Watch writes,

"Rare ceasefires, usually negotiated by representatives of Ahmad Shah Masood, SibghatullahMojaddedi or Burhanuddin Rabbani [the interim government], or officials from the International Committee of the Red Cross (ICRC), commonly collapsed within days" (IBPUSA, 2013).

Though Kabul remained under the government control, the security environment beyond the peripheries of Kabul was worrisome. There was complete pandemonium across the country.

Eventually, the chaos that prevailed provided ample opportunity for Taliban to gain foothold.

Rise of Taliban

Significantly, at that point of time Southern Afghanistan was neither under the control of foreign-backed militias nor the interim Government in Kabul. It was 'governed' by Gul Agha Sherzai.

Sensing an opportunity, Mullah Mohammad Omar [a Pashtun] began his movement [known as Taliban Movement] with fewer than 50 armed *madrassa* students in his hometown of Kandaharin 1994. The Taliban forces in 1994 captured the city of Kandhar from a local warlord (IBPUSA, 2013) and achieved many more 'victories'.

Emboldened by the successes, the Taliban launched firing at Kabul in early 1995, but were crushed by forces of the Islamic State government under Ahmad Shah Masood. Nevertheless, Taliban returned with more firepower and established its Islamic Emirate of Afghanistan in September 1996.

Establishment of Islamic Emirate of Afghanistan

After facing reverses in battle for Kabul, Taliban started concentrating on the outer periphery. In September 1995, Taliban captured the important city of Herat. It gradually started inching closer towards Kabul.

Realising the imminent defeat Masood pulled out his forces from Kabul. Eventually, on September 27, Mullah Mohammad Omar became the de facto Head of State. Afghanistan became Islamic Emirate of Afghanistan. Only Saudi Arabia, Pakistan and the United Arab Emirates recognised it.

However, for the rest of the international community, Rabbani's Government continued as the legitimate government.

Bloody Conflict under Taliban

The Taliban Government began with a barbaric act. Significantly, in the afternoon of September 26, 1996, Massod sent one of his senior Generals to request Najibullah to leave with the retreating government troops, assuring him safe passage to the North (IBPUSA, 2013), but he refused the offer. He was brutally killed. As Rashid writes, On September 27, the day the Emirate was established,

"The Taliban walked upto Najibullah's room, beat him and his brother senseless and then bundled them into a pick-up and drove them to the darkened Presidential Palace. There they castrated Najibullah, dragged his body behind a jeep for several rounds of the Palace and then shot him dead. His brother was similarly tortured and throttled to death. The Taliban hanged the two dead men from a concrete traffic control post just outside the Palace, only a few blocks from the UN compound" (Rashid, 2002).

This first act was the precursor of the barbaric rule that Afghanistan witnessed under Taliban. The Taliban movement which had started with an "aim to cleanse society" and provide safety to the people, started targeting the civilians opposed to their idea. The Hazara Shia population was the worst victim of the onslaught.

Indeed, the *Human Rights Watch* in report titled *Massacres of Hazaras in Afghanistan*, released on February 20, 2001, noted that mass killings of Hazars are taking place. Sidney Jones, Asia director of HRW, on the occasion stated, "The international focus on Afghanistan in recent months has been almost exclusively on the Taliban's reported support for terrorism abroad. The same energy should be directed to stopping the killings of civilians inside Afghanistan." The report quoted eyewitnesses in many villages describing Arab fighters carrying long knives used for slitting throats and skinning people.

In one incident of massacre, after taking over Mazar-i-Sharif in 1998, the Taliban executed about 4,000 civilians and tortured many more. Evidently, barbarism was at its peak during Taliban rule.

Osama bin Laden's al Qaeda was as repressive as the Taliban and was spreading its wing under the tutelage of Taliban government. Meanwhile, the Taliban refused to hand over Laden (later killed in an US operation inside Pakistan in May 2011) to the US. The US had claimed that he was involved in acts of terror across the globe through his network.

Nonetheless, the Taliban continued to spread and by some accounts, by the time the *Operation Enduring Freedom* began in 2001, the Taliban was in control of almost the entire country barring some areas in North.

However, they lost public support. According to the US *Congressional Research Service* (CRS) report dated October 9, 2014.

The Taliban lost international and domestic support as it imposed strict adherence to Islamic customs in areas it controlled and employed harsh punishments, including executions. The Taliban authorised its 'Ministry for the Promotion of Virtue and the Suppression of Vice' to use physical punishments to enforce strict Islamic practices, including bans on television, Western music, and dancing. It prohibited women from attending school or working outside the home, except in healthcare, and it publicly executed some women for adultery. In what many consider its most extreme action, and which some say was urged by Bin Laden, in March 2001 the Taliban blew up two large Buddha statues carved into hills above Bamiyan city, considering them idols.

Resistance to Taliban Movement

Realising the growing threat from Taliban, Hikmatyar and the Burhanuddin Rabbani Government joined hands. The duo on March 7, 1996, signed an agreement where they agreed to take military action against the Taliban. However, they failed to stall the Taliban March.

Soon after the establishment of the Emirate there emerged a coalition of *mujahideen* militias, "United Islamic Front for the Salvation of Afghanistan, usually referred to as Northern Alliance" (Leverett, 2009). It included, top leaders of the Islamic State of Afghanistan, particularly, president in exile, Burhanuddin Rabbani and former Defense Minister Ahmad Shah Masood. The powerful forces of Abdul Rashid Dostum had also joined the Alliance. Initially it included mostly Tajiks but by year 2000, it emerged as a multiethnic Alliance.

The Northern Alliance resisted Taliban move in Northern Afghanistan. Consequently, the two sides fought bitterly, and it went on till the time a new government was formed in Kabul. Nevertheless, a large swath of land in the Northern part remained under the Alliance's control till the very end of Taliban rule.

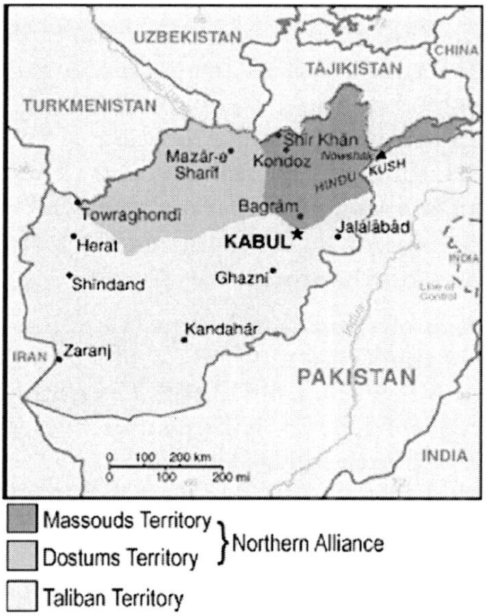

Source: Political Map of Afghanistan (1996), Landkarten & Stadtplan Index http://www.landkartenindex.de/weltatlas/? p. 2425.

Figure 4.2.Political Map of Afghanistan (1996).

Not surprisingly, scores of people were killed in the fighting.

Meanwhile, after the US-led invasion in the aftermath of 9/11, and the establishment of the Hamid Karzai Government in December 2001, the Northern Alliance broke apart and different political parties were formed.

Al Qaeda in Afghanistan

According to the SATP, Al Qaeda, or 'The Base', was formed in 1988 by Osama bin Laden and his associate Mohammed Atef to bring together Arabs who fought in Afghanistan against the Soviet invasion.

From 1988 until in or about 1991, the al Qaeda was headquartered in Afghanistan and Peshawar. In 1992, the al

Qaeda leadership as also its military command shifted its headquarters to Khartoum, the capital city of Sudan, in North Africa. With increasing USA pressure on Sudan, Laden reverted to Afghanistan in 1996, by which time the Taliban regime were controlling a major portion of that country's territory. From his hideouts in Taliban-controlled Afghanistan, Laden provided financial and other material support, religious fervour and 'inspiration' to thousands of al Qaeda cadres and affiliates throughout the world.[15]

With the aim of spreading Islamic Caliphate as against the influence of the West, al Qaeda evolved considerably to emerge as a primary umbrella outfit. The outfit carried out several attacks world over killing scores of people. The September 2001 attacks (also referred as 9/11) proved the deadliest and it eventually led to change of regime in Afghanistan.

September 11 Attacks

It was a coordinated and first of its kind attack. On September 11, 2001, 19 terrorists hijacked four fuel-loaded commercial airlines which were to go for west coast destinations. At 8:46 am American Airlines Flight 11 (travelling from Boston to Los Angeles) strikes the north tower of the World Trade Center (WTC) in New York City. At 9:03 am, United Airlines Flight 175 (travelling from Boston to Los Angeles) strikes the south tower of the WTC in New York City. At 9:37 am American Airlines Flight 77 (travelling from Dulles, Virginia to Los Angeles) strikes the Pentagon Building (the headquarters of the United States Department of Defense) in Washington. At 10:03 am, United Airlines Flight 93 (travelling from New York, New Jersey to San Francisco) crashes in a field near Shanksville in Pennsylvania.[16]

A total of 2,977 people were killed. At the WTC, 2,753 people were killed. Of those who killed during the early part of attacks and the consequent collapses of the towers, 343 were New York City firefighters, another 23 were New York City police officers and 37 others were officers at the Port Authority. At the Pentagon in Washington, 184 people were killed. Near Shanksville in Pennsylvania, 40 passengers and crew members aboard United Airlines Flight 93 die when the plane crashes into a field. It is supposed that the terrorists crashed the plane in that location, rather than their unknown target, after the passengers and crew attempted to retake control of the flight deck.[17]

Subsequently, on December 13, 2001, the US government released a tape in which Osama bin Laden took responsibility for the attacks[18].

Operation enduring Freedom

Significantly, K. P. S. Gill, the former Director General of Police credited for wiping out terror in Indian State of Punjab, in a statement released on the day of attack had stated,

> "The enormity of the events of September 11, 2001, in New York and Washington, will have reverberations across the world in the days and years to come, and will certainly transform the attitudes of ambivalence towards terrorism that have been reflected in policies and practices of the Western world till now" (Gill, 2001).

The Police official was apt in his assessment.

Indeed, the US President George W. Bush in his address to the Congress and the nation on September 20, 2001, stated:

> "Tonight we are a country awakened to danger and called to defend freedom. Our grief has turned to anger, and anger to resolution. Whether we bring our enemies to justice, or bring justice to our enemies, justice will be done. On September the 11th, enemies of freedom committed an act of war against our country. Americans have many questions tonight. Americans are asking: Who attacked our country? The evidence we have gathered all points to a collection of loosely affiliated terrorist organisations known as al Qaeda. This group and its leader — a person

named Osama bin Laden — are linked to many other organisations in different countries, including the Egyptian Islamic Jihad and the Islamic Movement of Uzbekistan. There are thousands of these terrorists in more than 60 countries. They are recruited from their own nations and neighbourhoods and brought to camps in places like Afghanistan, where they are trained in the tactics of terror. They are sent back to their homes or sent to hide in countries around the world to plot evil and destruction. The leadership of al Qaeda has great influence in Afghanistan and supports the Taliban regime in controlling most of that country. In Afghanistan, we see al Qaeda's vision for the world. The United States respects the people of Afghanistan — after all, we are currently its largest source of humanitarian aid — but we condemn the Taliban regime. It is not only repressing its own people, it is threatening people everywhere by sponsoring and sheltering and supplying terrorists. By aiding and abetting murder, the Taliban regime is committing murder. And tonight, the United States of America makes the following demands on the Taliban: Deliver to United States authorities all the leaders of al Qaeda who hide in your land. Release all foreign nationals, including American citizens, you have unjustly imprisoned. Protect foreign journalists, diplomats and aid workers in your country. Close immediately and permanently every terrorist training camp in Afghanistan, and hand over every terrorist, and every person in their support structure, to appropriate authorities. Give the United States full access to terrorist training camps, so we can make sure they are no longer operating. These demands are not open to negotiation or discussion. The Taliban must act, and act immediately. They will hand over the terrorists, or they will share in their fate. Our war on terror begins with al Qaeda, but it does not end there" (Presidents Statement in the US Congress).

As Taliban, expectedly, failed to meet US demand, Bush while addressing to the nation on October 7, 2001, declared:

> "On my orders, the United States military has begun strikes against al Qaeda terrorist training camps and military installations of the Taliban regime in Afghanistan. These carefully targeted actions are designed to disrupt the use of Afghanistan as a terrorist base of operations, and to attack the military capability of the Taliban regime. We are joined in this operation by our staunch friend, Great Britain. Other close friends, including Canada, Australia, Germany and France, have pledged forces as the operation unfolds. More than 40 countries in the Middle East, Africa, Europe and across Asia have granted air transit or landing rights. Many more have shared intelligence. We are supported by the collective will of the world. More than two weeks ago, I gave Taliban leaders a series of clear and specific demands: Close terrorist training camps; hand over leaders of the al Qaeda network; and return all foreign nationals, including American citizens, unjustly detained in your country. None of these demands were met. And now the Taliban will pay a price. By destroying camps and disrupting communications, we will make it more difficult for the terror network to train new recruits and coordinate their evil plans. Initially, the terrorists may burrow deeper into caves and other entrenched hiding places. Our military action is also designed to clear the way for sustained, comprehensive and relentless operations to drive them out and bring them to justice. The name of today's military operation is Enduring Freedom. We defend not only our precious freedoms, but also the freedom of people everywhere to live and raise their children free from fear. The battle is now joined on many fronts. We will not waver; we will not tire; we will not falter; and we will not fail. Peace and freedom will prevail."[19]

Within months, the operation yielded results. The Taliban was ousted from power.

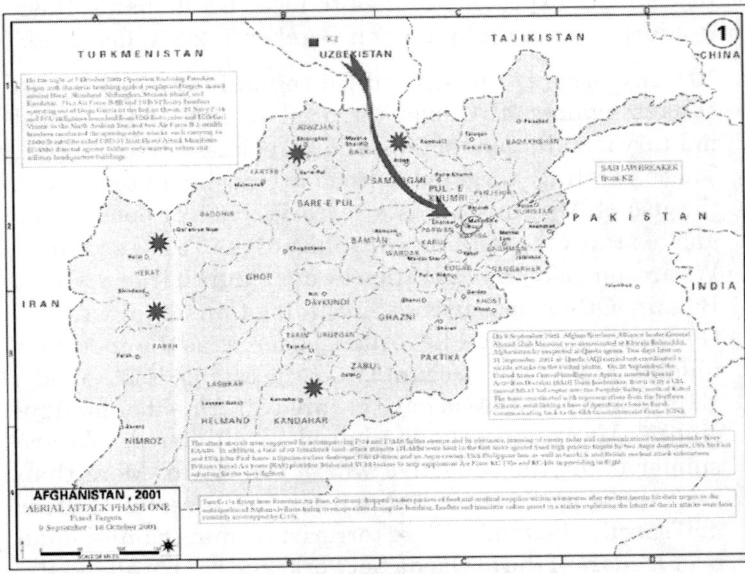

Source: History Map of Afghanistan 2001, Emerson Kent.com http://www.emersonkent.com/map_archive/afghanistan_2001.htm

Figure 4.3.Afghanistan 2001.

Conflict Resolution

The end of the Cold War and the subsequent demise of Soviet Union created a New World order. The state of Afghanistan was at a critical juncture. Her neighbouring states like Pakistan and Iran took advantage of it and made sincere efforts to influence the Afghan situation according to their own needs. However, neither the big powers like the USA and Russia nor the world organisations like the UN had shown keen interest in Afghanistan. The September 11 incident drew the attention of the world community towards Afghanistan. The Taliban misrule, ethnic strife, Islamic fundamentalism and terrorist infrastructure in Afghanistan compelled the world leaders, policy-makers and security analysts to describe it as a "failed state". The world community gave importance to state structuration and reconstruction in Afghanistan after the downfall of Taliban.

Soon, on the 5th of December 2001 several Afghan factions met under the sponsorship of the United Nations, in Bonn Germany, to end the conflict in Afghanistan, promote national reconciliation, and plan a pathway for governing the country. Afghan representatives from the Northern Alliance, the Peshawar Group - representing Afghan refugees in Pakistan, the Rome Delegation - representing former King Mohammad Zahir Shah, and the Cyprus Group - representing a group of exiles in Iran, signed in the presence of the UN Special Representative of the Secretary-General (SRSG) the 'Agreement on Provisional Arrangements in Afghanistan Pending the Re-Establishment of Permanent Government Institutions', which became known as the 'Bonn Agreement'.[20]

Notably, the Bonn Agreement initiated a democratic state building process. Since no Afghan government has been recognised by the whole nation since 1979, it was necessary to first establish an Interim Administration during a transition period until a permanent government was elected. The Bonn Agreement facilitated this process. On 9 October 2004, Presidential elections were held.[21] Karzai emerged winner and became President. The 2005 parliamentary elections were also successful.

The processes of final resolution thus begin.

Meanwhile, after the ouster of the Taliban from power in 2001, the ethnic conflict that had pushed the nation at the brink of structural collapse took the form of Islamist terrorism. The situation though was not alarming in early years.

Regrettably, however, the Taliban with the help of people at the helm of affairs in Islamabad regrouped. In fact, Islamabad took the advantage of the fact that the international community became less focused on Afghanistan after the collapse of Taliban regime. Islamist militancy picked up. Taliban was on surge.

Perturbed by the resurgence of Taliban, the US President Barack Obama in December 2009 called for surge in Forces strength. In his address to the nation on the 'Way Forward in Afghanistan and Pakistan', Obama stated on December 1, 2009,

> "This review is now complete. And as Commander-in-Chief, I have determined that it is in our vital national interest to send an additional 30,000 U.S. troops to Afghanistan. After 18 months, our troops will begin to come home. These are the resources that we need to seize the initiative, while building the Afghan capacity that can allow for a responsible transition of our forces out of Afghanistan."[22]

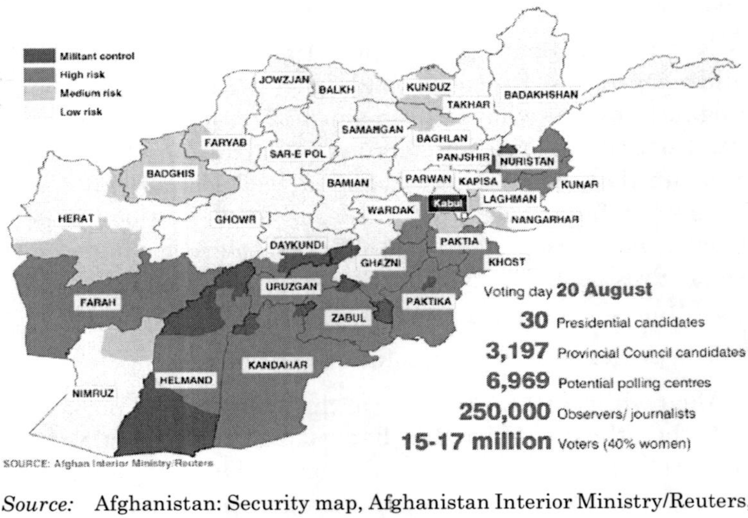

Source: Afghanistan: Security map, Afghanistan Interior Ministry/Reuters, http://news.bbc.co.uk/2/hi/south_asia/8194230.stm

Figure 4.4: Afghanistan Security Map 2009.

In fact, the new AfPak policy of Obama backfired. His call for surge in Forces along with the assertion that troops withdrawal will begin emboldened the spirits of Taliban. The Taliban felt that they have succeeded in defeating the foreign forces and now they have the chance to 'strengthen' their hold. They upped their ante.

Indeed, thousands of people are being killed on a yearly basis in terrorism related violence that is going unabated.

The latest report, titled *Protection of Civilians in Armed Conflict*, released by the *United Nations Assistance Mission in Afghanistan* (UNAMA), in July 2014, quoted Jan Kubis, United Nations Special Representative of the Secretary-General in Afghanistan, as saying,

"Civilians continue to bear the brunt of violence in Afghanistan. More efforts are required to protect civilians from the harms of conflict and to ensure accountability for those deliberately and indiscriminately killing them."[23]

The report further states,

> In the first half of 2014, the armed conflict in Afghanistan took a dangerous new turn for civilians. For the first time since 2009 when UNAMA began systematically documenting civilian casualties in Afghanistan, more civilians were found to have been killed and injured in ground engagements and crossfire between Anti-Government Elements and Afghan national security forces than any other tactic. In previous years, the majority of civilians were killed and injured by improvised explosive devices.

Despite 'repeated assurances', the Taliban continued to target civilians through the first half of 2014. Out of the 147 attacks claimed by the Taliban in which UNAMA recorded civilian casualties, 75 attacks appeared to have been directed at military targets, while 72 attacks deliberately targeted civilian objectives, including tribal elders, civilian government and justice sector employees, and civilians in public places. Out of the 4,853 civilian casualties (1,564 civilian deaths and 3,289 injuries) in the first half of 2014, the Taliban publicly claimed responsibility for 553 civilian casualties (234 killed and 319 injured). During the same period in 2013, out of

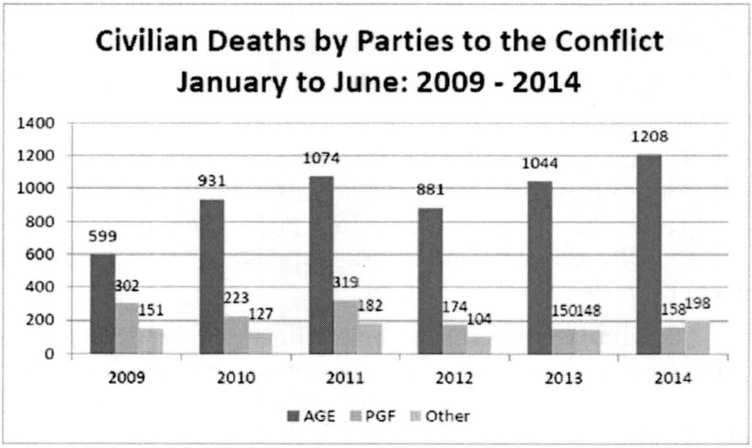

Source: Protection of Civilians in Armed Conflict midyear Report 2014 Afghanistan, UNAMA
http://unama.unmissions.org/Portals/UNAMA/human%20rights/English%20edited%20light.pdf

Figure 4.5: Civilian Deaths.

3,919 civilian casualties (1,342 civilian deaths and 2,577 injured), the Taliban claimed responsibility for 571 civilian casualties (166 civilians killed and 405 injured) in a total of 52 attacks. Significantly, there is an increase of 17 per cent in civilian deaths and 28 per cent in civilian injuries (24 per cent overall increases in civilian casualties) in 2014, as compared to the corresponding period in the previous year.

More worryingly, for the first time since 2009 when UNAMA began systematically documenting civilian casualties in Afghanistan, more civilians were found to have been killed and injured in ground engagements and crossfire between terrorists and SFs than any other tactic. Between January 1 and June 30, 2014, UNAMA documented 1,901 civilian casualties (474 civilian deaths and 1427 injuries) from ground engagements, as against 1,004 civilian casualties (219 civilian deaths and 785 injuries) in the corresponding period of 2013, an 89 per cent increase. Ground engagements include kinetic ground operations, crossfire, stand-off attacks and armed clashes between parties to the conflict that encompass attacks or operations in which small arms, heavy weapons and/or area weapon systems such as mortars and rockets are fired. Earlier, improvised explosive device (IED) explosions were the most preferred tactic.

The gigantic increase in ground engagements between the terrorists and SFs is, according to UNAMA, directly related to, the closure and transfer of more than 86 International Security Assistance Force (ISAF) bases in the last half of 2013. Obviously, the Afghan National Defense Security Force (ANDSF), which now controls almost 93 per cent of Afghan territory and leads 97 per cent of all security operations across the country, has failed to stem the spread of the Taliban, who are increasing their physical presence across wider areas. Despite ANDSF demonstrating their capabilities in a number of successful operations, tremendous vulnerabilities are increasingly visible. Indeed, varying media sources estimate that the Taliban has regrouped and now dominates an estimated 40 to 60 per cent of Afghanistan.

According to an unpublished partial data compiled by the New Delhi based *Institute for Conflict Management*, which maintains the largest database on terrorism related incidents in South Asia (www.satp.org), a total of 19492 civilians have been killed since 2007. It is not only the civilians who are facing the brunt of this mindless mayhem. As per the data, a total of 8379 ANDSF personnel, comprising of Afghan National Army (ANA), Afghan National Police (ANP) and Afghan Air Force, have been killed since 2007. The number of militants killed during the corresponding period stands at whopping 33415.

Table 1: Terrorism-related Fatalities in Afghanistan: 2007-2014

Year	*Afghan National Army*	*Afghan National Police*	*ISAF*	*Civilian*	*Militant*	*Total*
2007	278	688	232	1523	4500	7221
2008	259	724	295	2118	5000	8396
2009	292	639	521	2412	4610	8474
2010	821	1292	711	2777	5225	10826
2011	511	569	566	3021	4275	8942
2012	229	262	402	2754	2716	6363
2013	171	1082	161	2959	2702	7075
2014	282	280	65	1928	4387	6942
Total*	2843	5536	2953	19492	33415	64239

* Data till October 3, 2014.

Source: Compiled by this researcher on the basis of data obtained from various media sources and Government agencies

The numbers clearly suggest that Afghanistan is currently under the hold of Islamist terrorism. The Taliban have returned and now controls large swathe of Afghan territory. Indeed, varying media sources estimate that the Taliban now dominates an estimated 40 to 60 per cent of Afghanistan. Moreover, there are at least 25,000 Taliban militants operating within Afghanistan. These include about 3000 Haqqani Network militants and 1000 HIG militants[24].

America's 'drawdown' is taking place at a time when a troubled Afghanistan has been tainted by large-scale corruption (the country ranked 174th out of 176 in the 2012 Corruption Perceptions Index), and capacities for governance remain deeply suspect. Though apprehensions of an abrupt collapse, comparable to events in the aftermath of the Soviet withdrawal in 1989, have receded, the uncertainties of the situation are monumental. Worse, the future of Afghanistan remains as intimately tied to global peace and stability as has been its recent past. If the Western powers leave chaos behind in this unfortunate country, it is likely to follow them home in their baggage trains.

References

1. Hafizullah Amin, Encyclopedia Britannica, http://www.britannica.com/EBchecked/topic/20639/Hafizullah-Amin
2. Tajbeg Palace - Abandoned in Afghanistan, 25 July, 2012, http://www.worldabandoned.com/2012/07/tajbeg-palace.html, accessed on September 5, 2014.
3. Constitutional History of Afghanistan, Encyclopedia, Iranica, http://www.iranicaonline.org/articles/constitutional-history-of-afghanistan , accessed on September 6, 2014.
4. The Constitution of Afghanistan 1990, History, Afghanistan Online, http://www.afghan-web.com/history/const/const1990.html
5. Burhanuddin Rabbani, Military, Global Secuirty.org, http://www.globalsecurity.org/military/world/afghanistan/rabbani.htm
6. This portion has been taken from the description on Anti-Soviet Mujahedeen groups available at Global Security.org, http://www.globalsecurity.org/military/world/para/mujahideen.htm
7. Mujahideen, Encyclopedia Britannica, http://www.britannica.com/EBchecked/topic/396634/mujahideen , accessed on July 5, 2014.
8. How Not to End a War, The Washington Post, http://www.washingtonpost.com/wp-dyn/content/graphic/2007/07/17/GR2007071700070.html
9. 1985: Perestroika and Glasnost, Seventeen Moments in Soviet History, thttp://soviethistory.macalester.edu/index.php?page=subject&SubjectID=1985perestroika&Year=1985, accessed on August 15, 2014.
10. Ahmad Shah Massoud, National Radio Television of Afghanistan, http://rta.org.af/en/index.php/figures/430-ahmad-shah-massoud, accessed on June 26, 2014.
11. *Ibid.*
12. *Ibid.*
13. *Ibid.*
14. Crisis of Impunity - The Role of Pakistan, Russia, and Iran in Fueling the Civil War in Afghanistan, Human Rights Watch, refworld, http://www.refworld.org/docid/3bd540b60.html
15. Al Qaeda, South Asia Terrorism Portal, http://www.satp.org/satporgtp/usa/Al_Queda.htm
16. http://edition.cnn.com/2013/07/27/us/september-11-anniversary-fast-facts
17. *Ibid.*
18. *Ibid.*

19. Text: Bush Announces Strikes Against Taliban, The Washington Post, October 7, 2001, http://www.washingtonpost.com/wp-srv/nation/specials/attacked/transcripts/bushaddress_100801.htm, Accessed on August 12, 2013.
20. From the Bonn Agreement to the 2005 Wolesi Jirga and Provincial Council Elections, General Backgrounder, http://web.archive.org/web/20090305155438/http://www.unama-afg.org/news/_parelection/_factsheets/_english/JEMBS%20PO%20BG%20General%20BG%20final%202005-4-1%20eng.pdf
21. *Ibid.*
22. Remarks by the President in Address to the Nation on the Way Forward in Afghanistan and Pakistan, Office of the Press Secretary, The White House, December 1, 2009, http://www.whitehouse.gov/the-press-office/remarks-president-address-nation-way-forward-afghanistan-and-pakistan
23. Protection of Civilians in Armed Conflict, Mid Year Report 2014, Afghanistan, http://unama.unmissions.org/default.aspx?tabid=13941&language=en-us
24. Afghanistan: Post-Taliban Governance, Security, and U.S. Policy, Congressional Research Service, January 17, 2014, http://fpc.state.gov/documents/organisation/221259.pdf

Chapter - 5

External Conditioning of the Conflict

For the outside world Afghanistan, the 'land of the Afghans', has always remained strategically a vital area. Located on the ancient Silk Road, which carried trade from Mediterranean to China, Afghanistan has often been described by scholars as a 'gateway to India'. Some other scholars have even called Afghanistan the 'Central Asian roundabout'.

Meanwhile, over and again it has been emphasised that Afghanistan stands in a dangerous neighbourhood. Unsurprisingly, the prevalence of political instability and misery of its people is due to the fact that peripheral as distant powers "seeking to realise their own strategic, ideological, and economic interests in the country" have interfered in the country on numerous occasions in the past. These powers have on some occasions" acted on behalf of domestic clients" and have controlled and equipped them to dictate terms over large swath of the country. Although famous for resisting intruders, Afghans cannot be pardoned of accountability for much of the "fratricide and destruction" that has taken place within the country in recent decades. Still, the infuriating position of external powers, near and far, has proved more lethal in sustaining the conflict (Weinbaum, 2006).

Corroborating with the fact, the Head of the United Nations Mission in Liberia (UNMIL) field Office in Maryland, Corinna Vigier, writes the following:

> "Afghanistan has a history of invasions from foreign forces which have all resulted in the retreat of these invaders because of fierce Afghan resistance. This legacy of having to defend oneself against international aggressors benefits agitators and recruiters from the insurgency in mobilising people against international forces in the country. Afghanistan has a long history of serving as a battlefield for proxy wars, involving interference by foreign countries such as the British Empire/UK, USSR/Russia, Iran, Pakistan, the USA and Saudi Arabia. While Afghan men played the main role in fighting in these wars, international support provided a majority of the required funds and equipment and thus contributed to the prolonging and / or the escalation of the conflicts" (Vigier, 2009).

The current state of affairs in Afghanistan is the outcome of a long history of events that contains a significant amount of influence of foreign powers.

Similarly, while assessing the role of foreign powers in Afghanistan, Pakistani expert Rahul Bakshi Rais, points out that the country has emerged as the playing field of a new 'great game' among the "regional powers". Indeed, Iran, Pakistan and some of the Central Asian States have their own conflicting interests in bringing an end to the civil war in the country. At the bottom of foreign meddling of the regional powers is "political polarisation among the Afghan groups and the civil war, which pushes them to seek external support to counterbalance their internal adversaries" (Rais, 1999).

Last year on September 21, 2013, former President Hamid Karzai stated that "his administration was emphasising on the US to guarantee peace and stability in Afghanistan as part of the Bilateral Security Agreement (BSA) because the war in Afghanistan has external factors" (Fitri, 2013). Karzai stressed that the "three decades old conflict had been imposed on the Afghans, devastating their country and continuing to unleash misfortunes on them" (Fitri, 2013).

Source: Afghanistan and Its Neighbours, An Ever Dangerous Neighbourhood, Special Report, United States Institute of Peace, http://www.usip.org/sites/default/files/sr162.pdf

Figure 5.1.Afghanistan and Its Neighbours.

Different Phases of Intervention

As mentioned earlier the strategic location of Afghanistan in the Central Asian region has for long drawn the attention of World Powers. In the nineteenth century it was the war of supremacy between the two imperialist powers – Great Britain and Tsarist Russia - which embroiled Afghanistan into a protracted conflict. When both these powers withdrew from the scene due to the changing world environment, Afghanistan began its new journey.

Afghanistan was drawn into another protracted conflict when the two 'Super Powers' – the US and the USSR – were involved in the Cold War stand-off that brought the world to the brink of destruction. Once more, with the end of the Cold War, situation in Afghanistan changed. However, this change forced Afghanistan into a conflict that is still going on. Notably, during this round of external intervention there were many players apart from the two 'Super Powers'. These players primarily included Pakistan, Iran, Saudi Arabia, China, and others.

There was a phase when none of the major powers showed interest in Afghanistan and the resultant vacuum was utilised to their 'benefit' by the neighbours, primarily Pakistan. At present, a large segment of the world community is engaged in Afghanistan, but not involved in destabilising act. They are involved in nation building. Nevertheless, countries like Pakistan and Iran continue their subversive act.

During all these three phases the internal weaknesses of Afghanistan helped the external 'aggressors'. Despite the well-known fact that the Afghans are freedom loving people and they never want to be subjugated, for a long period now they have remained under the shadow of foreign powers because of the existing disunity among various ethnic and tribal groups.

The First Great Game[1]

The two imperial powers – Great Britain and Tsarist Russia – were involved in territorial expansion in Central Asia because of their political and commercial needs. It was also because they were involved in struggle for supremacy world over.

Though the history of Afghanistan dates back to early periods, Afghanistan which we presently know has come into being only in the middle of the 18th century. Before eighteenth century, people of Afghanistan had never been firmly united to claim a separate political identity. A measure of unity was achieved during the reign of Ahmad Shah

Durrani, who after his coronation took the title of "Durr-i-Durran" (Noelle, 1997). But once he left the scene the country once again lost its way, which made it vulnerable to outside forces. The Tsarist Russia and British India took advantage of it.

The Russians made many attempts to gain influence in Afghanistan and to capture the territory south of Oxus. This was the logical next move to its Central Asian conquests. To forestall an invasion of India, the British promoted strife among the Afghans and urged Iran to recover the long lost province of Herat from the Afghans. The British succeeded in preventing an invasion of India in spite of changes of fortune and reversal of alliances. Yet their fears on that score never entirely disappeared. From then onwards, they looked upon the land of Afghans as either a buffer against, or a political base for, such an invasion.

The removal of Napolean from the scene, who was the first one to draw Afghanistan into modern international politics, complicated the Afghan syndrome. The British and Russian positions shifted from that of an alliance against France to rivalry between both the imperial powers. Gradual expansion of Tsarist Russia towards the Caspian and Asia Minor was viewed by the British rulers as an eventual threat to India. According to the British planners, Tsarist incursions into Afghanistan and finally into India would occur through Iran via Herat and Kandhar.

The first move of the Britishers to counter the Russians, therefore, was to encourage the Iranian monarch Fatah Ali Shah Qajar to attack the Russian positions. He was encouraged to attack the Russian positions around the Caspian in order to recover his lost territory. On the Afghan front the British signed a mutual defence treaty with Shah Shoja in 1809. The treaty ensured British support to Afghan King against external aggression and also obtained Afghan assurance of leaving the British alone in India.

Meanwhile, having acquired tremendous influence in the Persian court, the Russians turned their attention towards

Afghanistan. In 1837, the Persian troops attacked the western Afghan province and took siege of the city of Herat. They were aided by a Russian regiment under the command of General Sampson. While keeping their military pressure on a major Afghan city, the Russians also showed an eagerness to send an envoy to Kabul to seek political concessions from the Afghan ruler.

The developments in western Afghanistan were serious enough to upset the British. The defiant attitude of Amir Dost Mohammad added to their distress. Shah Shoja who had lost throne soon after he signed the treaty was living in India as an exile. To settle their differences with Amir Dost Mohammad, British Prime Minister, Lord Palmerston, and his Governor-General in India, Lord Auckland, sent Captain Alexander Burnes to Kabul in 1837. Apparently it was to investigate the potentials of commercial relations between India and Central Asia, but in reality it was to negotiate British-Afghan differences, and to conclude a mutual security agreement with the Amir Dost Mohammad, based on the 1809 treaty.

Getting an inkling of the British mission, the Russians sent their envoy to Kabul, Captain Ivan Victorivich. He, too, came to discuss 'commerce', but his real purpose, like that of Burnes, was also political. Amir Dost Mohammad showed preference towards the British, but he was getting nowhere in enlisting the British support to recover his territory from the Sikhs. Similarly, Burnes failed to extract the anti-Russian treaty from the Amir Dost Mohammad. At one time, Burnes issued ultimatum to Amir Dost Mohammad.

With this ultimatum, British-Afghan negotiations ended in a deadlock, and as the British envoy turned to India, the Amir Dost Mohammad opened talks with the Russian envoy. Earlier the Amir had informed the British about the subjects he had been discussing with the Russians; now he informed the latter the substance of his conversations with the British. The Russians too offered an alliance to the Afghan ruler. But as the British won't promise him Peshawar, the Russians declined any statement over Herat's settlement.

In the meantime, Lord Palmerston and Auckland were running out of patience over the Herat situation. Consequently, an ultimatum was served on the Persian Shah to the effect that the British regarded his Russian aided siege of Herat as a potential threat to India, and that if the siege was not lifted, the British would declare war on Persia. The ultimatum worked. Qajar Shah and his Russian allies packed up and returned home.

However, that was not enough. To secure India against the Russian threat, the British must have had a ruler of their own choice in Kabul who would toe the imperial line. Therefore, it was decided to remove the independent-minded Amir Dost Mohammad and install the old Shah Shoja, who was virtually a British captive. Under instructions from London, Lord Auckland raised an army consisting of British and Indian soldiers to invade Afghanistan. The invading troops were christened as the army of Indus and put under the command of General Sir John Kean.

The first Afghan War had begun. General Kean led his troops through Sindh, interestingly the Sikhs had refused passage through Punjab, into Balochistan and crossed into Kandhar by April 1839. The Afghan army led by Haider Khan, son of Amir Dost Mohammad, met the army of Indus at Ghazni. Haider Khan fought bravely, but lost and the British moved into Kabul. Amir Dost Mohammad fled towards the north. Shah Shoja, the British puppet, was installed as *Amir* of Afghanistan. The Army of Indus stayed on to keep the puppet on the Kabul throne.

As history has demonstrated repeatedly, a puppet ruler anywhere is seldom able to gain support and command the respect of his people. It is almost impossible to do so in Afghanistan. In Afghanistan, tribal customs regard bravery, manhood and independence as essential virtues of a chief or an *Amir*. As the British troops stayed on, resentment built-up against them and their underling Shah Shoja. The British fled from the Afghan capital in a hurry. In the ensuing days, Shah Shoja was assassinated and the British completely withdrew from Afghanistan. Their old antagonist Amir Dost Mohammad regained power. Thus, the first Afghan war failed to destroy Afghan independence and thereby the Britishers failed to gain strategic advantage over the Russians.

As the British had viewed every Russian advance in Central Asia as potential threat to the British Indian Empire, the Russians interpreted the British invasion of Kabul as a threat to their Asian exploits. Thus, in 1839, the Tsarist troops invaded Khiva, a Muslim Khanate 500 miles North of Kabul, which they had tried but failed to conquer earlier on. Interestingly the Russian expedition to Khiva met the same fate as did the British in Afghanistan. Out of 5,000 men, 10,000 camels and 12,000 Kirghiz porters, only 1,000 men survived the Khiva adventure.

The reverse suffered by the two great powers between 1839 and 1842 postponed their confrontation in Central Asia leaving a buffer zone of independent states between the Russian in the Kirghiz steppes and the British in India. In the next decade, the Ottoman Empire was the theatre of the Anglo-Russian Conflict, leading the two powers to the Crimean war. As a consequence of Russia's defeat, its activity in Balkans declined.

The 'Pendulum Theory' of Russian expansion referred by the scholars and diplomats states, 'when checked in West, Russia turns east and vice versa'. After the Treaty of Paris, Russian expansion towards west was no longer possible. It was only beyond the Caspian sea, i.e. in the east that Russia could expand without fear of European intervention. Within two decades after the Treaty of Paris, the Russian invaders trampled the great Islamic Khanates of Central Asia. In 1865, the important city of Tashkent was occupied; in 1868, the two outstanding cultural centres of Islam, Bokhara and

Samarkand were subjected; Khanates of Khiva fell in 1873 and Khokand in 1876.

Prince A. M. Gorchakov, a well-known Russian diplomat of that era, put forth the theory to justify Russian advances in Central Asia. The Tactical Theory propounded by Prince Gorchakov brought the Russian troops at the doorsteps of Afghanistan. The worried Amir Sher Ali urged the British to assist. Sher Ali asked for two things: Guarantee of his boundaries against Russian advance and, Recognition of his descendants as the legitimate heirs of Kabul throne.

British Viceroy's response for both these demands was vague and indefinite. Lord Mayo was the Viceroy. On the other hand, the British Foreign office sought and obtained an assurance from Russian Ambassador Prince Gorchakov in London that Afghanistan laid 'completely outside the sphere which Russia might be called upon to exercise influence'. This assurance was given in 1869, and four years later, in 1873, a roughly drawn boundary was agreed upon. According to the agreement, Oxus or the Amu Darya was to form the boundary in the North. As to the borders on the south, a separate commission would deal with that.

Despite the border agreement, Sher Ali remained skeptic of the Russian intentions and made another attempt to secure British support, in writing, against possible aggression from the North. The British, however, had more faith in the 1873 border agreement than the Amir. Disappointed by the British, Amir Sher Ali turned to the Russians and tried in vain to improve ties with the rival power.

In the meantime, the government was changed in England. It introduced new concepts. Earlier the British government had no truce with the 'masterly inactivity' school. Instead it launched what came to be known as the 'Forward Policy' for the containment of Russians beyond Afghan frontier. The basic elements of the new policy were-Establish permanent British presence in the principal Afghan cities to watch the Russian moves; Annex Afghan areas near the Indian frontier and convert those into strong military bases; Control and guide Afghan foreign policy.

The Sher Ali was asked to accept British mission in Herat. He refused to do so citing different reasons. Viceroy Lytton was busy arguing back and forth with Sher Ali. In the meantime, the Russians attacked Turkey. To demonstrate opposition, the British dispatched 5,000 Indian troops to Malta. The Russians replied by dispatching a mission to Kabul. It was accompanied by large scale military activity on the Afghan border. The Pendulum Theory was at work. The alarmed Afghan Amir was forced to receive the Russian mission in Kabul. The British could not be left far behind.

Lytton arranged to dispatch his own mission to Kabul with a warning to Sher Ali that 'refusal to grant it a free passage and an honourable reception as has been accorded to the Russian mission will be considered as a hostile act'. Sher Ali rejected the warning and again refused to receive the British. Insulted and infuriated Lytton resorted to military action. Afghanistan was attacked. The second Anglo-Afghan war started in 1878. Upon the news of defeat reaching Kabul, Sher Ali's authority collapsed and he fled northward to Afghan Turkistan. On May 26, 1879, his Son Yakub Khan signed a treaty with British at a place called Gandamak. The Treaty of Gandamak had apparently yielded the desired objective of 'Forward Policy'.

Both the first and second Afghan wars were designed to checkmate the Russians, but both were ironically fought against the Afghans and not the Russians. Aftermath of the Second Afghan war was no different than the first. Afghan people rose again under the leadership of Mushak-i-Alam Akhondzadah. The throne of Kabul fell to the lot of warrior statesman Amir Abdur Rahman (1880-1901). The British immediately extended recognition to the new *amir*.

Encouraged by the setback to their rivals, the Russians started new adventures around Afghanistan. In 1880, the Russians marched into Turkoman but were defeated. In 1884, the Russians broke through the Tekke formations and captured their city and fort of Merv. The British strategist who had long held the view that Russian invasion of India would come from the western side of Afghanistan via Herat, were shaken by the fall of Merv. The distance to Herat from Central Asia was now shortened.

There were now only two options opened to the British: Meet the Russians in force at Merv or draw a mutually agreed boundary line which the Russians won't cross. The new British Government under Gladstone chose the latter course. It was supported by the Indian establishment. British overtures on the demarcation of boundary found positive response from the Russian foreign office, and both sides agreed that the boundary between Merv and Afghanistan be delimitated by a commission on the spot. In the meantime, Russians started advancing towards Panjdeh and finally occupied it. It generated angry reverberations from Kabul to London. The situation became volatile. As the pressure mounted the Russians agreed to neutralise Panjdeh until the Boundary Commission finds a solution.

A boundary line after protracted negotiations was drawn in 1885. It was known as the 'Ridgeway Line'. It divided Afghan territory and Russian Turkomania on the northwest, as an earlier line (1873) had separated the two countries in the northeast. The border between India and Afghanistan was too agreed in 1893. Durand, who enjoyed personal relations with Amir Abdur Rahman, was able to negotiate the border agreement within four weeks. It came to be known as "Durand Line". The actual boundary line was drawn in 1895.

An independent and well-defined state of Afghanistan came into existence. With the demarcation of these boundaries, the British extended recognition to the Russian conquests in Central Asia. Similarly, the Russians conceded the paramountcy in the territories lying east of Russian Afghan border. With the demarcation of Indo-Afghan border, expansion of British India to the north had come to an end, as had the Russian Afghan boundary ended the expansion of Tsarist Russia towards the East. Thus, the power vacuum, which had made possible the expansion of both the empires, was eliminated. Along with this, what Kipling called 'The Great Game' seemed over. Afghanistan emerged as a buffer between the two powers.

However, this entire saga weakened the Afghan state, which was already under disarray after the era of Ahmad Shah Durrani, further.

Indeed, it was during this phase, for the first time since Afghanistan took the shape of a modern nation that foreign troops landed on Afghan land. The Afghans were forced to fight. The bitter fight though resulted in Afghans 'victory', as the foreign troops failed to capture Afghanistan; it had adverse impact on Afghan polity and resultantly on the nation as a whole.

Significantly, it was during this phase that Afghanistan witnessed rule of puppet Governments for the first time. The installation of puppet Governments led to strong distrust among the masses against the ruling class and they started fighting against the establishment. The process is still continuing.

The Second Great Game

With the end of rivalry between the imperial powers – Great Britain and Tsarist Russia – ended the direct involvement of foreign powers in Afghanistan. However, it did not take long to start another kind of rivalry between two new powers – US and the USSR.

Once again, Afghanistan due to its strategic location became the fighting ground. Nonetheless, this time, it was more intense and bloody. There were more players too.

USSR

The Tsarist Russia had failed to gain much in Afghanistan. On the other hand, the new entity – USSR, which came into emergence after the Bolshevik Revolution, in initial days was busy with "institutionalising aid relationships" with the newly formed communist countries. Significantly, communist set of guidelines during the early 1950s normally" ruled out aid to nonaligned, less developed countries like Afghanistan" (Weinbaum, 2006).

However, with the death of Joseph Stalin in 1953 and the adoption of the policy to "contain local alliances" by John Foster Dulles brought a significant reorientation. The Soviet Union initiated the policy of mobilising non-ideological support "through aid to countries, most of them less developed states that could be weaned away from Western influences". The countries of the third world, like Afghanistan, became the testing ground for this new policy. Unsurprisingly, the USSR provided extensive development and military assistance to Afghanistan thereafter (Weinbaum, 2006).

Meanwhile, as discussed earlier, it was during this phase the country's Marxists got opportunities to organise and, significantly, to infiltrate the military ranks. It later culminated into the *Russian intervention.*

US

While the USSR initially overlooked Afghanistan because of its policy to 'help the new communist countries first', the US showed little interest in an economically and socially backward Afghanistan as it was "engaged in trying to prevent European countries from falling within the Soviet orbit" (Weinbaum, 2006). Nevertheless, once the Red Army invaded Afghanistan in 1979, the USA became worried. It looked for a policy to checkmate the Russians.

According to the Central Intelligence Agency (CIA) Library document after the Soviet invasion, US President Jimi Carter directed the CIA to support the Afghan *mujahidin*. CIA during the course observed that native Afghan resistance to the Soviets was "less an organised movement than widespread opposition by villages and tribes"[2].

Consequently, the CIA decided to fund the *mujahideen* and deliver weapons, medical supplies, and communications equipments through Pakistan. It was done, initially, with the aim to "drain Soviet resources by keeping their forces bogged down". In 1985, CIA changed its idea of grinding down to one that would help the mujahideens win. One of the crucial periods came in September 1986, when the *mujahidin* used CIA-provided Stinger missiles to bring down three Soviet Mi-24D helicopter gunships. President Ronald Reagan issues new direction that put "CIA into more direct contact with rebel commanders, beginning an era of CIA interaction with tribal and local leaders that continues through the post-9/11 era"[3].The Soviet withdrawal in 1989 eradicated the vital interest that the United States had shared with the mujahidin.

Pakistan

Since 1947, when Pakistan became an independent nation, its relations with Afghanistan have always been controversial. The bone of contention is the border issue. Significantly, the border drawn by the British Indian Empire during its rivalry with Tsarist Russia divided Afghanistan's principal ethnic group, the Pashtuns, into two parts – half with British Indian Empire (now with Pakistan) and half with Afghanistan, without Afghans consent. Consequently, when the Britishers left, Afghanistan wanted to have a united 'Pashtun land'. The new nation Pakistan opposed it.

Expectedly, Afghanistan opposed Pakistan's UN membership. Unsurprisingly, Pakistan responded with closed its border, on several occasions creating severe economic problems for Afghanistan. It is a known fact that being a land locked country Afghanistan depends upon its neighbours to trade with other countries. However, Pakistan got engaged in direct disruptive act in Afghanistan subsequent to Russian invasion. Notably, it was at this juncture, the US in its design to defeat Russian Forces allied with Pakistan and Saudi Arabia.

While the US started providing arms and ammunition, Pakistan began training Afghan *mujahideens* who had crossed over into Pakistan. Moreover, the establishment in Pakistan promoted Pakistani nationals to join the jihad against Russians in Afghanistan. A key organisation in this regard is the ISI, which was not only involved in the distribution of funds to Afghan resistance groups, but also providing training to them.

According to the *Institute for the Study of War*, "The Afghan resistance coalescing in Pakistan was a combination of nationalist and religious parties. At the outset, they were divided into over a hundred groups. In 1980, the ISI reorganised them into bigger units and it officially recognised seven of these Peshawar-based parties. Anyone wishing to receive aid from Pakistan, the US, the Arabs, and others, had to join one of these groups. The largest of these factions were the ethnic Tajik-dominated Jamiat-e Islami, led by Burhanuddin Rabbani and Ahmad Shah Massoud, and Gulbuddin Hekmatyar's Hezb-e Islami. Hezb-e Islami was favoured by ISI and had close ties to Zia's backers in Jamaat-e-Islami. It was also one the most radical of the groups. Gulbuddin's Hizb ultimately received the bulk of the foreign aid (mostly American and Saudi) during the Afghan resistance. Pakistan provided the mujahideen with weapons, supplies, training, and bases from which to operate; and Pakistani units, disguised as mujahideen, also participated directly in the fighting"[4].

In fact, since then, the commando bases for all major anti-governmental elements appear to be on Pakistani soil.

Iran

Afghanistan and Iran (Persia) always had frosty relations. Iran was adamant on having a pro-Iran Government in Afghanistan to counter Pakistani influence. Not surprisingly, when the Russians invaded and US and Pakistan began supporting Sunni mujahideen groups, it extended help to Shia Hazra groups to counter them.

Despite the fact that Iran was busy fighting Iraq during the course of 1980s, it never uncared for Afghanistan. Its responses to the Soviet interference were dissimilar from many of the other countries, particularly Pakistan. Unlike Pakistan which "organised, sheltered and supported a large network of armed resistance groups", it concentrated to the politics and military capabilities of the Shia groups in the central region of Hazarajat. Notably, after the Islamic revolution in Iran, one of the most important objectives of Iran's foreign policy is to work for the protection, welfare and empowerment of the Shias worldwide (Rais, 2009).

Also, Iran had a long-term purpose of preparing the Afghan Shias for a potential political and military responsibility in the post-Soviet Afghanistan. Consequently, it spent much of its energies to their unity, training, equipment and organisational matters (Rais, 2009). To be more precise, Iran was pursuing three objectives in Afghanistan, "Limiting the influence of the axis of Washington-Riyadh-Islamabad and possibly strengthening Wahabi significance in the Afghan resistance; Enhancing the position of the Afghan Shiites in the future distribution of power; Installing a government with pro-Iranian attitudes in Kabul" (Wilde, 2006).

Saudi Arabia

Soon after the Red Army's invasion in Afghanistan, the Americans were in search of partners in fighting against their rival. Saudi Arabia became a willing partner in this 'crusade' along with Pakistan. Saudi Arabia in alignment with other Arabic Gulf states was in charge of financing the resistance parties, and provided particular support to the Ittihad-iIslami [led by Prof. Abdulraab Rasul Sayyaf]. With this financial backing from Saudi Arabia, the comparably small Ittihad-iIslami became a wealthy and influential group within the resistance (Wilde, 2006).

India

Since ancient times, India and Afghanistan have enjoyed

strong bonding. The bonding always remained the same, as the Afghans trust India. India on its part has always remained neutral to Afghanistan's internal problem and has tried to provide assistance as and when required. However, according to some accounts, India did support "pro-Soviet regimes in Kabul during the 1980s" (Weinbaum, 2006). India at no point of time was playing a destructive role.

Neighbours exploiting the Vacuum

Soon after the Russian withdrawal and subsequent disintegration of USSR, Afghanistan lost global attention. Afghanistan plunged into deeper internal crisis as the government failed to deliver. Rebellious forces again raised their heads and fought against the government. More alarmingly, they fought against each other. It was chaos everywhere. This allowed the neighbouring nations, particularly Pakistan and Saudi Arabia to take control of the situation. They got engaged in their design to form a government of their own choice.

Pakistan

With Afghanistan plunging into deeper chaos as the *mujahideens* fought among themselves, Islamabad got indulged in its nefarious design of having control over the country with the help of groups closer to it. It took "sponsorship of a group of religious students seeking to overthrow the Kabul regime". This group took the form of 'movement' called the Taliban and by 1996, this group, controlled much of the country and captured Kabul, "thanks in no small part to Pakistan's poorly disguised military assistance (Weinbaum, 2006).

The Taliban obtained financial resources from Pakistan. Islamabad offered the Taliban USD 30 million in aid from 1997-1998 with USD 6 million earmarked to pay for the "salaries of the Taliban leadership". This assistance was made in the form of "hard currency, food, fuel, arms, ammunition, maintenance, spare parts, and infrastructure development"

(Rashid, 2000). The height of Pakistani participation is manifested by the fact that "Afghan cities under Taliban rule could be reached by dialling Pakistani telephone prefixes" (Crews and Tarzi, 2009).

A large number of Pakistani 'volunteers' fought in Afghanistan during this phase of war. In August 1999, it was estimated that 80,000-100,000 Pakistanis were fighting alongside Taliban. Indeed, Pakistani 'volunteers' were critical to Taliban's military capability (Alikuzai, 2013).

A US State Department document released in 1998 authenticates that "20-40 per cent of [regular] Taliban soldiers are Pakistani". The parents of those Pakistani nationals knew nothing about their child's armed participation with the Taliban "until their bodies were brought back to Pakistan" (IBPUSA, 2013). It was former Pakistani President General (retired) Pervez Musharraf who was largely accountable for sending Pakistanis to fight "alongside the Taliban and Bin Laden against the forces of Massoud". Masood himself had stated:

> "The Taliban are not a force to be considered invincible. They are distanced from the people now. They are weaker than in the past. There is only the assistance given by Pakistan, Osama bin Laden and other extremist groups that keep the Taliban on their feet. With a halt to that assistance, it is extremely difficult to survive" (IBPUSA, 2013).

It was in December 2000 that the UN Security Council adopted the Resolution 1333, which imposed a mandatory arms embargo.[5]

Earlier, according to an October 22, 1999, *UN Security Council Press Release*, the Council had "expressed deep distress over reports indicating that thousands of non-Afghani nationals — some younger than 14 years old — were involved in the fighting on the Taliban side. Stating that outside interference in Afghanistan's internal affairs should cease immediately, the Council called on all States to prohibit their military personnel from planning and participating in combat in Afghanistan; withdraw personnel immediately; and halt the supply of ammunition and other war-making material"[6]. It was indirect indictment of Pakistani involvement.

According to *The Washington Times* report dated July 2, 2001, the US officials had told Pakistani Foreign Minister Abdul Sattar during his visit to Washington that the White House had a 'growing body of evidence' that Islamabad was in infringement of UN sanctions because of its military help to the Taliban.[7]

Iran

Iran began supporting Rabbani Government despite the fact that he had lost his legitimacy as he continued to be in power beyond the tenure set in the Peshawar Accord. It was in contrast to Iran's pledge that it will help implement the Accord. The primary reason for this change in policy seems to be Iran's anxiety over increasing support of Islamabad to anti-establishment forces. Even when the Rabbani government lost Kabul in September 1996, Iran increased its assistance to the Northern Alliance, which includes Tajiks, Hazaras, and Uzbeks. Iran supplied massive amounts of weapons and money to keep this alliance going" (Rais, 2009). It continued assisting the Northern Alliance till the ouster of the Taliban Government.

Weainbaum concludes, "*Regional competition between Pakistan and Iran carries over into Afghanistan. While the interventions of other countries have come and gone when expedient, these two neighbours have remained perennial meddlers in Afghanistan's internal affairs*" (Weinbaum, 2006).

Saudi Arabia

Saudi Arabia played an important role in Taliban's rise to power in Afghanistan. It helped Taliban providing "fuel, money, and hundreds of new vehicles" (Crews and Tarzi, 2009).

The Taliban also got financial aid from the Saudi community during the late 1990s through a variety of informal channels reinforced by ties of "shared ideology in regards to Deobandism and Wahhabism. Saudi Arabia also officially recognised the Taliban regime as the government of Afghanistan" (Kaplan and Bruno, 2008). On the other hand, through a large period of 1998, the 'official government' support for the Taliban (both financial and political) reduced as Taliban refused to hand over bin Laden to Saudi authorities (Sinno, 2008). It is because of the fact that al Qaeda questioned its leading role in Muslim world (Vigier, 2009).

China

China which shares only a small mountainous boundary with Afghanistan that is practically impenetrable and barely inhabited. Nevertheless, Beijing's involvement with Afghanistan increased during the Taliban rule, after Chinese Uighurs trying to fuel an insurgency among southwest China's Muslim population took refuge and training among the Afghans. Some Uighurs also fought along with the Taliban and al Qaeda (Weinbaum, 2006).

Central Asian Countries

Post their emergence the Central Asian countries also played their role in influencing Afghanistan's internal situation. While Turkmenistan followed the neutral policy, Uzbekistan and Tajikistan became vigorously occupied in the Afghan conflict. They had two fundamental interests: ethnicity and security. Notably, the Tajiks and Uzbeks are the second and third largest ethnic groups in the country. But none of the Central Asian Countries are interested in redrawing of the state boundaries, along ethnic lines, as they panic about their "own territorial integrity" (Rais, 2009).

Other Countries

The Russians along with India and some other countries tried to stall Taliban's March by helping out the Northern

Alliance. Russia became sensitive to Islamic extremism earlier than the USA due to the fact that it considered Islamists' calls for the liberation of Central Asia's Muslims – and thus (former) parts of the Soviet Union – as a threat to its control and stability in the region. With the rise of the Taliban, Russia started supporting a coalition of some of the very same commanders that it fought against a few years earlier: the Northern Alliance (Vigier, 2009). However, they found it very difficult to stall the Taliban progression as Pakistan continued to replenish Taliban's arms and ammunition stock by diverting its own military equipment which it used to get from the USA.

Meanwhile, the US did not recognise the Taliban government and openly criticised their human rights violations after 1997. Islamist terrorist attacks on USA targets, including the first bomb attack on the World Trade Centre (WTC) in 1993 and the US Embassy bombings in 1998, increased US attention on the region again, leading to cruise missile strikes on camps in Afghanistan in 1998 (Vigier, 2009).

Referring to the US policy towards Taliban, a CRS report (October 9, 2014) says,

The Clinton Administration opened talks with the Taliban after it captured Qandahar in 1994, and engaged the movement after it took power. However, the Administration was unable to moderate the Taliban's policies and relations worsened. The United States withheld recognition of Taliban as the legitimate government of Afghanistan, formally recognising no faction as the government. The United Nations continued to seat representatives of the Rabbani government, not the Taliban. The State Department ordered the Afghan embassy in Washington, DC, closed in August 1997.

Meanwhile, a *mujahideen* government formed in Kabul in 1992 attempted to get rid of Pakistani manipulation, and therefore soon after it sought India's support as a counterweight to their former patron. [India did support the Government, but] this policy rapidly ended with the fall of

Kabul in 1996 to the Pakistan-backed Taliban insurgency (Weinbaum, 2006).

Post 9/11

The international community was aghast by the magnitude of terrorists reach after the 9/11 attacks. There was unanimity across the globe to fight terror. The world had realised that Afghanistan has become the safe sanctuary of al Qaeda and its affiliates. Foreign troops once again landed in Afghanistan, but like at earlier occasions, have so far failed to bring peace in the country.

US

As discussed in the previous chapter, the US launched *Operation Enduring Freedom* soon after the 9/11 attacks. It was also joined by almost 50 nations in its endeavour to topple Taliban Government. It "forced Pakistan to co-operate with efforts to eliminate al Qaeda and bring regime change in Afghanistan" (Weinbaum, 2006). It is entirely a different matter that Pakistan never really effectively fought against the Taliban regime.

Russia

This time around Russia remained more or less aloof as it neither took direct participation in the operations nor did help the Taliban Government. It reluctantly, hover, joined the international community in the formation of a Government in Afghanistan. According to the CRS Report, "Since 2002, Russia has only been providing small amounts of humanitarian aid to Afghanistan".

Pakistan

Despite claiming to have joined the 'war on terror', and even as the Taliban were falling, Islamabad was openly recruiting young Pakistani men to "fight in Afghanistan against the Northern Alliance and the Americans"

(Weinbaum, 2006). Afghan officials on a regular basis accused Pakistan of militant recruitment, training camps, and arms depots on its territory. In its most recent assessment on Pakistani role in the Afghan conflict, CRS report highlights the following:

> DOD [US Department of Defence] reports on Afghanistan's stability repeatedly have identified Afghan militant safe haven in Pakistan as a threat to Afghan stability. Pakistan's main goal is that Afghanistan not align with or be unduly influenced by rival India, and potentially provide Pakistan strategic depth against India. These goals lead many experts to assert that Pakistan privately wants proxy or friendly factions such as the Taliban to have major influence in post-2014 Afghanistan. Pakistan's goal in allowing some militant groups to have relative safe haven may be to develop leverage with Afghanistan to support Pakistan's policies. At the same time, Pakistan apparently believes that instability in Afghanistan would rebound to Pakistan's detriment. Pakistan apparently strongly preferred Ghani to Dr Abdullah as successor to Karzai, but Abdullah's substantial role in the Ghani government might have diluted the benefits to Pakistan of Ghani's becoming president.

Moreover, other international agencies have blamed Pakistan for the problem in Afghanistan. Major General Stephen Townsend, who commands US and North Atlantic Treaty Organisation (NATO) Forces in eastern Afghanistan, noted, "Until the Pakistanis do something about the safe havens, that's going to be a problem. (Terrorists) can recruit and train and equip and prepare to launch in Pakistan" (Ryan and Stewart, 2014).

Iran

Not surprisingly, Iranian involvement in Afghanistan is far less "obvious" than that of Pakistan. While Iranian weapons were found in the possession of insurgent fighters, security officials believed that non-governmental, criminal or terrorist networks were behind it (instead of the official Iranian government). The main counter-argument given is that it would be very risky for mainly Shiite Iran to support a predominantly Sunni resistance force. Also, most of the more complex improvised explosive devises are believed to stem from non-governmental Iranian sources. There are, however, tensions between Afghanistan and Iran regarding Afghan refugees and illegal immigrants in Iran. Also the use of the water from shared rivers is a source of conflict between the two countries (Vigier, 2009).

Assessing the role of Iran in the present times, the CRS report notes:

> Despite its relations with the Afghan government, Iran, perhaps attempting to demonstrate that it can cause U.S. combat deaths in Afghanistan, is allegedly arming militants there. The State Department report on international terrorism for 2012, released May 30, 2013, repeats language in prior reports that the Qods Force of the Islamic Revolutionary Guard Corps of Iran provides training to the Taliban on small unit tactics, small arms, explosives, and indirect weapons fire, and that it has shipped arms to militants in Qandahar. This phrasing implies that Iran is arming Pashtun Taliban militants in the core of the combat zone in Afghanistan. Weapons provided, according to the State Department report, include mortars, 107 mm rockets, rocket-propelled grenades, and plastic explosives. On March 9, 2011, NATO said it had seized 48 Iranian-made rockets in Nimruz Province, bound for Afghan militants; the 122 mm rockets have a range (13 miles) greater than those previously provided by Iran. On August 3, 2010, the Treasury Department, acting under Executive Order 13224, named two Qods Force officers as terrorism supporting entities, freezing any U.S.-based assets.

Saudi Arabia

Saudi Arabia hosted talks between Afghan government officials and (former/moderate) Taliban in Mecca in September 2008. Some experts assume that Saudi Arabia's interests in these negotiations are primarily to reduce conflicts among Sunnis which could otherwise led to greater influence for mainly Shiite Iran in the Muslim world (Vigier, 2009).

China

Of late China is primarily engaged in using diplomatic means to frustrate an "open-ended US military presence in Afghanistan and the region" (Weinbaum, 2006). According to Cotter, "China's historical alliance with Pakistan and antipathy toward India, as well as its competition with Russia for a dominant position on the Asian continent colour its views of an Afghan solution" (Cotter, 2001).

Foreign *Jihadis*

While during all this period foreign countries individually or jointly tried to influence situation in Afghanistan, they were supported by radicals from across the Muslim World.

After the Soviet invasion, Arab and other non-Afghan volunteers joined the *jihad* to fight the presence of non-Muslim military forces in Afghanistan. These fighters came from countries like Saudi Arabia, Jordan, Algeria, Tunisia, Egypt or Israel/Palestine, but also Indonesia and Malaysia. The relationship between Afghans and their non-Afghan comrades-in-arms was not without tension. They came from a different culture, spoke different languages and followed a different interpretation of Islam. Interestingly, in the 1980s, suicide attacks were only advocated by these foreign resistance fighters whereas the Afghans denounced them (Vigier, 2009). According to Coll, "The Afghans whom Yousaf trained uniformly denounced suicide attack proposals as against their religion. It was only the Arab volunteers - from Saudi Arabia, Jordan, Algeria and other countries - who later advocated suicide attacks. Afghan jihadists, tightly woven into family, clan, and regional social networks, never embraced suicide attacks in significant numbers" (Coll, 2004). Significantly, Brigadier General Mohammad Yousaf was an ISI man.

In 1986, Osama bin Laden opened his first training camp for Arab volunteers in the Afghan province of Paktia and by 1989, the CIA estimated that there were about 4,000 Arab volunteers in Afghanistan, mainly organised under Sayyaf's (Islamist Mujahedin leader having strong support from Saudi Arabia; today leader of the political party Dawat-e Islami]) leadership (Coll, 2004). As Vigier writes, "Besides Arabs, there are individuals from the Caucasus and Central Asia (Chechens, Tajik, Uzbek...) fighting in Afghanistan and Pakistan today. Also, several waves of Arabs settled in Waziristan during the mujahedin wars against the Soviets and, more recently, after the U.S. and Northern Alliance overthrow of the Taliban regime" (Vigier, 2009).

International Forces

While during the 'First Great Game', it was the British Indian Forces which fought with Afghans in Afghanistan, it was the turn of Soviet Forces to fight Afghans in Afghanistan during the course of the 'Second Great Game'. The role of these two Forces, which acted in their own individual capacity, in affecting the conflict in Afghanistan has been discussed earlier. Post 9/11, however, the international community sent joint Forces to operate in Afghanistan.

Operation Enduring Freedom (OEF) Forces

Though the *Operation Enduring Freedom* (OEF) began on October 7, 2001, with the then US President George W. Bush announcing that the USA and British forces have begun airstrikes on Taliban and al Qaeda targets in Afghanistan[8], it was on October 19, 2001, that the Pentagon reported that the US forces have searched a compound used by Taliban leader Mullah Mohammed Omar and, hence, it "first acknowledged ground action of OEF."[9] The US troops were on Afghan land.

According to the Global Security Website, the first US troops to land in Afghanistan were Special Operation Forces, specialists in unconventional combat tactics alongside enemy forces; in this case, anti-Taliban groups. Despite the fact that particulars about these clandestine operations at the start were not made public, "it did not take long for images of horse-mounted soldiers riding with Northern Alliance troops to hit the airwaves."[10]

The US Forces were subsequently joined by the Forces from Britain, Turkey, Australia, Canada, German, Italy, Netherlands, France, and Poland. On December 20, 2001, the United Nations authorises the ISAF to provide security support to the Afghans. The United Kingdom agrees to lead the force initially.[11]

Subsequently, the US troops were stationed in Afghanistan were divided under two heads: Under Direct US command within OEF and as part of the ISAF. The OEF in Afghanistan comprises out of two different commands: Combined Security Transition Command Afghanistan (CSTC-A), which is responsible for strategic training, advising and mentoring of the ANA and the ANP, in "part through Embedded Training Teams". The second is the Combined Joint Task Force 101 (CJTF-101) which is stationed mainly in the East and the South of Afghanistan along the Pakistani border "as counter-terrorism comb mission" (Vigier, 2009).

International Security Assistance Force (ISAF)

The ISAF is working in tandem with the OEF Forces. The ISAF was formed in agreement with the Bonn Conference in December 2001.[12] According to the ISAF Website, "These agreements paved the way for the creation of a three-way partnership between the Afghan Transitional Authority, the United Nations Assistance Mission in Afghanistan (UNAMA) and ISAF"[13].

ISAF's mandate was originally limited to facilitate security in and around Kabul. In October 2003, the United Nations extended ISAF's mandate to cover the whole of Afghanistan (UNSCR 1510), paving the way for an expansion of the mission across the country. On August 11, 2003, NATO assumed leadership of the ISAF operation, ending the six-month national rotations. The Alliance became accountable for the "command, coordination and planning of the force, including the provision of a force commander and headquarters on the ground in Afghanistan". This new leadership ended the difficulty of a recurrent search to find new nations to lead the mission and the problems of setting up a new headquarters every six months in an intricate environment. A continuing NATO headquarters also enables small countries, less likely to take over leadership responsibility, to play a strong role within a multinational headquarters.[14]

International Security Assistance Force

Troop Contributing Nations

Country	Troops	Country	Troops	Country	Troops
Albania	22	Germany	1.599	Poland	304
Armenia	121	Greece	9	Portugal	37
Australia	273	Hungary	101	Romania	327
Austria	3	Iceland	2	Slovakia	277
Azerbaijan	94	Ireland	7	Slovenia	2
Bahrain	0	Italy	1,411	Spain	181
Belgium	160	Jordan	526	Sweden	13
Bosnia & Herzegovina	8	Republic of Korea	50	The former Yugoslav Republic of Macedonia [1]	152
Bulgaria	320	Latvia	11	Tonga	0
Croatia	153	Lithuania	84	Turkey	393
Czech Republic	227	Luxembourg	1	Ukraine	10
Denmark	145	Malaysia	2	United Arab Emirates	35
El Salvador	0	Mongolia	40	United Kingdom	3,906
Estonia	4	Montenegro	25	United States	28,970
Finland	88	Netherlands	30	Total	41,124
France	88	New Zealand	1		
Georgia	755	Norway	57		

Note on numbers: Numbers of troops should be taken as indicative as they change daily.

1 Turkey recognises the Republic of Macedonia with its constitutional name

2 In line with ISAF's planning and in coordination with NATO, Singapore has completed its contribution to ISAF on 22 June 2013, Canada on 31 March 2014

3 September 2014

Source: Troop numbers and contributions http://www.isaf.nato.int/troop-numbers-and-contributions/index.php

Figure 5.2. ISAF Troop Numbers and Contributions.

Describing the mission of the Force, the ISAF says, "In support of the Government of the Islamic Republic of Afghanistan, ISAF conducts operations in Afghanistan to reduce the capability and will of the insurgency, support the growth in capacity and capability of the ANDSF, and facilitate improvements in governance and socio-economic development in order to provide a secure environment for sustainable stability that is observable to the population"[15].

The foreign troops began their stipulated withdrawal. From the peak of 132,457 troops on July 26, 2011, the number came down to mere 41,124 as on September 3, 2014. Moreover, almost the entire foreign contingent is in non-combat role now.

This followed "the *Inteqal* (Transition) Framework defined at the London (UK) and Kabul conferences on Afghanistan in 2010. Under the *Inteqal* Framework, the international community's civilian and military representatives decided to shift their responsibilities to the Afghans, and to increasingly limit themselves to a supporting, mentoring, and eventually sustaining role in security, governance and development" (Singh, 2013). Indeed, "on 22 March 2011, President Karzai announced the first set of Afghan provinces and districts to start the transition. On 18 June 2013, Karzai announced the fifth and final tranche of transition"[16]. On June 18, 2013, he made it to the public that his country's armed forces were taking over the lead for nationwide security from the United States (US)-led NATO coalition. Karzai immediately declared that 'from tomorrow all of the security operations will be in the hands of the Afghan security forces'. The ANDSF having an estimated strength of 350,000 troops thereafter leads operations in "all 403 Districts of Afghanistan's 34 Provinces"[17].

The ISAF moved entirely into a supporting role, and now provides support to ANDSF on the battlefield when they require it. Explaining the future role of NATO forces, NATO Secretary-General Anders Fogh Rasmussen observe that 'as your [Afghan] forces step forward across the country, the main effort of our forces is shifting from combat to support. We will continue to help Afghan troops in operations if needed. But we will no longer plan, execute or lead those operations. And by the end of 2014, our combat mission will be completed. At that time, Afghanistan will be fully secured by Afghans. From 2015, a new chapter will begin. Together with our partners, we are planning a new and different mission. The goal of the new mission is to train, advise and assist Afghan forces. We will also play our part in the broader international efforts, to ensure the long-term sustainment of the Afghan security forces.

As of September 3, 2014, the total number of ISAF personnel stationed inside Afghanistan stands at 41,124. The number of contributing countries stands at 48[18]. The maximum number of ISAF troops stationed in Afghanistan stood at 132, 457 (July 26, 2011)[19]. At one point of time, the number of countries contributing troops stood at 50.

International Private Security Firms

A series of international private security firms including DynCorp and Blackwater are also active in Afghanistan. DynCorp is officially tasked with training of policemen and is in part also responsible for the security of prominent members of government. Blackwater's role in Afghanistan appears to be less transparent and there are various rumors circulating about its activities (Vigier, 2009).

The external forces, thus, have indeed played a big role in the emergence of conflict in Afghanistan. They have in fact got the opportunity to do so as Afghanistan for most part of its existence has lacked unity among its people. All these interventions - political and military - have an adverse impact on the conflict in Afghanistan. While the first great game involving Afghanistan drew Afghanistan in a war which was not all in its own creation, the second great game pushed the country in the prolonged conflict. The landing of the foreign troops in the aftermath of the 9/11 attacks complicated the situation further as the policy was not well implemented.

In the meantime, the continuous inflow of foreign jihadis multiplies the problem further.

To correct their fault the international community, mainly the distant powers, is engaged in the restructuring of Afghanistan.

International Countries' Pledges for Afghanistan, 2002-2012 (USD in millions)[20]

United States	79,879
Japan	13,150
European Union	2,880
Germany	2,680
Asian Development Bank	2,270
Britain	2,220
World Bank	2,140
Total	**104,776**

Source: Afghanistan Ministry of Finance (MoF), Development Cooperation Report 2012; Congressional Research Service Report for Congress.

Note: Table includes international donors of over USD 2,000 million only.

However, similar to the military interference in 2001 which failed to control terrorism, the flow of economic aid has failed to boost Afghan economy. Though there are several indicators to prove the point, in a most damning assessment the *World Food Programme: Fighting Hunger Worldwide* notes:

> With an estimated total population of 27 million, Afghanistan still faces enormous challenges after more than three decades of war and civil unrest. Despite recent progress, millions of Afghans still live in severe poverty with limited access to food and other basic requirements. According to the findings of the 2011/2012 National Risk and Vulnerability Assessment, 7.6 million people, roughly one-third of the population, are food-insecure, and a further 14 per cent are considered to be borderline food-insecure.

To conclude, the conflict in Afghanistan aided and abetted by the external forces has failed to be subsided despite the role reversal of many of the players. It is mainly because of the fact that some forces inimical to Afghan interest continue to operate well within Afghanistan and closer to its border well in tandem.

References

1. Some portion of this section has been taken from this researcher's own M.Phil. Dissertation titled, *Emergence of Afghanistan as a Buffer State between Tsarist Russia and British Indian Empire (19th C.)* submitted to the Jawaharlal Nehru University in 2003.
2. Afghanistan, Devotion to Duty, Library, Central Intelligence Agency, https://www.cia.gov/library/publications/additional-publications/devotion-to-duty/afghanistan.html
3. *Ibid.*
4. Pakistan and Afghanistan, Institute for the Study of War, http://www.understandingwar.org/pakistan-and-afghanistan.
5. Case study: The Taliban, 2000–2006, United Nations Arms Embargoes Their Impact on Arms Flows and Target Behaviour, Stockholm International Peace Research Institute 2007http://books.sipri.org/files/misc/UNAE/SIPRI07UNAETal.pdf
6. Security Council, In Presidential Statement, Condemns Afghanistan's Taliban For July Military Offensive, Sheltering Terrorists, Press Release, Security Council, United Nations, 22 October 1999, http://www.un.org/press/en/1999/19991022.sc6743.doc.html
7. U.S. presses for bin Laden's ejection, The Washington Times, July 2, 2001,http://www.washingtontimes.com/news/2001/jul/2/20010702-024109-5365r/?page=all
8. Operation Enduring Freedom Fast Facts, CNN Library, September 30, 2014, http://edition.cnn.com/2013/10/28/world/operation-enduring-freedom-fast-facts
9. *Ibid.*
10. Operation Enduring Freedom - Operations, Military, Global Secirty.org http://www.globalsecurity.org/military/ops/enduring-freedom-ops.htm
11. Operation Enduring Freedom Fast Facts, CNN Library, September 30, 2014, http://edition.cnn.com/2013/10/28/world/operation-enduring-freedom-fast-facts

12. History, About ISAF, International Security Assistance Force, http://www.isaf.nato.int/history.html
13. *Ibid.*
14. *Ibid.*
15. Mission, About ISAF, Internal Security Assistance Force, Afghanistan, http://www.isaf.nato.int/mission.html
16. Inteqal: Transition to Afghan lead, North Atlantic Treaty Organisation, October 13, 2014, http://www.nato.int/cps/in/natolive/topics_87183.htm
17. Karzai: Afghan forces take security lead from NATO, USA Today, June 18, 2013, http://www.usatoday.com/story/news/world/2013/06/18/afghanistan-bombing/2433495/
18. International Security Assistance Force (ISAF): Key Facts and Figures, International Security Assistance Force, http://www.isaf.nato.int/images/media/PDFs/140904placemat.pdf
19. International Security Assistance Force (ISAF): Key Facts and Figures, International Security Assistance Force, http://www.isaf.nato.int/images/stories/File/Placemats/Revised%2026%20June%202011%20Placemat%20(Full).pdf
20. Salih Dogan, International Aid to Afghanistan and its Importance in the Post-2014 Era, February 2014, The Washington Review of Turkish & Eurasian Affairs, http://www.thewashingtonreview.org/articles/international-aid-to-afghanistan-and-its-importance-in-the-post-2014-era.html#_ftnref15

Chapter - 6

Conclusion

This doctoral thesis entitled "The Ethnic Conflict and State Structure in Afghanistan (1989-2001), which has been discussed and analysed in the preceding chapters, has attempted to bring out various factors responsible for the growth of ethnic conflict and its repercussions on the State structure in Afghanistan. To that end, one may find that the theory of ethnic conflict and theory of structuration has been examined in a broader framework to apply in the case of Afghanistan so as to understand the whole scenario of Afghan society and state during the period of this research study and its aftermath.

The conclusions that can be drawn here indicate that today most of the nations, across the world, are engaged in one conflict or the other, though a large number of these conflicts are ethnic in nature. A multi-ethnic nation, Afghanistan, which has plunged into an ethnic conflict in the beginning of 1990s has since been looking for a resolution to become a peaceful society and state without having any prejudices whatsoever. While dealing with different aspects of ethnic conflicts in South Asia in general and Afghanistan in particular, this research study has discovered that the whole South Asian region has for long faced a complex ethnic conflict. Whereas some of these conflicts have subsided with the passage of time there are many which still have the potential to destabilise the whole region. The conflict in Afghanistan is one of them. The partial survey of available literature has established the fact that despite having innumerable pioneering work in the field, dearth of substantive work continues to exist.

After studying ethnic conflict in theoretical perspective several findings have been made. First, it has been reaffirmed that the complexity involved with the term 'ethnicity' has not been resolved in totality. The various attempts to reach to a definite definition, consequently, have also failed. Secondly, after surveying various theories and approaches of ethnicity, it has been found that no single theory is complete in itself and a combination of various theories can only help us understand better the phenomenon of ethnic assertions. In turn, no universally accepted theory of ethnicity has been propounded. Moreover, scholars have failed to bring forward a universally accepted theory of ethnic conflict which can be made applicable to all ethnic conflicts. Consequently, these theories fail to tell us when an ethnic conflict will break out in one particular region. This proves that ethnic conflict is a complex phenomenon.

The analysis of the state, society and polity in Afghanistan has emphasised the fact that the fragmented society of Afghanistan has always remained an obstacle in the formation of a strong united nation state. The country has witnessed interregnum quite often than not. However, for the first time in Afghanistan's checkered political history there has been a transfer of power which is truly democratic following the recent presidential elections. As the new government is a truly multi-ethnic government as President Ghani belongs to the dominant Pashtun group, while the Chief Executive Abdullah Abdullah is a Tajik, it now seems Afghanistan at last is on the path of formation of a democratic State in which the polity will be truly representative of all the sections of the society. Nevertheless, there is a long way to go for the conflict resolution.

The research findings point to the understanding that the conflict that has engulfed Afghanistan has its root in the developments that took place during the later years of President Mohammad Daud Khan. The deteriorating ties between Daud and the USSR resulted in a Soviet backed coup in 1978. The Coup changed the dynamics of Afghan polity and subsequently Afghanistan plunged into a conflict with compounding complexities. Ethnic conflicts in Afghanistan, which were not so prominent during the Soviet occupation of the country, are entirely different from the conflicts in other country in the region. Notably, while most of the other conflicts have either subsided, the conflict in Afghanistan continues to endanger the peace in the region. All attempts to conflict resolution seem to have failed as Afghanistan continues to be in turmoil. Evidently, while the rest of the world has focused its attention towards bloodbath in the Arab World, where the Islamic State of Syria and al Sham (ISIS), now rechristened as Islamic State, has created havoc, Afghanistan is plunging deeper into chaos.

Indeed, external forces have played a big role in the emergence of conflict in Afghanistan. They have, in fact, got the opportunity to do so as Afghanistan for most part of its existence has lacked unity among its people. All these interventions - political and military - have an adverse impact on the conflict in Afghanistan. While the first great game involving Afghanistan drew Afghanistan in a war which was not all in its own creation, the second great game pushed the country in the prolonged conflict. The landing of the foreign troops in the aftermath of the 9/11 attacks complicated the situation further as the policy was not well implemented. In the meantime, the continuous inflow of foreign *jihadis* multiplies the problem further.

America's 'drawdown' is taking place at a time when a troubled Afghanistan has been tainted by large-scale corruption (the country ranked 174th out of 176 in the 2012 Corruption Perceptions Index), and capacities for governance remain deeply suspect. Though apprehensions of an abrupt collapse, comparable to events in the aftermath of the Soviet withdrawal in 1989, have receded, the uncertainties of the situation are monumental. Worse, the future of Afghanistan remains as intimately tied to global peace and stability as has been its recent past. If the Western powers leave chaos behind in this unfortunate country, it is likely to follow them home in their baggage trains.

As already emphasised, this study brings into sharp focus some key points which concerned with the period beyond the purview of this thesis, i.e., aftermath the 2001. Post-2001 period is significant in the sense that any study on ethnic conflict and state structure in Afghanistan would remain incomplete unless it is examined in the context of current scenario so as to reach a conclusion for the possible solution of the conflict. As it is, the research findings suggest that after the ouster of the Taliban from power in 2001, the ethnic conflict that had pushed the Afghan nation at the brink of structural collapse took the form of Islamist terrorism. The situation though was not alarming in early years. Regrettably, however, the Taliban with the help of people at the helm of affairs in Islamabad regrouped. In fact, Islamabad took the advantage of the fact that the international community became less focused on Afghanistan after the collapse of Taliban regime. Islamist militancy picked up. Taliban was on surge. Perturbed by the resurgence of Taliban, the US President Barack Obama in December 2009 called for surge in Forces strength. In fact, the new AfPak policy of Obama backfired. His call for surge in Forces along with the assertion that troops withdrawal will begin emboldened the spirits of Taliban. The Taliban felt that they have succeeded in defeating the foreign forces and now they have the chance to 'strengthen' their hold. They upped their ante.

The situation in Afghanistan highlights the fact that thousands of people are being killed on a yearly basis in terrorism-related violence that is going unabated. The numbers clearly suggest that Afghanistan is currently under the hold of Islamist terrorism. The Taliban have returned and now controls large swathe of Afghan territory. Indeed, varying media sources estimate that the Taliban now dominates an estimated 40 to 60 per cent of Afghanistan. Despite this harsh reality, the foreign troops began their stipulated withdrawal. From the peak of 132,457 troops on July 26, 2011, the number came down to mere 41,124 as on September 3, 2014. Moreover, almost the entire foreign contingent is in non-combat role now. Despite ANDSF demonstrating their capabilities in a number of successful operations, tremendous vulnerabilities are increasingly visible. It has failed to stem the spread of the Taliban.

Meanwhile, ending months of uncertainty, a day after the formation of the National Unity Government, on September 30, 2014, Afghanistan signed two separate security pacts with the US and the NATO. The pacts which will allow the US and the NATO Forces to continue training and advising the ANDSF, as well as to continue assisting the ANDSF in counterterrorism operations, were eagerly awaited by the world community which was worried over the negative repercussions of premature withdrawal of troops. Article 2 of the agreement between the US and Afghanistan, known as BSA, stating the purpose and the scope stresses:

> "The Parties shall continue to foster close cooperation to strengthen security and stability in Afghanistan, counter terrorism, contribute to regional and international peace and stability, and enhance the ability of Afghanistan to deter internal and external threats against its sovereignty, security, territorial integrity, national unity, and its constitutional order. Unless otherwise mutually agreed, United States forces shall not conduct combat operations in Afghanistan. To that end, the United States shall undertake supporting activities, as may be agreed, in close cooperation and coordination with Afghanistan, to assist ANDSF in developing capabilities required to provide security for all Afghans, including as may be mutually agreed: advising, training, equipping, supporting, and sustaining ANDSF...developing intelligence sharing

capabilities. The Parties recognise that ANDSF are responsible for securing the people and territory of Afghanistan. The Parties shall work to enhance ANDSF's ability to deter and respond to internal and external threats. Upon request, the United States shall urgently determine support it is prepared to provide ANDSF in order to respond to threats to Afghanistan's security. The Parties acknowledge that U.S. military operations to defeat al-Qaida and its affiliates may be appropriate in the common fight against terrorism. The Parties agree to continue their close cooperation and coordination toward those ends, with the intention of protecting U.S. and Afghan national interests without unilateral U.S. military counter-terrorism operations. U.S. military counter-terrorism operations are intended to complement and support ANDSF's counter-terrorism operations, with the goal of maintaining ANDSF lead, and with full respect for Afghan sovereignty and full regard for the safety and security of the Afghan people, including in their homes"[1].

Finally, the agreement has made it clear by stating:

"This Agreement shall enter into force on January 1, 2015, after the Parties notify one another through diplomatic channels of the completion of their respective internal legal requirements necessary for the entry into force of this Agreement. It shall remain in force until the end of 2024 and beyond, unless terminated pursuant to paragraph 4 of this Article"[2].

Interestingly, the agreement nowhere mentions about the strength of US Forces that will remain within Afghanistan after December 31, 2014, when the process of withdrawal will be completed. It is, however, assumed that around 10,000 US troops will remain stationed. Notably, US President Barack Obama, on May 27, 2014, had announced, "Today, I want to be clear about how the United States is prepared to advance those missions. At the beginning of 2015, we will have approximately 9,800 U.S. service members in different parts of the country, together with our NATO allies and other partners. By the end of 2015, we will have reduced that presence by roughly half, and we will have consolidated our troops in Kabul and on Bagram Airfield. One year later, by the end of 2016, our military will draw down to a normal embassy presence in Kabul, with a security assistance component, just as we've done in Iraq"[3].

Meanwhile, on the same day, September 30, 2014, Afghanistan signed an agreement with the NATO. The agreement, called Status of Forces Agreement (SOFA), again did not mention the number of NATO personnel that will remain in Afghanistan after December 31, 2014. However, as per various media reports, around 2000 NATO troops will remain stationed. It means the number of foreign troops operating in Afghanistan will come down to around 12,000 from the current 41,000, mostly in non-combat role. Consequently, it remains a huge challenge for the much depleted Foreign Forces to assist the ANDSF to take on the Taliban.

It is in this context that what is important to address the biggest concern for peace in Afghanistan is - Pakistan's nefarious design in Afghanistan. The USA need to realise the Pakistani game. It is pertinent to mention here that the man who was responsible for the 9/11 attacks, al Qaeda founder Osama bin Laden was found and killed not in the rugged terrains of Afghanistan, where he was believed to have taken shelter, but deep inside Pakistan. In this regard, Ajai Sahni, writes the following:

> "After an unrelenting effort spanning more than a decade, Osama bin Laden, the *amir* and ideological fountainhead of al Qaeda, its founder, and the architect of the 9/11 attacks in the US, was killed in the intervening night of May 1-2, 2011, in a US operation in the garrison town of Abbottabad, less than 62 kilometres from Islamabad, and a stone's throw from the Pakistan Military Academy, the country's top training established for officers, and the local

> Army Brigade Headquarters. Barely a week earlier, on April 23, 2011, Pakistan's Army Chief, General Ashfaq Kayani, had driven by this location to the Kakul Military Academy, just over half a kilometre away, to boast, in his address to cadets there, that 'the terrorists' backbone has been broken' by his Forces. Over the past years, the Pakistan establishment, including two successive Presidents – General Pervez Musharraf and Asif Ali Zardari – have actively spread a smokescreen over the al Qaeda leadership's presence on Pakistani soil, repeatedly asserting that bin Laden, in particular, was either dead or holed up in some caves in Afghanistan" (Sahni, 2011).

In his final address to Afghanistan's Parliament on March 15, 2014, Karzai declared, in an obvious reference to Pakistan, that the US could bring peace to Afghanistan if it went after terrorist sanctuaries and countries that supported terrorism. Also, on several occasions in the past the US officials have acknowledged that Pakistan is engaged in destabilising role. Major General Stephen Townsend, who commands US and NATO Forces in eastern Afghanistan, noted, "Until the Pakistanis do something about the safe havens, that's going to be a problem. (Terrorists) can recruit and train and equip and prepare to launch in Pakistan."

It seems the BSA has taken note of that. As per Annexure A of the agreement, "Agreed Facilities and Areas", include Kabul, Bagram, Mazar-e-Sharif, Herat, Kandahar, Shorab (Helmand), Gardez, Jalalabad, and Shindand[4]. Notably, most of these areas are close to Pakistani territory. Also, the BSA has brought this aspect of Afghan problem within its ambit under the head External Aggression (Article 6),

> "On a regular basis, the Parties shall consult on potential political, diplomatic, military, and economic measures that could form part of an appropriate response in the event of such external aggression or the threat of external aggression against Afghanistan. Consultations shall seek

to develop a list of political, diplomatic, military, and economic measures"[5].

The BSA alone, however, cannot ensure peace in Afghanistan given the extent of Pakistani involvement.

On the other hand, the US feels that it needs Pakistan's help to exit from the land-locked Afghanistan at any cost. In return, it is trying to give some legitimacy to Pakistan's Taliban proxies – the 'Pakiban' as some commentators now describe them – in Kabul, via their recognition in Doha. Kabul did make an indirect reference to Pakistan's role in the context of the Doha office controversy, noting, 'the latest developments show that foreign hands are behind the Taliban's Qatar office'. The US, however, publicly acknowledged, on June 21, 2013, the 'constructive role' played by Pakistan in bringing Taliban and the US administration closer to reconciliation. The US Ambassador to Pakistan Richard Olson stated that 'We are working closely with Pakistan. Pakistan played a constructive role in the opening of Taliban office in Doha. This is a big step and we greatly appreciate Pakistan's support'.

Over the long term, the US seeks an assurance from the Taliban too that its Forces will not attack convoys carrying equipment and weapons of US Forces who are preparing to leave Afghanistan. The present US initiatives are driven, overwhelmingly, by fears of a chaotic flight of its Forces in the last phases of the drawdown, under focused attack by the Taliban. In its moment of desperation Washington has, once again, fallen back on its unreliable 'principal ally', Pakistan, restoring the prime supporter of the Taliban and of terrorism in Afghanistan to a central role at the most sensitive phase of the 'transition'. Though there are arguments that 'the Taliban is changing', as claimed by Masoom Stanikzai, head of the Afghan Government's High Peace Council secretariat, it is useful to recall that the Malim Shah Wali, the head of the High Peace Council in the southern Province of Helmand, was killed by the Taliban as recently as on May 1, 2013. The US faith in Pakistan and a 'peaceful' Taliban is wishful thinking, and will only plunge Afghanistan, and the wider South Asian region, into a deeper and lasting chaos.

Unless the Taliban's safe sanctuaries and infrastructure of support in Pakistan are dismantled, Pakistan-backed Islamist extremists will continue to wreak havoc in Afghanistan. Similarly, the political stability is the need of the hour. The lack of political sagacity on the part of the new National Unity Government will prove more disastrous for the socio-economic condition of the country.

Significantly, according to the *United Nations World Food Programme* (WFP), food insecurity in Afghanistan increased from 29 per cent in 2007 to 33 per cent in 2012, with 20 per cent of the population "severely food-insecure". "The situation in Afghanistan will become more challenging as international troops withdraw, aid levels decline and elections take place. The resulting insecurity could impede humanitarian access to 8.8 million food-insecure and undernourished people, a third of the population", WFP said. On January 15, 2014 Afghanistan's Ministry of Finance signed a USD 50 million grant agreement with the World Bank for a project that provides technical and financial support to thousands of the country's poorest households to help lift them out of extreme poverty by 2018.

What we find during this research is that Afghanistan is the largest producer and cultivator of opium in the world, accounting for 74 per cent of the global opium production in 2012. Launched by President Hamid Karzai in 2007, the Good Performers Initiative, which is supported by the United States, has been rewarding provinces which show progress in their eradication efforts with $1 million for development projects annually. Until last year, 17 of Afghanistan's 34 provinces were each awarded USD 1 million for being poppy-free. However, by the end of 2013, two northern provinces - Balkh and Faryab - lost their poppy-free status, according to a joint report by the United Nations Office on Drugs and Crime and the Government of Afghanistan, released in November 2013.[6]

In the fragile state index for 2014, Afghanistan stands at seventh out of 178 countries[7]. Similarly, according to Corruption Perception Index, 2013, Afghanistan is at eighth position out of 177 countries and territories.[8]

To sum up, ethnic conflict is not a new phenomenon as it is considered to be as old as the mankind. Ethnic conflict has leapt onto centre stage due to the structural changes brought about by the end of the Cold War and colonialism. These structural changes have promoted ethnic conflict. The colonial powers and the independent states succeeding them declared that each and every person had an "ethnic identity" that determined his or her place within the colony or the postcolonial system. Since ethnic conflict is a complex phenomenon,there is no single approach that will work to its resolution. In fact, it is a case-by-case story. In the case of Afghanistan, ethnic conflicts, which were not so prominent during the Soviet occupation of the country, are now entirely different from the conflicts in other country. There have been cultural and external factors that had prompted the ethnic divisions in Afghanistan.

One may agree that the State plays an important role in resolving ethnic conflict. From time to time, the international system reorders itself normally in the aftermath of a major conflict. Recent events indicate that a new ordering principle is required. A state facing ethnic conflict (or for that matter any conflict) needs to be structured and for that a definite way has to be adopted. Afghanistan is a country in which nationalism is a sentiment expressed only in the face of great external pressures. On the individual level, an Afghan is torn between the one direction enforced by his society and the other by his faith. Islam, though the most prominent example of a common identity, has served as a weak foundation for national unity and has presented certain moral contradictions to the individual. One might argue that these circumstances have had the greatest impact on the contemporary history of Afghanistan.

During the period of this research it is hard to find any clear-cut resolution to the Afghan conflict, though recent political developments in Afghanistan, particularly after the election, points to a positive future scenario. However, we must not forget that even in the absence of foreign threat, the country is riddled with inner division and conflict. Any plan of action, therefore, must work from the inside out; meaning we must first solicit a change in the Afghan identity before we can expect any change in the behaviour that it creates. Only a strong nation-state will be able to create any sense of national identity. The world community must make every effort to help Afghanistan create such an entity. Hope for Afghanistan lies in its unification, and hence through changes in identity and loyalty, its people can hopefully experience some period of peace after so much conflict. Today, Afghanistan is at the cross road. If the world community fails to address the issues concerning Afghanistan in an appropriate manner there is every likelihood of Taliban's or its proxies returning to power in Kabul. If it happens, the country might plunge into another round of ethnic conflict.

References

1. Text of Security and Defense Cooperation Agreement Between the Islamic Republic of Afghanistan and the United States of America, Ministry of Foreign Affairs, Islamic Republic of Afghanistan, http://mfa.gov.af/en/news/text-of-security-and-defense-cooperation-agreement-between-the-islamic-republic-of-afghanistan-and-the-united-states-of-america.
2. *Ibid.*
3. Statement by the President on Afghanistan, Office of the Press Secretary, The White House, May 27, 2014, http://www.whitehouse.gov/the-press-office/2014/05/27/statement-president-afghanistan.
4. Text of Security and Defense Cooperation Agreement Between the Islamic Republic Of Afghanistan and the United States of America, Ministry of Foreign Affairs, Islamic Republic of Afghanistan, http://mfa.gov.af/en/news/text-of-security-and-defense-cooperation-agreement-between-the-islamic-republic-of-afghanistan-and-the-united-states-of-america.

5. *Ibid.*
6. Afghan authorities expand award scheme for poppy-free provinces, 27 January 2014, http://www.unama.unmissions.org/default.aspx?ctl=Details&tabid=12254&mid=15756&ItemID=37652.
7. Fragile Sates Index 2014, http://ffp.statesindex.org/rankings-2014.
8. Corruption Perceptions Index 2013, Transparency International, http://www.transparency.org/cpi2013/results.

References

(* indicates primary sources)

Abbi, Anvita, Gupta, R. S. Gupta and Kidwai, Ayesha (2001), *Linguistic Structure and Language Dynamics in South Asia,* New Delhi: Shri Janendra Press.

Adamec, Ludwig (1997), Historical *Dictionary of Afghanistan*, 2nd edition, Lanham: Scarecrow Press.

*Address by HE President Mahinda Rajapaksa at the ceremonial opening of Parliament, Sri Jayawardhanapura - Kotte, May 19, 2009, Sri Lanka, Sri Lanka Parliament (2009), Sri Lanka President Website [Online: web] accessed on on 5 Sept. 2014, URL: http://www.president.gov.lk/speech_ New.php?Id=74

*Ahmad Shah Massoud, National Radio Television of Afghanistan, [Online: web] accessed on 26 June 2014, URL: http://rta.org.af/en/index.php/figures/430-ahmad-shah-massoud

*Afghan authorities expand award scheme for poppy-free provinces, 27 January 2014, UNAMA, [Online: web] accessed on 3 August 2014, URL: http://www.unama.unmissions.org/default.aspx?ctl=Details&tabid=12254&mid=15756&ItemID=37652

Afghan Election 2014, [Online: web] accessed on 20 October 2014, URL: http://www.afghanwarnews.info/events/election2014.htm .

*Afghan (Ethnonym), World Heritage Encyclopedia, [Online: web] accessed on 15 September 2014, URL: http://www.worldheritage.org/articles/Afghan_(ethnonym)

*Afghanistan Midyear Report 2014 Protection of Civilians in Armed Conflict, UNAMA, [Online: web] accessed on 3 September 2014, URL: http://unama.unmissions.org/Portals/UNAMA/human%20rights/English%20edited%20light.pdf

*Afghanistan and the United Nations, *UN News Centre*, [Online: web] accessed on 20 September 2014, URL: http://www.un.org/News/dh/latest/afghan/un-afghan-history.shtml

*Afghanistan Constitutions of the Past (1990), Afghanistan Online, [Online: web] accessed on 16 September 2013, URL: http://www.afghan-web.com/history/const/const1990.html

*Afghanistan: Devotion to Duty 2013, Central Intelligence Agency, [Online: web] accessed on 5 September 2014, URL: https://www.cia.gov/library/publications/additional-publications/devotion-to-duty/afghanistan.html

*Afghanistan in Brief, *Embassy of Afghanistan*, Washington DC, [Online: web] Accessed on 5 September 2014, URL: http://www.embassyofafghanistan.org/page/afghanistan-in-brief

*Afghanistan: Politics, Elections, and Government Performance (2014), Congressional Research Service, [Online: web] accessed on 22 September 2014, URL: http://fas.org/sgp/crs/row/RS21922.pdf

*Afghanistan: Post-Taliban Governance, Security, and U.S. Policy, Congressional Research Service, [Online: web] accessed on January 30, 2014, URL: http://fpc.state.gov/documents/organisation/221259.pdf

*Afghanistan: The World Factbook 2014, Central Intelligence Agency, [Online: web] accessed on 5 September 2014, URL: https://www.cia.gov/library/publications/the-world-factbook/geos/af.html

*Afghanistan 1843-1878: Sources in the India Office Records, British Library, [Online: web] accessed on 18 September 2013,URL:http://www.bl.uk/reshelp/findhelpregion/asia/

afghanistan/afghanistancollection/1843to1878/sources1843to1878.html

Ahadia, A., The Decline of Pashtuns in Afghanistan, Asian Survey, July, 1995, 35(7), pp. 621-35.

Ahmed, Azam and Zahori, Habib (2014), "Afghan Ethnic Tensions Rise in Media and Politics", *New York Times,* [18th February 2014].

Ahmed, Ishtiaq (1996), *State, Nation and Ethnicity in Contemporary South Asia,* New York: Wellington House Publication.

Allen, I.L. (1983), *The Language of Ethnic Conflict,* New York: Columbia University Press.

*Amin, Hafizullah, Encyclopedia Britannica 2014, [Online: web] Accessed on 5 September 2014, URL: http://www.britannica.com/EBchecked/topic/20639/Hafizullah-Amin

Anderson, E.W., and Dupree, N.H., *The Cultural Basis of Afghan Nationalism*, London: Pinter Publishers.

Armstrong, John A., Nations before Nationalism (Chapel Hill: University of North California Press, 1982)

Aronson, Elliot, Wilson, Tim and Akert, Robin (2009), *Social Psychology.*

Asthana, N. C. and Nirmal, Anjali (2009), *Urban Terrorism: Myths and Realities,* Jaipur: Pointer Publication.

Auriat, Nadia and Bonneuil, Noel, Fifty Years of Ethnic Conflict and Cohesion, 1945-1994, Journal of Peace Research, 37(5), September, 2000, pp. 563-81.

*Bangladesh: The World Factbook 2014, Central Intelligence Agency, [Online: web] accessed on 5 September 2014, URL: https://www.cia.gov/library/publications/the-world-factbook/geos/bg.html

*Bangladesh: Foreign travel advice, Governmnet.UK, [Online: web] accessed on 6 October 14, URL: https://www.gov.uk/foreign-travel-advice/bangladesh/safety-and-security

Banks, M. (ed.), Conflict in World Society (Brighton: Wheatsheaf, 1984).

Banting, Erinn (2003), *Afghanistan - The People,* New York: Crabtree Publishing Company.

Basir, Khwaja and Fitri, Ahmad (2013), "External factors behind Afghan war: Karzai", Pajhwok *Afghan News,* 21st September 2013, [Online: web] accessed on 30 September 2014, URL: http://www.pajhwok.com/en/2013/09/21/external-factors-behind-afghan-war-karzai

Bell, Wendell and Freeman, Walter E. (eds.) (1974), *Ethnicity and Nation-Building: Comparative International and Historical Perspectives*, Beverly Hills: Sage Publications.

Berghe, Pierre L. van den (1981), *The Ethnic Phenomenon*, New York: Elsevier.

Bezhan, Frud, "Controversial ID Cards Expose Ethnic Divisions in Afghanistan", [Online: web] accessed on 5 September 2012, URL: http://www.sabawoon.com/articles/index.php?page=ID_Card

Bhutan Backgrounder (2008), South Asia Terrorism Portal, [Online: web] accessed on 5 August 2013, URL: http://www.satp.org/satporgtp/countries/bhutan/backgrounders/index.html .

*Bhutan: The World Factbook 2014, Central Intelligence Agency, [Online: web] accessed on 5 September 2014, URL: https://www.cia.gov/library/publications/the-world-factbook/geos/bt.html

Boucher, Jerry (1987), *Ethnic Conflict: International Perspectives*, Newbury Park: Sage Publications.

Boudon, Raymond (1971), *The Uses of Structuralism*, London: Heinemann, 1971.

Brass, Paul (ed.) (1985), *Ethnic Groups and the State*, Tottawa New Jersey: Barnes and Noble.

Brass, Paul R. (1991), *Ethnicity and Nationalism: Theory and Comparison*, New Delhi: Sage Publications.

Brown, Michael E. ...[et al] (2001), *Nationalism and Ethnic Conflict*, Cambridge: The MIT Press.

Burhanuddin Rabbani, Military, Global Security.org, [Online: web] accessed on 9 September 2014 http://www.globalsecurity.org/military/world/afghanistan/rabbani.htm

Bukhari, Dr Syed Mussawar Hussain and Ahmad, Mr Riaz (2013), "Ethnic conflicts and South Asian security", *Institute of Interdisciplinary Business Research,* 5(1): 779-794.

*Call for violence probe in Bangladesh's Chittagong Hill Tracts, Islamic Republic News Agency, [Online: web] accessed on 6 October 2014, URL: http://www.irinnews.org/fr/report/98515/call-for-violence-probe-in-bangladesh-s-chittagong-hill-tracts

Carberry, Sean (2013), "Afghans Confront Sensitive Issue of Ethnicity", NPR, [Online: web] accessed on 5 September 2012, URL: http://www.npr.org/2013/05/08/179079930/afghans-confront-senstive-issue-of-ethnicity%20l%20.

Carlstein, T. (1981), *The Sociology of Structuration in Time and Space: A Time Geographic Assessment of Gidden's Theory, Swedish Geographical Year Book*, Lund: Lund University Press.

Castillo, Graciana Del (2014), *Guilty Party: The International Community in Afghanistan*, United State of America (USA).

Cederman Lars-Erik, Wimmer Andreas, and Min Brian (2010), "Why Do Ethnic Groups Rebel? New Data and Analysis", *World Politics,* 62 (1).

Chadda, Maya, Ethnicity, State and Nation, World Affairs, 4(3), July- September, 2000, pp. 98-109.

*Crisis of Impunity - The Role of Pakistan, Russia, and Iran in Fueling the Civil War in Afghanistan, Human Rights Watch, Refworld, [Online: web] accessed on 3 September 2014, http://www.refworld.org/docid/3bd540b60.html

Clark, Kate, Afghanistan: the Ethnic Conflicts, Middle East International, 559, 26 September, 1999, pp. 17-18.

Clifford, Geertz (1963), "The Integrative Revolution: Primordial Sentiments and Civil Politics in the New States" [Online: web] accessed on 5 August 2013, URL: http://faculty.washington.edu/charles/562_f2011/Week%2010/Geertz%20The%20Integrative%20Revolution.pdf .

Coll, Steve (2001), "*Ghost Wars: The Secret History of the CIA, Afghanistan, and Bin Laden, from ...*" New York: The Penguin Press.

*Concepts and Definitions, Ethno cultural characteristics United Nations Statistics Division, [Online: web] accessed on 1 October 2014, URL:http://unstats.un.org/unsd/demographic/sconcerns/popchar/popcharmethods.htm

*Constitutional History of Afghanistan, Encyclopedia Iranica, [Online: web] accessed on August 6, 2014, URL: http://www.iranicaonline.org/articles/constitutional-history-of-afghanistan

Corinna, Vigier (2009), "Conflict Assessment Afghanistan", [Online: web] accessed on 5 Sept. 2014 URL: http://afsc.org/sites/afsc.civicactions.net/files/documents/Afghanistan% 20-%20Conflict%20Assessment.pdf

Cotter, Michal W (2001), "Afghanistan and its Neighbours", *American Diplomacy* (December 2001).

Crews Robert D. Crews and Amin Tarzi, *The Taliban and the Crisis of Afghanistan,* Cambridge, MA: Harvard University Press, 2008: 29.

Crocker, Chester A., Engaging Failing States, Foreign Affairs, 82(5), September- October, 2003, pp. 32-44.

Crocker, Chester A., How to Think about Ethnic Conflict, ORBIS, 43(4), Fall, 1999, pp. 613-20.

Cunningham, William G (1998), "Theoretical Framework for Conflict Resolution" [Online: web] accessed on 12 September. 2012, URL: http://cain.ulst.ac.uk/conflict/cunningham.htm

Cutler, Robert M., Policy Options for Resolving Post-Soviet Ethnic Conflict, Central Asian Survey, 19(3/4), September-December, 2000, pp. 451-68.

Dhillon, Rupinder Kaur, Nation-Building and State-Formation in Multi-Ethnic Societies: Focus on South Asia, BIISS Journal, 22(2), April, 2001, pp. 209-44.

Dil, Shaheen F., Cabel in Kabul: Great Power Interaction in Afghanistan; American Political Science Review; 71 (2); June, 77; pp. 468-76.

Dobson, George Davis (1895), *Russia's Railway Advantages in Central Asia; Notes on a Journey from St. Petersburg to Samarkand,* London: Nabu Press.

Doðan, Salih (2014), "Afghan Presidential Election and Future of US-Afghan Relations" *Strategic Outlook* [5th April 2014].

Dogan, Salih (2014), International Aid to Afghanistan and its Importance in the Post-2014 Era, The Washington Review, [Online: web] accessed on 6 June 2014, URL: http://www.thewashingtonreview.org/articles/international-aid-to-afghanistan-and-its-importance-in-the-post-2014-era.html#_ftnref15

Donini, Antonio; Niland, Norah and Wermester, Kenin (eds.), Nation-Building Unraveled?: Aid, Peace and Justice in Afghanistan (Bloomfield: Kumarian Press, 2004).

Dunaway, Wilma A. (2003), "Ethnic Conflict in The Modern World System: The Dialectic of Counter- Hegemonic Resistance in an Age of Terrorism", *Journal of World-Systems Research*, 9(1): 3-34.

Dupree, Louis, Afghan and British Military Tactics in the First Anglo-Afghan War (1838-1842); Army Quarterly and Defence Journal; 107(2); April; 77; pp. 214-21.

Dupree, Louis, Inside Afghanistan: Yesterday and Today: A Strategic Appraisal; Strategic Studies; 2 (3); Spring. 79; pp. 64-83.

Edwardes, Michael; The West In Asia; New York: G. P. Putnam; 1967.

Epstien, A.L., *Ethos and Identity: Three Studies in Ethnicity*, London: Tavistock Publications.

Eriksen, Thomas Hylland (2002), *Ethnicity and Nationalism: Anthropological Perspective*, London: Pluto Press.

Eriksen, Thomas Hylland (2014), *The Kea Concept of Globalisation*, London (UK): Bloomsbury Publishing Plc.

Eriksen, Thomas Hylland (1991), "Ethnicity versus Nationalism", *Journal of Peace Research,* 28(3): 263-278.

Ethston, Percy T., In the Heart of Asia; Boston: Houghton Miffin; 1926.

*Ethnocultural characteristics, United Nations Statistics Division, [Online: web] accessed on 5 Sept. 1995, URL: http://unstats.un.org/unsd/demographic/sconcerns/popchar/popcharmethods.htm#E

Ewans, Martin (2013), *Afghanistan - A New History,* London: Routledge.

Fearon, James D and Laitin, David D (1996), "Explaining Interethnic Cooperation" *The American Political Science Review* , 90 (4): 715-735.

Fitzgerald, Paul and Gould, Elizabeth (2011), "Gulbuddin Hekmatyar, the Messiah of Darkness", *Politics* (6th May 2011).

Fitzmaurice, Lord Edmond, The Life of Granvile George Leveson Gower; Second Earl Granvile; Vol. II; London; Longman Green and Co.; 1905.

Fletcher, Arnold, Afghanistan: Highroad of Conquest; Ithaca: Cornwell University Press; 1965.

Fox, Jonathan, Rise of Religious Nationalism: Ethnic Conflict and Revolutionary Wars, 1945-2001, Journal of Peace Research, 41(6), November, 2004, pp. 715-31.

Fraser- Tytler, W. K., Afghanistan: A Study of Political Development in Central Asia and South Asia, rev. by M. C. Gillet, London; Oxford University Press; 1967.

*From the Bonn Agreement to the 2005 Wolesi Jirga and Provincial Council Elections, UNMA, [Online: web] accessed on 1 October, 2014, URL: http://web.archive.org/web/20090305155438/http://www.unama-afg.org/news/_parelection/_factsheets/_english/JEMBS%20PO%20BG%20General%20BG%20final%202005-4-1%20eng.pdf

Gellner, E., Nations and Nationalism (Oxford: Blackwell, 1983).

Ghosh, Partha Sarathy (1995), *Cooperation and Conflict in South Asia*, New Delhi: Manohar Publications.

Giddens, Anthony, The Constitution of Society: Outline of the Theory of Structuration (Cambridge: Polity Press, 1984).

Gladstone, Cary (2001), *Afghanistan Revisited,* New York: Nova Science Publishers.

Glaser, Charles L and Kaufmann, Chaim (1998), "What is the offense-defense balance and can we measure it? (Offense, Defense, and International Politics)" *International Security,* 22(4): 39-44.

Glazer, Nathan and Moynihan, Daniel P. (eds.), Ethnicity: Theory and Experience (Cambridge: Harvard University Press, 1978).

Goldscheider, Calvin (ed.), Population, Ethnicity, and Nation-Building (Oxford: Westview Press, 1995).

Goldstein (2009), *Principle of International Relations*, Washington: Content Technology Inc. Publications.

Green, Elliott D (2006), "Redefining Ethnicity", London School of Economics and Political Science [Online web] accessed on 5 August 2013, URL: http://personal.lse.ac.uk/greened/ISA.pdf

Green, Katherine (2012), "The Symbolic Politics Theory of Ethnic War", E-International Relations Students, [online web] accessed on 2 September. 2012, URL: http://www.e-ir.info/2012/03/13/the-symbolic-politics-theory-of-ethnic-war/.

Gurr, T.D. and Hurff, B., Ethnic Conflict in World Politics: Dilemmas in World Politics (Boulder: Westview, 1994).

Gurtz, Clifford, The Interpretation of Cultures (London: Fontana, 1973).

Harrison, Emma Graham (2014), "Afghanistan election guide: everything you need to know", *The Guardian* [3rd February 2014].

Heredia, Rudolf C., Ethnicity, Class and Nation: Inter-relationships in a Multi- Cultural State, Economic and Political Weekly, 32(19), 10-16 May. 1997, pp. 1010-15.

*History, About ISAF, International Security Force Assistance, [Online: web] accessed on 15 March 15 2014, URL http://www.isaf.nato.int/history.html,

Hobsbawm, Eric, Nations and Nationalism: Since 1780 (Cambridge: Cambridge University Press, 1990).

Hodder, Rupert (2000), *Development Geography*, New York: Routledge.

Holdich, T. H., The Use of Practical Geography by Recent Frontier Operations; The Geographical Journal, Vol. 13, no. 5, May 1899

Horowitz, Donald L (1998), "Structure and Strategy in Ethnic Conflict", The World Bank, [Online: web] accessed on 5 August 1998, URL: http://siteresources.worldbank.org/DEC/Resources/84797-1251813753820/6415739-1251813951236/horowitz.pdf.

Horowitz, Donald L., Ethnic Groups in Conflict (California: California University Press, 2001).

How not to End War, The Washington Post, [Online: web] accessed on 12 September 2012, URL: http://www.washingtonpost.com/wp-dyn/content/graphic/2007/07/17/GR2007071700070.html,

Howard, E., India's Defence as an Imperial Problem, Journal of Central Asian Society, London, Vol. 13, pt. 2, 1926.

*Human Development Report 2004, Human Development Reports, United Nations Development Programme, [Online: web] accessed on 8 September 2014, URL: http://hdr.undp.org/en/content/human-development-report-2004

*Human Development Report 2014, Human Development Reports, United Nations Development Programme, [Online: web] accessed on 8 September 2014, URL: http://hdr.undp.org/en/content/human-development-report-2014

Hutchinson, John and Smith, Anthony D (1996), *Ethnicity*, New York: Oxford University Press.

IBPUSA (2013), *Afghanistan Country Study Guide Volume 1 Strategic Information and Developments*, USA: Int'l Business Publications.

*India: The World Factbook 2014, Central Intelligence Agency, [Online: web] accessed on 5 September 2014, URL: https://www.cia.gov/library/publications/the-world-factbook/geos/in.html

*International Security Assistance Force (ISAF): Key Facts and Figures, International Security Assistance Force, [Online: web] accessed on 27 July 2014, URL: http://www.isaf.nato.int/images/media/PDFs/140904placemat.pdf, accessed on March 10, 2014

*Inteqal: Transition to Afghan lead, North Atlantic Treaty Organisation, [Online: web] accessed on 6 October 2014, URL: http://www.nato.int/cps/in/natolive/topics_87183.htm

Isajiw, Wsevolod W. (1992), "Definition and Dimensions of Ethnicity: A Theoretical Framework", University of Toronto, [Online: web] accessed on 5 August 2013, URL: https://tspace.library.utoronto.ca/bitstream/1807/68/3/Def_DimofEthnicity.pdf.txt

Jalalzai, Musa Khan, Sectarianism and Ethnic Violence in Afghanistan (Lahore: Vanguard, 1996).

John, M.S., Ethnic Conflict Resolution: In Search of Alternative Strategies, Man and Development, 25(4), December, 2003, pp. 85-102.

Kanbur, Ravi (2009), "Ethnic Diversity and Ethnic Strife: An Interdisciplinary Perspective", Cornell University, [Online web] accessed on 5 August 2013, URL: http://kanbur.dyson.cornell.edu/papers/EthnicitySymposiumOverview.pdf .

Khalizad, Zalmay, The Politics of Ethnicity in South West Asia: Political Development or Political Decay, Political Science Quarterly, 99(4), Winter, 1984-85, p. 669.

Khan, Dr Borhan Uddin (2009), *Protection of Minorities: A South Asian Discourse,* Dhaka (Bangladesh): Eurasia Net.

Kharwal, Meena K., Religion, Psyche and Ethnic Conflict, Perspectives in Education, 19(1), January, 2003, pp. 5-9.

Khitab, Muhammad Hassan (2014), *New ID cards to be issued in a month: Ministry*, *Pajhwok Afghan News* (7th January 2014) [Online: web] accessed on 3 October 2014, URL: http://www.pajhwok.com/en/2014/01/07/new-id-cards-be-issued-month-ministry

Kurth, James, Religion and Ethnic Conflict in Theory, ORBIS, 45(2), Spring, 2001, pp. 281-94.

Lentz, Harris M.(2013), "Heads of States and Governments Since 1945" New York: Routledge.

Leverett, Hillary Mann (2009), "The Real Winner of Afghanistan Election", *FP Magazine* (31st August 2009).

Liberation Tigers of Tamil Eelam (LTTE), Terrorist Groups, Sri Lanka, South Asia Terrorism Portal [Online: web] accessed on 5 February 2014, http://www.satp.org/satporgtp/countries/shrilanka/terroristoutfits/LTTE.HTM,

*List of Banned Terrorist Organisations Under Section 35 of Unlawful Activities (Prevention) Act, 1967 (As On 27-01-2014), Ministry of Home Affairs, Government of India [Online: web] accessed on 1 October 2014, URL: http://mha.nic.in/BO

Louis, Andrews, Understanding Multi-Ethnic Politics, The Occidental Quarterly, 2(4), Winter, 2002/2003.

Lowie, Robert, The Origin of the State (New York: Harcourt, 1927).

MacColl, Malcolm, The Eastern Question; London, Longman, 1877.

MacDonald, Kevin, "An Integrative Evolutionary Perspective on Ethnicity", CSU-Long Beach [Online: web] accessed on 10 August 2014, URL: http://www.csulb.edu/~kmacd/paper-ethnicity.html.

MacDonald, Kevin, Numbers Game: Ethnic Conflict in the Contemporary World, Population and Environment, 21(4), March, 2000, pp. 413-25.

Mackenzie, R. and Mccurrys, S., Afghanistan's Uneasy Peace, National Geographic, 184(4), October-December, 1993, pp. 58-89.

Magocsis, Paul, R (1999), *Encyclopedia of Canada's Peoples*, Toronto: Canadian Publication.

Malcolm, Sir John; History of Persia; two volumes; London; John Murray; 1815.

*Maldives: The World Factbook 2014, Central Intelligence Agency, [Online: web] accessed on 5 September 2014, URL: https://www.cia.gov/library/publications/the-world-factbook/geos/mv.html

Malleson, Col. G.B., History of Afghanistan; London; Allen; 1878.

Malleson, Col. G.B., The Russo-Afghan Question; London; Routledge; 1885.

Malleson, Col. G.B; Herat; London; Allen; 1880.

Mandal, Monika (2011), "Ethnic Conflict in Nepal", *the IUP Journal of International Relations*, 5(2): 22-40.

Maria Montserrat Guibernau i Berdún, and John Rex (2010), *The Ethnicity Reader: Nationalism, Multiculturalism and Migration*, United Kingdom: Polity Press.

May, Stephen; Madood, Tariq and Squires (eds.), Judith, Ethnicity, Nationalism and Minority Rights (Cambridge: Cambridge University Press, 2004).

Mazhar, Muhammad Saleem, Khan, Samee Ozair and Goraya,Naheed S (2012), "Ethnic Factor in Afghanistan", *Journal of Political Studies*, 19 (2): 97:109.

Mehrotra, O.N., Ethno-Nationalism in the Contemporary World, Strategic Analysis, 22(6), September, 1998, pp. 829-40.

Mehta, Jagat S., The March of Folly in Afghanistan: 1978-2001 (New Delhi: Manohar Publishers and Distributors, 2002).

Mendoza, Kristin (2003), *Islam and Islamism in Afghanistan*, New York: Harvard Publication.

Minda, Ababu (2004), *An African Indian Community in Hyderabad Siddi Identity, Its maintenance and Change*, Gottingen: Die Deutsche Bbliothek verzeichent diese Publication.

Mission, About ISAF, Internal Security Assistance Force, Afghanistan, [Online: web], accessed on 16 September 2014, URL:http://www.isaf.nato.int/mission.html

Mukarji, Apratim, Afghanistan: From Terror to Freedom (New Delhi: Sterling Publishers, 2003).

Mukarji, Apratim, Challenges to Democratisation: Peace and Stability in Afghanistan, Himalayan and Central Asian Studies, 8(2-3), April-September, 2004.

Muni, S.D., "Ethnic conflict, federalism, and democracy in India", United Nations University, [Online: web] accessed on 5 August 2013, URL: http://archive.unu.edu/unupress/unupbooks/uu12ee/uu12ee0j.htm .

*Mujahideen, Encyclopedia Britannica, [Online: web] accessed on 15 Sept. 2014, URL: http://www.britannica.com/EBchecked/topic/396634/mujahideen

Narang, Amarjit S (1987), *Indian government and politics,* New Delhi: Gitanjali Publishing House.

*Nepal: The World Factbook 2014, Central Intelligence Agency, [Online: web] accessed on 5 September 2014, URL:https://www.cia.gov/library/publications/the-world-factbook/geos/np.html

Nevittee, N. and Kennedy, C.H., Ethnic Preference and Public Policy in Developing State (Boulder: Lynne Rienner, 1986).

*Nuristanis, World Directory of Minorities and Indigenous People, [Online: web] accessed on 1 October 2014, URL: http://www.minorityrights.org/5448/afghanistan/nuristanis.html

Nyrop, Richard F. and Donald M. Seekins (1986), "Afghanistan: country study", *Foreign Area Studies*, Washington.

Nyrop, R.S., and Seekings, D.M., (eds.), Afghanistan a Country Study, Area Hand Book Series (Washington D.C.: Department of The Army, 1986).

*Operation Enduring Freedom Fast Facts, CNN, [Online: web] accessed on 2 October 2014, URL: http://edition.cnn.com/2013/10/28/world/operation-enduring-freedom-fast-facts, accessed on October 1, 2014

Operation Enduring Freedom- Operations, Global Secuirty.org, [Online: web], accessed on 5 June 2014, URL: http://www.globalsecurity.org/military/ops/enduring-freedom-ops.htm

Origin of Wakhi Ethnic Group, Gojal, News Forum Magazine, [Online: web] accessed on 12 October 2014, URL: http://www.gojal.net/history_wakhies.htm

Pace, Eric (1996), "Babrak Karmal, Afghanistan's Ex-President, Dies at 67", *New York Times* (6th December, 1996).

Pacione, Michael (2014), *Urban Geography,* London, UK: Routledge.

*Pakistan, World Report 2014, Human Rights Watch, [Online: web], accessed on 5 September 2014, URL: http://www.hrw.org/world-report/2014/country-chapters/pakistan

*Pakistan Country of Origin Information (COI) Report, COI Service, UK Border Agency, [online: web] accessed on 6 September 2013, URL: https://www.gov.uk/government/uploads/system/uploads/attachment_data/file/310424/Pakistan_COI_report_june_2012.pdf

Pakistan and Afghanistan, Institute for the Study of War, [Online: web], accessed on 6 July 2014, http://www.understandingwar.org/pakistan-and-afghanistan

Pakistan Backgrounder, South Asia Terrorism Portal, [Online: web] accessed on 4 October 2013, URL: http://www.satp.org/satporgtp/countries/pakistan/backgrounders/index.html

*Pakistan: The World Factbook 2014, Central Intelligence Agency, [Online: web] accessed on 5 September 2014, URL: https://www.cia.gov/library/publications/the-world-factbook/geos/pk.html

Paullada, Leon, B., The Pashtun Role in Afghan Political System, Occasional Paper No. 1 (New York: Asian Society, 1970).

*Present status of Peace process in Northeast, Ministry of Home Affairs, Government of India [Online: web] accessed on 5 Sept. 2014, URL: http://mha.nic.in/sites/upload_files/mha/files/Peaceprocess-300813.pdf

Psalidas-Perlmutter, Foulie, Ethnic Conflict: Interplay of Myths and Realities, ORBIS, 44(2), Spring, 2000, pp. 237-44.

Rais, Rashul Baksh, Conflict in Afghanistan: Ethnicity, Religion and Neighbours, [Online: web] accessed on 5 Sept. 2014, URL: http://webcache.googleusercontent.com/search?q=cache:http://necsi.edu/afghanistan/pdf_data/Afghanistan-_Rais,ESR,Jan_1999.doc

Rashid Ahmed Rashid, *Taliban*, New Haven, CT: Yale University Press, 2000: 25.

Reed, John Shelton (1986), *The Enduring South*, Washington: Heath and Company.

Reeves, Hugh (2014), "Identity and Conflict in Afghanistan", Kabul Pen, [Online: web] accessed on 5 August 2013, URL: http://www.kabulpen.net/articles/english/afghanistan/2007/01/04/1988.html

Regmi, Rishikeshav, "Ethnicity and Identity", University of Cambridge, [Online: web] accessed on 5 September 2013, URL: http://himalaya.socanth.cam.ac.uk/collections/journals/opsa/pdf/OPSA_08_01.pdf

*Remarks by the President in Address to the Nation on the Way Forward in Afghanistan and Pakistan (2009), The White House, [Online: web] accessed on 5 Sept. 2014, URL: http://www.whitehouse.gov/the-press-office/

remarks-president-address-nation-way-forward-afghanistan-and-pakistan

Robert, Lindsay (2010), "Mutual Intelligibility Among the Turkic Languages", Robert Lindsay Word Press.com [Online: web] accessed on 5 September 2012, URL: http://robertlindsay.wordpress.com/2010/01/04/mutual-intelligibility-among-the-turkic-languages/ .

Roy, Pinaki (2010), "Bangladesh erupts in ethnic violence", Open Democracy [Online: web] accessed on 5 August 2013, URL: https://www.opendemocracy.net/author/pinaki-roy

Rex, J. and Mason, D. (eds.), Theories of Race and Ethnic Relations (Cambridge: Cambridge University Press, 1988).

Roosens, Eugeen E., Creating Ethnicity: The Process of Ethnogenesis (Newbury Park: Sage Publications, 1989).

Rubin, Barnett R., The Fragmentation of Afghanistan: State Formation and Collapse in the International System (New Haven: Yale University Press, 1995).

Rubin, Barnett R., The Search for Peace in Afghanistan: From Buffer State to Failed State (New Haven: Yale University Press, 1995).

Rushton, J. Philippe (2005), "Ethnic nationalism, evolutionary psychology and Genetic Similarity Theory", *Nations and Nationalism,* 11(4): 489-507.

Roberts, P. E.; History of British India under the Company and the Crown; Ed. III; compiled by TGP Spear; London; Oxford University Press; 1976.

Roberts, P. E.; India under Wellesley; Gorakhpur; Vishwavidyalaya Prakashan; 196.

Rostovsky, A Lobonov, Russia in Asia; London; McMillan; 1933.

Ryan, Stephen, Ethnic Conflict and International Relations (Aldershot: Dartmouth Publishing Company Limited, 1990).

Sadowski, Yaha, Ethnic Conflict, Foreign Policy, 111, Summer, 1998, pp. 12-23.

Saharani, Nazif M (2002), "War, Factionalism, and the State in Afghanistan," *American Anthropologist,* 104(3): 715-722.

Sahni, Ajai (2012), "Survey of Conflicts and Resolution in India's Northeast" [Online web] accessed on 5 August 2013 URL: http://www.satp.org/satporgtp/publication/faultlines/volume12/Article3.htm

Saideman, Stephen M., Overloading the Obvious: Bringing International Politics Back into Ethnic Conflict Management, Comparative Political Studies, 35(1), February, 2002, pp. 103-29.

Saikal, Amin, Afghanistan's Ethnic Conflict, Survival, 40(2), Summer, 1998, pp. 114-26.

*Saito, Mamiko (2007), "Second-generation Afghans in Neighbouring Countries, From Mohajer to Hamwatan: Afghans return home", Research was provided by the European Commission (EC) and United Nations High Commissioner for Refugees (UNHCR).

Schneckener, Ulrich, Making Power-Sharing Work: Lessons from Successes and Failures in Ethnic Conflict Regulation, Journal of Peace Research, 39(2), March, 2002, pp. 203-28.

Schöpflin, George (2000), *Nations, Identity, Power: The New Politics of Europe*, London (UK): C. Hurst and Co (Publishers) Ltd.

Security Council, In Presidential Statement, Condemns Afghanistan's Taliban For July Military Offensive, Sheltering Terrorists, Press Release, Security Council, 22 October 1999, [Online: web] accessed on 4 October 2011, URL: http://www.un.org/press/en/1999/19991022.sc6743.doc.html

Shah, Ikbal Ali, Modern Afghanistan; Lodon: Marston and Co. Ltd.; 1938.

Shawe, Keith (2013), "Afghanistan in 2013: A Survey of the Afghan People" Afghan Center for Socio-economic and Opinion Research (ACSOR), Kabul: The Asia Foundation.

Simonsen, Sven Gunnar, Ethnicising Afghanistan?: Inclusion and Exclusion in Post Bonn Institution Building, Third World Quarterly, 25(4), 2004, pp. 707-29.

Singh, Kumar Ajit (2014), "Afghanistan: Deepening Crisis", *South Asia Intelligence Review: Weekly Assessments and Briefings*, 13 (3).

Singh, Ajit Kumar (2011), "Nepal: Terai Simmering", *South Asia Intelligence Review: Weekly Assessments and Briefings*, 9 (39).

Singh, Ajit Kumar (2011), "Endgame in Sri Lanka" [Online web] accessed on 5 August 2013, URL: http://www.satp.org/satporgtp/publication/faultlines/volume20/Article%206.pdf

Singhal D.P., India and Afghanistan, 1876-1907: A Study in Diplomatic Relations; Queensland; University of Queensland Press; 1963.

Skrine, F.H., The Expansion of Russia (1815-1900); Cambridge: Cambridge University Press; 1915.

Smith, Anthony D., The Ethnic Origins of Nations (Oxford: Basil Blackwell, 1986).

Smith, Anthony D., The Ethnic Origins of Nations (Oxford: Blackwell, 1986).

Smith, Vincent, The Oxford History of India; Oxford: Oxford University Press; 1958.

Sollors, Werner; Cabot, Henry B. and Cabot, Anne M. (eds.), Theories of Ethnicity: A Classical Reader (Basingstoke: Macmillan, 1996).

Sommer, Judith (2009), *Ethnic Diversity and Conflict: The Role of Horizontal Inequalities*, Diploma Thesis: School of Business and Economics – Institute of Public Economics.

Sotiropoulou, Angeliki, "The role of ethnicity in ethnic conflicts: The case of Yugoslavia" [Online web] accessed on 25 September 2013 URL: file:///C:/Users/vcpl/Downloads/PN04.02%20(1).pdf .

*Sri Lanka: The World Factbook 2014, Central Intelligence Agency, [Online: web] accessed on 5 September 2014,

URL: https://www.cia.gov/library/publications/the-world-factbook/geos/ce.html

Stack, John F. (1986), *The Primordial challenge: ethnicity in the contemporary world,* Michigan: Greenwood Publishing Group.

Stephenson, Graham (1969), *History of Russia, 1812-1945,* New York: Routledge.

Stephenson, Graham, History of Russia: 1812-1945; London; McMillan; 1969.

Swinson, A., North-West Frontier People and Events, 1839-1947; New York: Praeger; 1967.

Sykes, Percy, A History of Afghanistan; Vol. I and II; London: Macmillan; 1940.

Tambiah, Stanley, Ethnic Conflict in World Today, American Ethnologist, 16(2), May, 1989, pp. 335-49.

Tang, Shiping (2011), "The security dilemma and ethnic conflict: toward a dynamic and integrative theory of ethnic conflict", *Review of International Studies,* 37(02): 511-536.

Taylor, Rupert (2009), *Consociational Theory*, New York: Routledge.

Terrorism was the problem: Krishna no need of solution now: Gotabhaya (2011), *Lanka newspaper*, [Online: web] accessed, 5 August 2013, URL: http://www.lankanewspapers.com/news/2011/8/69549_space.html

*Text of Security and Defence Co-operation Agreement Between the Islamic Republic of Afghanistan and the United States of America, Ministry of Foreign Affairs, Islamic Republic of Afghanistan, [Online: web] accessed on 1 October 2014, URL: http://mfa.gov.af/en/news/text-of-security-and-defense-cooperation-agreement-between-the-islamic-republic-of-afghanistan-and-the-united-states-of-america

*The Nepal Conflict Report, United Nation Human Rights, [Online: web] accessed on 5 Sept. 2014, URL: http://

www.ohchr.org/EN/Countries/AsiaRegion/Pages/NepalConflictReport.aspx

Thompson, Dennis L. and Ronen, Dov (eds.), Ethnicity, Politics, and Development (Boulder: Lynne Rienner Publishers, 1986).

Toft, Monica Duffy (2003), *The Geography of Ethnic Violence: Identity, Interests, and the Indivisibility of Territory*, Princeton: Princeton University Press.

*UNHCR 2011 Refugee Statistics: Full Data, The Guardian, [online: web] accessed on 5 October 2014, URL:http://www.theguardian.com/news/datablog/2011/jun/20/refugee-statistics-unhcr-data

*United Nations Arms Embargoes, SIPRI, [Online: web] accessed on 5 September 2014, URL: http://books.sipri.org/files/misc/UNAE/SIPRI07UNAETal.pdf, accessed on February 15, 2014

U.S. presses for bin Laden's ejection, The Washington Times, July 2, 2001, [Online: web] accessed on 3 October 2014, URL: http://www.washingtontimes.com/news/2001/jul/2/20010702-024109-5365r/?page=all

Vanhanen, Tatu (1999), "Ethnic Conflicts Explained by Ethnic Nepotism", *The Occidental Quarterly,* 2(4): 89-96.

Wade, Nicholas (2003), "A Prolific Genghis Khan, It Seems, Helped People the World", *The New York Times* [11th February 2003], [Online: web] accessed on 1 September, 2006, URL: http://www.nytimes.com/2003/02/11/science/a-prolific-genghis-khan-it-seems-helped-people-the-world.html

Weinbaum, Marvin G. (2006), "Afghanistan and its Neighbours", *United States Institute of Peace.*

Wienner, M. and Banuazizi, A., The Politics of Social Transformation in Afghanistan, Iran, and Pakistan (New York: Syracuse University Press, 1994).

Wimmer, Andreas (2008), "The Making and Unmaking of Ethnic Boundaries: A Multilevel Process Theory", *J Store,* 113(4): 970-1022.

Journals and Periodicals

American Ethnologist
Asian Survey
BIISS Journal
Central Asian Survey
Comparative Political Studies
Economic and Political Weekly
Foreign Policy
Journal of Peace Research
Man and Development
Middle East International
National Geographic
ORBIS
Perspectives in Education
Population and Environment
Strategic Analysis
Survival
Third World Quarterly
World Affairs

Newspapers

The Dawn
The Kabul Times
The Tribune
The New York Times
Frontier Post
National Herald
News Times
The Asian Age
The Hindu

Appendix

Security and Defence Co-operation Agreement between the Islamic Republic of Afghanistan and the United States of America

Preamble

The Islamic Republic of Afghanistan (hereinafter, "Afghanistan") and the United States of America (hereinafter, "the United States"), referred to collectively as "the Parties" and singularly as a "Party;"

Recognising the Enduring Strategic Partnership Agreement between the Islamic Republic of Afghanistan and the United States of America, signed May 2, 2012, (the "Strategic Partnership Agreement") and reaffirming that, as recognised in that Agreement, the Parties are committed to strengthen long-term strategic cooperation in areas of mutual interest, including: advancing peace, security, and stability; strengthening state institutions; supporting Afghanistan's long-term economic and social development; and encouraging regional cooperation;

Confirming the recognition in the Strategic Partnership Agreement that cooperation between the Parties is based on mutual respect and shared interests;

Emphasising also the Strategic Partnership Agreement's recognition that the Parties will go forward in partnership with confidence because they are committed to seeking a future of justice, peace, security, and opportunity for the Afghan people, as well as the reaffirmation of the Parties' strong commitment to the sovereignty, independence, territorial integrity, and national unity of Afghanistan;

Recognising the enduring partnership between Afghanistan and the United States, and affirming the mutual intent of the Parties to expand, mature, promote and further elevate their security and defense cooperation based on this Agreement;

Desiring to continue to foster close cooperation concerning defense and security arrangements in order to strengthen security and stability in Afghanistan, contribute to regional and international peace and stability, combat terrorism, achieve a region which is no longer a safe haven for al-Qaida and its affiliates, and enhance the ability of Afghanistan to deter threats against its sovereignty, security, and territorial integrity; and noting that the United States does not seek permanent military facilities in Afghanistan, or a presence that is a threat to Afghanistan's neighbours, and has pledged not to use Afghan territory or facilities as a launching point for attacks against other countries;

Recalling the Chicago Summit Declaration on Afghanistan, issued on May 21, 2012, by the Heads of State and Government of Afghanistan and Nations Contributing to the North Atlantic Treaty Organisation (NATO)-led International Security Assistance Force (ISAF), and specifically, the participants' renewed firm commitment to a sovereign, secure, and democratic Afghanistan and acknowledgment that ISAF's mission will be concluded by the end of 2014 and that their close partnership will continue beyond the end of the transition period including through NATO and Afghanistan's mutual commitment to work to establish a new NATO-led Mission to train, advise, and assist the Afghan National Defense and Security Forces (ANDSF), and noting here that such a mission will also need to be provided with the necessary authorities, status arrangements, and legal basis;

Reaffirming the continued support of the Parties for regional cooperation and coordination mechanisms, with a goal of increasing security and stability by reducing tensions, uncertainty, and misunderstanding;

Recalling the 2013 Consultative Loya Jirga's recognition that this Security and Defense Cooperation Agreement between Afghanistan and the United States is important for the security of Afghanistan;

Desiring to develop further the means of defense and security cooperation between the Parties, based on the principles of full respect for the independence, sovereignty, and integrity of their territories, and non-interference in the domestic affairs of each other, in order to promote security and stability in the region, and to combat terrorism;

Agreeing on the importance of co-operative relationships between Afghanistan and its neighbours conducted on the basis of mutual respect, non-interference, and equality and calling on all nations to respect Afghanistan's sovereignty and territorial integrity, and to refrain from interfering in Afghanistan's internal affairs and democratic processes; and

Affirming also that the Parties' co-operation is based on full respect for the sovereignty of each Party, the purposes of the United Nations Charter, and a shared desire to provide a framework for defense and security cooperation between the Parties; and reaffirming their strong commitment to the sovereignty, independence, territorial integrity, and national unity of Afghanistan, as well as respect for Afghan laws, customs, and traditions;

Have agreed as follows:

Article - 1
Definitions

1. "United States forces" means the entity comprising the members of the force and of the civilian component, and all property, equipment, and material of the United States Armed Forces present in the territory of Afghanistan.
2. "Member of the force" means any person belonging to the land, sea, or air services of the United States Armed Forces.
3. "Member of the civilian component" means any person employed by the United States Department of Defense (DoD) who is not a member of the force. However, "member of the civilian component" does not mean persons who are permanently resident in Afghanistan or Afghan nationals who normally reside in Afghanistan.
4. "Executive Agent" means Ministry of Defense (MoD) for Afghanistan and DoD for the United States. The Executive Agent serves as the principal contact for its respective Party for the implementation of this Agreement.
5. "United States contractors" means persons and legal entities who are supplying goods and services in Afghanistan to or on behalf of United States forces under a contract or subcontract with or in support of United States forces.
6. "United States contractor employees" means the employees of United States contractors.
7. "Agreed facilities and areas" means the facilities and areas in the territory of Afghanistan provided by Afghanistan at the locations listed in Annex A, and such other facilities and areas in the territory of Afghanistan as may be provided by Afghanistan in the future, to which United States forces, United

States contractors, United States contractor employees, and others as mutually agreed, shall have the right to access and use pursuant to this Agreement.

8. "Afghan National Defense and Security Forces" or "ANDSF" means the entity comprising the members of the security forces under the Ministry of Interior and the MoD of Afghanistan and, as appropriate, the National Directorate of Security, and other entities as mutually agreed.
9. "Taxes" means all taxes, duties (including customs duties), fees, and similar or related charges of whatever kind, imposed by the Government of Afghanistan which, for the purposes of this Agreement, means by governmental authorities of Afghanistan at any level, including provincial and district levels, and by the agencies of such governmental authorities.

Article - 2

Purpose and Scope

1. The Parties shall continue to foster close cooperation to strengthen security and stability in Afghanistan, counter terrorism, contribute to regional and international peace and stability, and enhance the ability of Afghanistan to deter internal and external threats against its sovereignty, security, territorial integrity, national unity, and its constitutional order. Unless otherwise mutually agreed, United States forces shall not conduct combat operations in Afghanistan.
2. To that end, the United States shall undertake supporting activities, as may be agreed, in close cooperation and coordination with Afghanistan, to assist ANDSF in developing capabilities required to provide security for all Afghans, including as may be mutually agreed: advising, training, equipping,

supporting, and sustaining ANDSF, including in field engineering, countering improvised explosive devices, and explosive ordnance disposal; establishing and upgrading ANDSF transportation and logistics systems; developing intelligence sharing capabilities; strengthening Afghanistan's Air Force capabilities; conducting combined military exercises; and other activities as may be agreed. The Parties will continue to work on the details of ANDSF development as set forth in the Afghan Programme of Record, adopted at the Chicago Summit in 2012, and in the context of the Afghanistan-United States Bilateral Security Consultative Forum.

3. The Parties recognise that ANDSF are responsible for securing the people and territory of Afghanistan. The Parties shall work to enhance ANDSF's ability to deter and respond to internal and external threats. Upon request, the United States shall urgently determine support it is prepared to provide ANDSF in order to respond to threats to Afghanistan's security.
4. The Parties acknowledge that U.S. military operations to defeat al- Qaida and its affiliates may be appropriate in the common fight against terrorism. The Parties agree to continue their close cooperation and coordination toward those ends, with the intention of protecting U.S. and Afghan national interests without unilateral U.S. military counter-terrorism operations. U.S. military counter-terrorism operations are intended to complement and support ANDSF's counter-terrorism operations, with the goal of maintaining ANDSF lead, and with full respect for Afghan sovereignty and full regard for the safety and security of the Afghan people, including in their homes.
5. In furtherance of the activities and operations referred to in this Article and for other purposes and missions as may be mutually agreed, and consistent with the

authorisations as detailed in this Agreement, United States forces may undertake transit, support, and related activities, including as may be necessary to support themselves while they are present in Afghanistan under the terms of this Agreement, and such other activities as detailed in this Agreement, or as may be mutually agreed.

6. This Agreement, including any Annexes and any Implementing Agreements or Arrangements, provides the necessary authorisations for the presence and activities of United States forces in Afghanistan and defines the terms and conditions that describe that presence, and in the specific situations indicated herein, the presence and activities of United States contractors and United States contractor employees in Afghanistan.

Article - 3
Laws

1. It is the duty of members of the force and of the civilian component to respect the Constitution and laws of Afghanistan and to abstain from any activity inconsistent with the spirit of this Agreement and, in particular, from any political activity in the territory of Afghanistan. It is the duty of United States forces authorities to take necessary measures to that end.
2. The Parties' respective obligations under this Agreement, and any subsequent arrangements, are without prejudice to Afghan sovereignty over its territory, and each Party's right of self-defense, consistent with international law. Cooperation and activities relating to implementation of this Agreement shall be consistent with the Parties' respective commitments and obligations under international law.

3. United States forces shall not enter Afghan homes for the purpose of military operations and searches except under extraordinary circumstances involving the urgent risk to life and limb of U.S. nationals. United States forces shall not arrest or imprison Afghan nationals, nor maintain or operate detention facilities in Afghanistan.

Article - 4
Developing and Sustaining Afghanistan's Defence and Security Capabilities

1. With full respect for Afghanistan's sovereignty, the Parties recognise Afghanistan's current requirement for continued international security assistance, and share the goal of Afghanistan taking increasing and, ultimately full, responsibility for funding its defense and security needs and sustaining ANDSF.
2. Afghanistan shall make, consistent with its political and economic stability and its general economic condition, the full contribution permitted by its manpower, resources, and facilities to the development and sustainment of its own defense and security forces. Afghanistan shall take all necessary measures to develop and sustain its defense and security capacities.
3. So long as the Strategic Partnership Agreement so provides, and guided by the pledges set forth at the Chicago Summit in 2012, the United States shall have an obligation to seek funds on a yearly basis to support the training, equipping, advising, and sustaining of ANDSF, so that Afghanistan can independently secure and defend itself against internal and external threats, and help ensure that terrorists never again encroach on Afghan soil and threaten Afghanistan, the region, and the world. The United States shall consult with Afghanistan regarding

the amount of funding needed to accomplish the purposes of this Agreement, keeping in mind pledges made in Chicago, and shall take the results of those consultations into consideration in executing this obligation. Taking into account Afghanistan's annual priorities, the United States shall direct appropriate funds through Afghan Government budgetary mechanisms, to be managed by relevant Afghan institutions implementing financial management standards of transparency and accountability and procurement, audit, and regulatory oversight in accordance with international best practices.

4. The Parties recognise the importance of ANDSF having the necessary equipment and materiel to secure Afghanistan. To that end, the United States shall continue to cooperate with Afghanistan on providing equipment and material for ANDSF.
5. Afghanistan and the United States may cooperate and coordinate with other countries to strengthen ANDSF, as may be mutually agreed, including on equipping ANDSF.
6. In order to contribute effectively to the security of Afghanistan and the region, the United States agrees to cooperate with Afghanistan to continue the development of ANDSF capabilities consistent with Afghanistan's status as a Major non-NATO Ally.
7. The Parties recognise the benefits for Afghanistan's defense and security to be derived from developing defence capabilities and systems that are consistent with NATO standards and that promote interoperability with NATO. The Parties shall coordinate in the development of Afghanistan's defense and security forces, equipment, materiel, facilities, operational doctrine, and institutions to achieve standardisation and interoperability with NATO, in order to promote further the effective utilisation and maintenance of defense and security assistance

provided to Afghanistan, and to maximise the benefits of cooperation between ANDSF and United States forces. This coordination shall not preclude Afghanistan from procuring independently equipment and material for ANDSF from non-NATO countries with its own resources.

Article - 5

Defence and Security Co-operation Mechanisms

1. The Parties agree to direct the Afghanistan - United States Working Group on Defence and Security Co-operation, established under the Strategic Partnership Agreement, to:
   (a) Develop appropriate measures of effectiveness for the analysis and strengthening of Afghanistan's use of available defense and security resources, consistent with the purpose and scope of this Agreement;
   (b) Complete semi-annual assessments of actual performance against these measures to inform the Parties' respective resource allocation decisions and their cooperation in developing and sustaining Afghanistan's defense capabilities;
   (c) Develop a process consistent with the purpose and scope of this Agreement, for making timely, accurate, and effective cooperative assessments of internal and external threats to Afghanistan; and
   (d) Make specific recommendations on enhancing information and intelligence sharing and evaluation.
2. The Parties share the objective of continuing to improve their ability to consult on such threats, including considering how to establish secure or dedicated channels of communication.

Article - 6

External Aggression

1. Afghanistan has been subject to aggression and other uses of force inconsistent with the United Nations Charter by foreign states and externally based or supported armed groups. In the context of this Agreement, the Parties strongly oppose such uses of armed force or threats thereof against the territorial integrity or political independence of Afghanistan, including in this regard provision to armed groups of support, such as sanctuary or arms, by any state or other armed groups. The Parties agree to cooperate to strengthen Afghanistan's defenses against such threats to its territorial integrity, sovereignty or political independence.
2. The United States shall regard with grave concern any external aggression or threat of external aggression against the sovereignty, independence, and territorial integrity of Afghanistan, recognising that such aggression may threaten the Parties' shared interests in Afghanistan's stability and regional and international peace and stability.
3. On a regular basis, the Parties shall consult on potential political, diplomatic, military, and economic measures that could form part of an appropriate response in the event of such external aggression or the threat of external aggression against Afghanistan. Consultations shall seek to develop a list of political, diplomatic, military, and economic measures.
4. In the event of external aggression or the threat of external aggression against Afghanistan, the Parties shall hold consultations on an urgent basis to develop and implement an appropriate response, including, as may be mutually determined, consideration of available political, diplomatic, military, and economic

measures on the list developed pursuant to paragraph 3, in accordance with their respective constitutional procedures.

5. The Parties shall develop comprehensive procedures to promote the effective accomplishment of such regular and urgent consultations.
   (a) Such comprehensive procedures shall recognise consultations involving the participation of the Afghanistan Foreign Minister and the United States Secretary of State, the Afghanistan Defense Minister and the United States Secretary of Defense, and respective Ambassadors in Kabul and Washington, D.C., as primary channels to initiate urgent consultations in the event of external aggression, or threat of external aggression.
   (b) Such comprehensive procedures shall not, however, limit or prejudice the Parties' ability to consult each other in other channels or through other mechanisms, as urgency or exigency may require.
6. The Parties agree to direct the Afghanistan - United States Working Group on Defense and Security Cooperation to promote the effective implementation of this Article, including development of such comprehensive procedures, and review on a regular basis the list of measures developed pursuant to paragraph 3.

Article - 7

Use of Agreed Facilities and Areas

1. Afghanistan hereby provides access to and use of the agreed facilities and areas, as defined in paragraph 7 of Article 1, solely to implement the purpose and scope of this Agreement, taking into account locations

of ANDSF and the local Afghan population. Access to and use of such agreed facilities and areas for other purposes shall be as mutually agreed by the Parties.

2. Under this Agreement, Afghanistan hereby authorises United States forces to exercise all rights and authorities within the agreed facilities and areas that are necessary for their use, operation, defense, or control, including the right to undertake new construction works. United States forces may carry out such construction works with members of the force and the civilian component or by contract.
3. Afghanistan hereby authorises United States forces to control entry to agreed facilities and areas that have been provided for United States forces' exclusive use, and to coordinate entry with Afghan authorities at joint-use agreed facilities and areas, for the purposes of safety and security. Upon request, the United States shall provide to relevant authorities of Afghanistan access to any agreed facility or area that has been provided for United States forces' exclusive use. The Parties shall establish mutually agreed procedures regarding Afghan authorities' access to any agreed facility or area that has been provided for United States forces' exclusive use. Such procedures and access shall be established with due respect for United States forces operations and security requirements. Acknowledging that United States forces may conduct force protection activities at and in the vicinity of agreed facilities and agreed areas as are necessary, the Parties agree to coordinate and integrate their respective plans for force protection to ensure the safety of United States forces, with full respect for Afghan sovereignty and with full regard for the safety and security of the Afghan people. In furtherance of this objective, United States forces shall not target Afghan civilians, including in their

homes, consistent with Afghan law and United States forces' rules of engagement.

4. In pursuit of the purpose and scope of this Agreement, in particular United States efforts to train, equip, advise, and sustain ANDSF, Afghanistan shall provide all agreed facilities and areas without charge to United States forces.
5. United States forces shall be responsible for the construction, development, operations, and maintenance costs for agreed facilities and areas provided for their exclusive use, unless otherwise agreed by the Parties. Construction, development, operations, and maintenance costs for agreed facilities and areas provided for joint use, or otherwise used jointly by United States forces and ANDSF or other entities, shall be shared on the basis of proportionate use, unless otherwise agreed.
6. The United States confirms its commitment to respect relevant Afghan environmental and health and safety laws, regulations, and standards in the execution of its policies. United States forces operations and activities on agreed facilities and areas shall be conducted with due regard for the protection of the natural environment and human health and safety, with due respect for applicable Afghan laws and regulations, and in accordance with applicable United States laws and regulations and applicable international agreements.
7. United States forces operations and activities on agreed facilities and areas shall be conducted with full respect for Afghan laws and regulations for the protection of sites or artifacts of historic and cultural heritage. United States forces shall notify and consult immediately with appropriate Afghan authorities through the Joint Commission when sites or artifacts of historic and cultural heritage are discovered on an agreed facility or area.

Article - 8
Property Ownership

1. United States forces shall return to Afghanistan any agreed facility or area, or any portion thereof, including buildings, non-relocatable structures, and assemblies connected to the soil, including those constructed, altered, or improved by United States forces, when no longer needed for United States forces' use. United States forces shall keep the requirement for such agreed facilities and areas under periodic reassessment with a view toward such return. The Parties or their Executive Agents shall consult regarding the terms of return of any agreed facility or area. The Parties agree to pursue a preventative rather than reactive approach to environmental protection and human health and safety. The Parties recognise that the policies and practices of the United States are designed to avoid such damage and endangerment and to apply the more protective of either Afghan or United States standards. In accordance with United States forces policy, United States forces shall take prompt action to address a substantial impact to human health and safety due to environmental contamination that is caused by activities of United States forces and is located on an agreed facility or area.
2. All buildings, non-relocatable structures, and assemblies connected to the soil at the agreed facilities and areas, including those constructed, used, altered, or improved by United States forces, are for the exclusive use of United States forces, United States contractors, and United States contractor employees, and for others as mutually agreed. All such buildings, non-relocatable structures, and assemblies connected to the soil built by United States forces or provided to United States forces for their access and use may be modified by United States forces, and United States

forces may use them exclusively until they are no longer required by United States forces.

3. United States forces and United States contractors shall retain title to all equipment, material, supplies, relocatable structures, and other movable property they have installed in, imported into, or acquired within the territory of Afghanistan in connection with the presence of United States forces and United States contractors in Afghanistan. The Parties shall consult regarding the possible transfer to or purchase by Afghanistan of equipment determined to be excess, as may be authorised by United States laws and regulations.

Article - 9

Positioning and Storage of Equipment and Material

1. Afghanistan authorises United States forces to position the equipment, supplies, and material of United States forces within agreed facilities and areas, and at other locations as mutually agreed. United States forces shall maintain title to and control over the use and disposition of such equipment, supplies, and material that are stored in the territory of Afghanistan and shall have the right to remove such items from the territory of Afghanistan.
2. The United States confirms its commitment to respect relevant Afghan safety laws, regulations, and standards. United States forces shall take all necessary measures to protect and safely store equipment, supplies, and material of United States forces that are of a hazardous nature in accordance with applicable United States laws and regulations. In accordance with United States forces policy, United States forces shall take prompt action (1) to clean up

spills located on an agreed facility or area; and, (2) to address a substantial impact to human health and safety due to environmental contamination that is caused by activities of United States forces and is located on an agreed facility or area.

3. The United States, taking into account its obligations under the Convention on the Prohibition of the Development, Production, Stockpiling and Use of Chemical Weapons and on their Destruction, done at Paris on January 13, 1993, and the Convention on the Prohibition of the Development, Production and Stockpiling of Bacteriological (Biological) and Toxin Weapons and on their Destruction done at Washington, London, and Moscow on April 10, 1972, agrees that chemical and biological weapons shall not be stored in the territory of Afghanistan. The Parties affirm that the United States will not position or store nuclear weapons in the territory of Afghanistan.

Article - 10

Movement of Vehicles, Vessels, and Aircraft

1. Afghanistan has full sovereignty over its airspace, territory, and waters. Management of Afghanistan's airspace and transportation shall be exercised through relevant Afghan authorities.
2. With full respect for Afghan sovereignty and consistent with the purpose and scope of this Agreement, Afghanistan authorises United States government aircraft and civil aircraft that are operated by or exclusively for United States forces to enter, exit, overfly, land, take off, conduct aerial refueling, and move within the territory of Afghanistan. United States government aircraft and civil aircraft that are operated by or exclusively for United States forces shall not be subject to payment of overflight or

navigation fees, or landing or parking fees at government-owned airfields, or other charges. United States government aircraft shall be operated with full respect for the relevant rules of safety and movement in Afghanistan, including notification requirements. Civil aircraft being operated by or exclusively for United States forces are subject to notification requirements regarding their entry into and exit from the territory of Afghanistan as required by the civil aviation authorities of Afghanistan.

3. With full respect for Afghan sovereignty and consistent with the purpose and scope of this Agreement, Afghanistan authorises United States government vessels and vehicles and other vessels and vehicles that are operated by or exclusively for United States forces, to enter, exit, and move within the territory of Afghanistan. All such vessels and vehicles shall be operated with full respect for the relevant rules of safety and movement in Afghanistan. Members of the force and of the civilian component have a duty to respect Afghan motor vehicle regulations when operating official vehicles.
4. United States government aircraft, vessels and vehicles shall be free from boarding without the consent of United States forces authorities. United States government aircraft, vessels, and vehicles shall be free from inspection, regulation, or registration requirements within Afghanistan, except as otherwise provided in this Agreement or as otherwise agreed by the Joint Commission.
5. United States forces shall pay reasonable charges for services requested and received for United States government aircraft, vehicles, and vessels, free of taxes or similar charges.
6. The Parties agree to establish procedures to implement this Article. The Parties shall review and update, as

appropriate, such procedures, and shall address any issues immediately through the Joint Commission that may arise regarding such procedures.

Article - 11
Contracting Procedures

1. United States forces, in accordance with United States laws, may enter into contracts for the acquisition of articles and services, including construction, in the territory of Afghanistan. Afghanistan recognises that United States forces are bound by the laws and regulations of the United States in the solicitation, award, and administration of such contracts. United States forces shall strive to utilise Afghan suppliers of goods, products, and services to the greatest extent practicable, in accordance with United States laws and regulations.
2. United States contractors are subject to registration in Afghanistan, via an expedited process that shall include issuance of a business registration license valid for three years and payment of a reasonable, standard, one-time service charge to the Afghanistan Investment Support Agency as required by the laws and regulations of Afghanistan. United States contractors shall otherwise be exempt from all other Afghan licenses and similar requirements in relation to their entry into or execution of contracts and subcontracts with or on behalf of United States forces.
3. Recognising the importance of transparency, including through the sharing of information and consultations as may be mutually agreed, United States forces shall give due consideration to concerns and disputes expressed by Afghan authorities regarding United States contractors. The Parties will work together to improve transparency, accountability, and effectiveness

of contracting processes in Afghanistan with a view to preventing misuse and bad contracting practices.

4. Upon the request of either Party, the Parties shall consult immediately through the Joint Commission concerning any issues, including issues concerning the activities of United States contractors and United States contractor employees that may arise regarding implementation of this Article.

Article - 12
Utilities and Communications

1. United States forces may produce and provide services including but not limited to water, electricity, and other utilities for agreed facilities and areas and for other locations as mutually agreed. The production and provision of such services shall be notified to and coordinated with the Joint Commission on a periodic basis. United States forces and United States contractors may use Afghan public water, electricity, and other Afghan public utilities on terms and conditions, including rates or charges, no less favourable than those paid by ANDSF, less taxes or similar or related charges, unless otherwise mutually agreed. United States forces' or United States contractors' costs shall be equal to their proportionate use of such public utilities.
2. Afghanistan recognises that United States forces shall use the radio spectrum. The Afghan side shall allocate Afghan owned frequencies based on relevant Afghan regulations. The United States shall be allowed to operate its own telecommunications systems (as telecommunication is defined in the 1992 Constitution of the International Telecommunication Union), including the use of such means and services as required to ensure full ability to operate telecommunications

systems, and the use of radio spectrum allocated by appropriate Afghan authorities for this purpose. Use of radio spectrum shall be free of cost to the United States.

3. United States forces, in recognition of Afghan ownership and allocation of frequencies within Afghanistan and in the interest of avoiding mutually disruptive interference, shall coordinate with appropriate Afghan authorities for the allocation of frequencies for United States forces present in Afghanistan. United States forces shall respect frequencies in use by or reserved for local operators.
4. Use of telecommunications by United States forces shall be done in a manner that avoids interference with use of radio spectrum or other telecommunication equipment operated by the Afghan government and other organisations the Afghan government has granted permission to use radio spectrum and/or telecommunications equipment.

Article - 13
Status of Personnel

1. Afghanistan, while retaining its sovereignty, recognises the particular importance of disciplinary control, including judicial and non-judicial measures, by United States forces authorities over members of the force and of the civilian component. Afghanistan therefore agrees that the United States shall have the exclusive right to exercise jurisdiction over such persons in respect of any criminal or civil offenses committed in the territory of Afghanistan. Afghanistan authorises the United States to hold trial in such cases, or take other disciplinary action, as appropriate, in the territory of Afghanistan.

2. If requested by Afghanistan, the United States shall inform Afghanistan of the status of any criminal proceedings regarding offenses allegedly committed in Afghanistan by the members of the force or of the civilian component involving Afghan nationals, including the final disposition of the investigations or prosecution. If so requested, the United States shall also undertake efforts to permit and facilitate the attendance and observation of such proceedings by representatives of Afghanistan.
3. In the interests of justice, the Parties shall assist each other in investigation of incidents, including the collection of evidence. In investigating offenses, United States authorities shall take into account any report of investigations by Afghan authorities.
4. The United States recognises the critical role that Afghan law enforcement officials play in the enforcement of Afghan law and order and the protection of the Afghan people. Relevant Afghan authorities shall immediately notify United States forces authorities if they suspect a member of the force or of the civilian component is engaged in the commission of a crime so that United States forces authorities can take immediate action. Members of the force and of the civilian component shall not be arrested or detained by Afghan authorities. Members of the force and of the civilian component arrested or detained by Afghan authorities for any reason, including by Afghan law enforcement authorities, shall be immediately handed over to United States forces authorities.
5. Afghanistan and the United States agree that members of the force and of the civilian component may not be surrendered to, or otherwise transferred to, the custody of an international tribunal or any other entity or state without the express consent of the United States.

6. Afghanistan maintains the right to exercise jurisdiction over United States contractors and United States contractor employees.

Article - 14
Bearing of Arms and Wearing of Uniforms

1. When present in Afghanistan under this Agreement, members of the force and of the civilian component may possess and carry arms in Afghanistan as required for the performance of their duties and as authorised by their orders. When issuing such orders, United States forces authorities shall consider relevant Afghan officials' views regarding appropriate locations for the presence of arms, including considerations of public safety. In consideration of such views, United States forces shall not, for military operations, enter mosques or other sites of religious significance being used for religious purposes. Members of the force may wear uniforms while in Afghanistan. United States forces authorities shall take appropriate measures to ensure that members of the force and of the civilian component are mindful of their presence in public areas, including in the carrying of weapons.
2. The Parties agree that United States contractors and United States contractor employees are not permitted to wear military uniforms and may only carry weapons in accordance with Afghan laws and regulations.
3. United States contractors performing security services in Afghanistan are subject to all relevant requirements of Afghan laws and regulations.
4. Upon the request of either Party, the Parties shall consult immediately through the Joint Commission concerning any issues that may arise regarding implementation of this Article.

Article - 15
Entry and Exit

1. Members of the force and members of the civilian component may enter and exit Afghanistan at agreed facilities and areas at locations listed in Annex A, at official points of embarkation and debarkation as listed in Annex B, and at other areas as mutually agreed, with identification cards issued by the United States, and either collective or individual movement orders. Passports and visas shall not be required. Such personnel shall be exempt from Afghan laws and regulations on registration and control of foreign nationals.
2. United States contractors and United States contractor employees may enter and exit Afghanistan at the places of entry and exit described in paragraph 1 of this Article. Passports and visas shall be required in accordance with Afghan law. If a visa is required, and requested by a United States contractor or a United States contractor employee, it shall provide for multiple entries and exits and shall be valid for a period of not less than one year. The appropriate Afghan authorities may issue or decline to issue required visas expeditiously. In the event Afghanistan declines to issue such visa, the appropriate Afghan authorities shall notify the person concerned and United States forces authorities. For exceptional situations as may be agreed through the Joint Commission, Afghanistan shall seek to put in place and make available to United States contractor employees a process for the issuance of visas upon their arrival in Afghanistan.
3. The United States recognises the sovereign right of Afghanistan to request the removal of any member of the force or member of the civilian component from Afghanistan. United States forces authorities shall

take appropriate measures to remove expeditiously such persons from Afghanistan upon request by proper Afghan authorities.

4. The Parties agree to establish procedures to implement this Article. The Joint Commission shall periodically review and update procedures for appropriate Afghan authorities to process members of the force and of the civilian component who arrive at or depart from the places of entry and exit described in paragraph 1 of this Article, including coordination and inspection of documentation. Afghan authorities may develop lists of members of the force and of the civilian component entering and exiting Afghan territory at the agreed facilities and areas, as necessary.

Article - 16
Importation and Exportation

1. United States forces and United States contractors may import into, export out of, re-export out of and transport and use in Afghanistan any equipment, supplies, material, technology, training, or services. The authorisations in this paragraph do not cover the activities of United States contractors that are not related to the presence of United States forces in Afghanistan. Identifying documents shall be provided to indicate that such equipment, supplies, material, technology, training, or services being imported by United States contractors are for United States forces' purposes and not for any private commercial purposes.
2. Members of the force and of the civilian component, United States contractors, and those United States contractor employees who are not Afghan nationals, may import into, export out of, re-export out of and transport and use in Afghanistan personal effects. The imported quantities shall be reasonable and

proportionate to personal use. The property referred to in this paragraph may not be sold or otherwise transferred in Afghanistan to persons who are not entitled to import such items duty free unless such transfer is in accordance with agreed procedures, including on payment of any taxes or fees due as a result of such transaction, established by the Joint Commission.

3. United States forces authorities, working with relevant Afghan authorities, shall take appropriate measures to ensure that no items or material of cultural or historic significance to Afghanistan are being exported and that, as provided in United States Central Command General Order Number 1, no alcohol, pornography, illegal narcotics, or privately owned firearms, or other contraband or items as may be mutually agreed, are being imported using the authorisations provided in paragraphs 1 and 2 of this Article.
4. The importation, exportation, re-exportation, transportation, and use of any articles brought into Afghanistan pursuant to paragraphs 1 and 2 of this Article shall not be subject to restrictions, such as licensing, inspection, or verification, except as provided in this Article, or taxes and customs duties or other charges assessed by government authorities in Afghanistan within the territory of Afghanistan. If Afghan authorities suspect the abuse of the privileges granted in paragraph 2 of this Article to United States contractors and United States contractor employees, then relevant Afghan authorities reserve the right of inspection of such personal effects when arriving or departing from civilian airports in Afghanistan or in personal vehicles at border crossings.
5. The relevant Afghan authorities reserve the right of verification of any container imported by United States contractors and United States contractor employees

containing items for United States forces' purposes in Afghanistan or for personal use, as authorised in paragraphs 1 and 2 of this Article. Without causing undue delay, and upon presentation by the relevant Afghan authorities of information to United States forces authorities that a United States contractor is abusing the authority granted in paragraphs 1 or 2 of this Article, United States forces authorities shall open and verify suspected shipments or containers intended for import in the presence of the Afghan authorities. Afghan authorities shall consent to the security requirements of United States forces and upon request by United States forces authorities permit such verifications to take place within agreed facilities and areas or other areas as mutually agreed.

6. Sharing the common goal with Afghanistan of preventing the improper entry into Afghan markets of items imported into Afghanistan under the terms of this Agreement, United States forces authorities shall take measures to prevent abuse of the authorisations in paragraphs 1 and 2 of this Article, and shall conduct inquiries and assist the relevant Afghan authorities in the conduct of inquiries and the collection of evidence relating to the suspected improper importation, exportation, re-exportation, transfer, or disposition of goods by members of the force, members of the civilian component, United States contractors, and United States contractor employees.
7. Items imported into Afghanistan or purchased in Afghanistan pursuant to this Article may be disposed of in Afghanistan with due respect for Afghan laws and regulations.
8. Upon the request of either Party, the Parties shall review and consult immediately through the Joint Commission concerning any issues that may arise regarding implementation of this Article.

Article - 17
Taxation

1. The acquisition in Afghanistan of articles and services by or on behalf of United States forces shall not be subject to any taxes or similar or related charges assessed within the territory of Afghanistan.
2. United States forces, including members of the force and of the civilian component, shall not be liable to pay any tax or similar or related charges assessed by the Government of Afghanistan within the territory of Afghanistan.
3. United States contractors shall not be liable to pay any tax or similar or related charges assessed by the Government of Afghanistan within the territory of Afghanistan on their activities, and associated income, relating to or on behalf of United States forces under a contract or subcontract with or in support of United States forces. However, United States contractors that are Afghan legal entities shall not be exempt from corporate profits tax that may be assessed by the Government of Afghanistan within the territory of Afghanistan on income received due to their status as United States contractors.
4. United States contractors are subject to Afghan requirements regarding employer withholding of personal income tax from United States contractor employees who normally reside in Afghanistan and from United States contractor employees who are Afghan nationals for payment to Afghanistan as required by the laws and regulations of Afghanistan.
5. United States contractor employees who do not normally reside in Afghanistan and United States contractor employees who are not Afghan nationals shall not be liable to pay any tax or similar or related charges assessed by the Government of Afghanistan

within the territory of Afghanistan on their activities, and associated income, relating to a contract or subcontract with or in support of United States forces.

6. United States contractors and United States contractor employees are not exempt under this Agreement from paying taxes assessed by the Government of Afghanistan within the territory of Afghanistan on their activities in Afghanistan that are not associated with supplying goods and services in Afghanistan to or on behalf of United States forces under a contract or subcontract with or in support of United States forces.

Article - 18

Driving and Professional Licenses

1. Afghanistan agrees to accept as valid, without a driving test or fee, driving licenses or permits issued by United States authorities to members of the force or of the civilian component, United States contractors, and United States contractor employees for operation of vehicles, vessels, aircraft, or other equipment by or for United States forces within the territory of Afghanistan.
2. Afghanistan agrees to accept as valid all professional licenses issued by United States authorities to members of the force or of the civilian component and United States contractors or United States contractor employees in relation to the provision of services as part of their official or contractual duties.
3. United States forces authorities shall endeavour to ensure that members of the force or of the civilian component, United States contractors, and United States contractor employees have current, valid driving licenses and permits for operation of vehicles, vessels, aircraft, or other equipment by or for United

States forces within the territory of Afghanistan. The Joint Commission shall establish mechanisms to exchange information on United States licenses and permits. In response to requests from Afghan authorities, the United States shall seek to verify the validity of such licenses.

Article - 19

Motor Vehicles

Afghanistan agrees to accept as valid the registration and licensing by United States forces authorities of the official vehicles of United States forces. Upon the request of United States forces authorities, Afghan authorities shall issue, without charge, license plates for United States forces' official, non-tactical vehicles. United States forces' official, non-tactical vehicles shall display official Afghan license plates that are indistinguishable from other Afghan license plates, upon their provision by Afghanistan.

Article - 20

Service Support Activities

1. United States forces may directly or through contract establish and operate at agreed facilities and areas service support activities, including military post offices, banking services, military service exchanges, commissaries, recreational service areas, and telecommunications services, including broadcast services. It is not the United States' intention for broadcasting, media, and entertainment services to reach beyond the scope of the agreed facilities and areas. Taking into consideration Afghan laws, traditions, and customs, United States forces may continue to make available television and radio broadcast services such as media and entertainment

programming for the purposes of morale, welfare, and recreation of United States forces and other authorised recipients located on agreed facilities and areas.

2. United States forces shall take appropriate measures to limit broadcasting, television programmes, media, and entertainment services to authorised recipients and to agreed facilities and areas.
3. Access to service support activities shall be in accordance with United States regulations. United States forces authorities shall adopt appropriate measures to prevent the abuse of such service support activities and the sale or resale of goods or services to persons who are not authorised to patronise such service support activities or providers.
4. No license, permit, or inspection shall be required by Afghanistan for activities connected with such service support activities.
5. The activities, and any organisations undertaking the activities referred to in this Article, are integral parts of United States forces and shall be accorded the same fiscal and customs exemptions granted to United States forces, including those provided in Articles 16 and 17 of this Agreement. Such organisations and activities shall be maintained and operated in accordance with applicable United States regulations. Such activities shall not be required to collect or pay taxes or to pay other fees related to their operations. Access to these service support activities shall be restricted to members of the force, members of the civilian component, United States contractors and United States contractor employees, and others as may be authorised.
6. Mail shipped within the United States Military Postal Service transportation system shall be exempt from inspection, search, or seizure by Afghan authorities.

7. The Joint Commission shall periodically review the service support activities and resolve by mutual agreement questions arising in the course of implementation of this Article.

Article - 21

Currency and Exchange

The Parties agree to establish procedures regarding currency and exchange. The Parties shall review and update, as appropriate, such procedures and shall address any issues immediately through the Joint Commission that may arise regarding such procedures.

Article - 22

Claims

1. Each Party waives any and all claims (other than contractual claims) against the other for damage to, loss of, or destruction of its property or injury or death to members of ANDSF or United States forces, and their respective civilian components, arising out of the performance of their official duties in Afghanistan.
2. For claims not excluded under paragraph 1 of this Article, United States forces authorities shall pay just and reasonable compensation in settlement of meritorious third party claims arising out of acts or omissions of members of the force and of the civilian component done in the performance of their official duties and incident to the non-combat activities of United States forces. Such claims shall be expeditiously processed and settled by United States forces authorities in accordance with the laws and regulations of the United States and seriously

considering the laws, customs, and traditions of Afghanistan.

3. In settling third party claims, United States forces authorities shall take into account any report of investigation or opinion provided to them by Afghan authorities regarding liability or amount of damages.
4. The settlement or adjudication of contract claims shall be carried out in accordance with the terms of the contracts.
5. Upon the request of either Party, the Parties shall consult immediately through the Joint Commission concerning any issues that may arise regarding implementation of this Article.

Article - 23

Annexes

Any Annex appended to this Agreement shall form an integral part of this Agreement, and may be amended by written agreement of the Parties.

Article - 24

Disputes and Implementation

1. Any divergence in views or dispute regarding the interpretation or application of this Agreement shall be resolved through consultations between the Parties and shall not be referred to any national or international court, tribunal or other similar body, or any third party for settlement.
2. The Parties, or their Executive Agents including through the Joint Commission, may enter into Implementing Arrangements and procedures to carry out the provisions of this Agreement.

3. Cooperation under this Agreement is subject to the relevant laws and regulations of the respective Parties, including applicable appropriations laws.
4. United States forces authorities shall pay reasonable, fair market charges, minus any taxes, for goods or services they request and receive.

Article - 25

Joint Commission

1. The Parties hereby establish a Joint Commission to oversee implementation of this Agreement. The Joint Commission shall be co-chaired by representatives of the Executive Agents. The Joint Commission may include other governmental representatives requested by the Executive Agents and appointed by the Parties.
2. The Joint Commission shall determine its own procedures and arrange for such auxiliary organs, including the establishment of Working Groups and administrative services, as may be considered appropriate. Each Executive Agent shall bear the costs of its participation in the Joint Commission.
3. The Joint Commission shall coordinate and exchange information, as appropriate, with the Afghanistan - United States Working Group on Defense and Security Cooperation established under the Strategic Partnership Agreement.

Article - 26

Entry into Force, Amendment, and Termination

1. This Agreement shall enter into force on January 1, 2015, after the Parties notify one another through diplomatic channels of the completion of their

respective internal legal requirements necessary for the entry into force of this Agreement. It shall remain in force until the end of 2024 and beyond, unless terminated pursuant to paragraph 4 of this Article.

2. This Agreement, upon its entry into force, shall supersede the exchange of notes dated September 26, 2002, December 12, 2002, and May 28, 2003, regarding the status of United States forces in Afghanistan. This Agreement shall also supersede any prior agreements and understandings which the Parties mutually determine, through a subsequent exchange of diplomatic notes, to be contrary to the provisions of this Agreement.
3. This Agreement may be amended by written agreement of the Parties through the exchange of diplomatic notes.
4. This Agreement may be terminated by mutual written agreement or by either Party upon two years' written notice to the other Party through diplomatic channels. Termination of any Annex to or Implementing Arrangement under this Agreement does not result in termination of this Agreement. Termination of this Agreement in accordance with this paragraph shall, without further action, result in termination of all Annexes and Implementing Arrangements.

IN WITNESS WHEREOF, the undersigned, being duly authorised by their respective Governments, have signed this Agreement.

DONE at Kabul, this 30th day of September 2014 in duplicate, in the Pashto, Dari, and English languages, each text being equally authentic.

ANNEX - A

List of Locations in Afghanistan of Afghan Facilities and Areas Provided by Afghanistan for United States Forces Access and Use

("Agreed Facilities and Areas")

Kabul Bagram

Mazar-e-Sharif Herat

Kandahar

Shorab (Helmand) Gardez

Jalalabad Shindand

Agreed facilities and areas also include other facilities and areas, if any, of which United States forces have the use as of the effective date of this Agreement and other facilities and areas at other locations in Afghanistan as may be agreed and authorised by the Minister of Defence.

ANNEX - B

Official Points of Embarkation and Debarkation

Bagram Airbase

Kabul International Airport Kandahar Airbase Shindand Airbase

Herat International Airport

Mazar-e-Sharif Airport

Shorab (Helmand)

Land Ports:

Toorkham, Nangarhar Province

Spinboldak, Kandahar Province Toorghundi, Herat Province

Hairatan, Balkh Province

Sherkhan Bandar, Kunduz Province

Other official points of embarkation and debarkation as may be mutually agreed.

Index

B

D

E

F

N

O

P

Q

R

S